INTERPRETIVE SYNTHESIS

The Task of Literary Scholarship

INTERPRETIVE SYNTHESIS

The Task of Literary Scholarship

by JOST HERMAND

and EVELYN TORTON BECK

Frederick Ungar Publishing Co., New York

Translated from Jost Hermand's
Synthetisches Interpretieren: Zur Methodik der Literaturwissenschaft
© 1968 by Nymphenburger Verlagshandlung GmbH., München

This edition has been especially adapted for the
American reader and substantially brought up to date; the translation
is by Jost Hermand and Evelyn Torton Beck.

Library of Congress Cataloging in Publication Data
Hermand, Jost.
    Interpretive synthesis.
    "A revision and considerable expansion of the
German text by Jost Hermand, which appeared in 1968 under
the title: Synthetisches Interpretieren, zur Methodik
der Literaturwissenschaft."
    Bibliography: p.
    Includes index.
    1. Literature—History and criticism—Theory, etc.
I. Beck, Evelyn Torton, joint author. II. Title.
PN441.H413   801'.95   75-10102
ISBN 0-8044-2035-1

Contents

Prefatory Note

This collaborative effort is a revision and considerable expansion of the German text by Jost Hermand, which appeared in 1968 under the title *Synthetisches Interpretieren: Zur Methodik der Literaturwissenschaft*. The present volume is an adaptation for the English reader. Recent developments in the field of literary criticism have been added.

For the convenience of the reader, we have opted for expediency. Therefore, all book titles are offered in English; the titles of the original publication are given in the bibliography. Similarly, all quotations (unless stated otherwise) have been specially translated for this book; source notes refer to the original edition.

One final comment on the text: there is, regrettably, no third-person singular pronoun that refers to both sexes in statements referring to the scholar, the critic, or the artist. Although even today, for many cultural and political reasons, the vast majority of these are male, the pronoun "he" is used only for the sake of readability. According to established usage, it refers to both male and female.

The authors would like to take this opportunity to thank Susan Lanser and Audrey Roberts (graduate students at the University of Wisconsin) and the publisher, Frederick Ungar, for their careful reading of the manuscript and many helpful suggestions.

J.H./E.T.B.

Madison, Wisconsin, 1975

vii

Introduction

Whoever dares to add yet one more volume—be it ever so slim—to the overwhelming number of works on literary theory and method, must recognize in advance that he or she will be considered extremely ambitious. For what can anyone offer as "new" when already at hand are so many awe-inspiring volumes that boast such illustrious names as Croce, Kayser, Wellek, Lukács, and Frye? To come up with a new perspective in this much-studied field, one must surely have made a sensational discovery. Indeed, in the last decades, such a multitude of scholarly methods have been developed that it hardly seems possible to offer an original approach in the area of aesthetics. Slogans abound: sociology of literature, thematology, psychoanalysis, Marxism, generation theory, new humanism, new criticism, the art of interpretation, textual analysis, genre studies, the mutual illumination of the arts, existentialism, *Geistesgeschichte*, history of problems and ideas, literary morphology, phenomenology, linguistics, formalism, and most recently, structuralism. Of what use is yet another "ism"? Are we not sated with what we have at hand? Each one of these critical approaches has produced such an abundance of essays on method that not only the novice and the more advanced student, but even the expert, no longer knows where to begin.

Nevertheless, we need not despair, for as yet no method has succeeded in doing away with that basic historical, biographical approach that was simply known as "literary studies" in the nineteenth century. In spite of all methodological experimentation, we observe that none of the humanities have been willing to completely relinquish those inter-disciplinary connections that bind each to each. As soon as we give these up and pursue our discipline only in terms of a single method, we move toward obscurantism. Unfortunately, some scholars have applied their approaches narrowly, apparently oblivious to the fact that in so doing they lose sight of the broad, universal implications of art. At times, it becomes obvious that the scholar is delighted to have found a new twist, so original and so specialized, that no other critic feels adequate to challenge it. The sparks generated by some of the more flashy theories often give off more heat than light. The logical consequence of this methodological uncertainty is an irritating cacophony of schools, each equipped with its own terminology. In the realm of *Geistesgeschichte*, we have "continual becoming" and "primal experience"; the existentialists favor "revealed being" and "authenticity"; the vocabulary of the formalists centers around "text," "symbol," "particle of narration," and "information value." These terms, artificially inflated by clever advertising, eventually take on the character of well-established brand names whose worth is no longer questioned.

To find a place for oneself in this chaos of opinion, it is tempting to take an extremely narrow approach. After all, no one wishes to have spoken in vain; everyone wants to be heard. Therefore, we ought not to be surprised at the forced originality shown by so many scholars trying to establish themselves in the academy. This is understandable, perhaps even unavoidable. Unfortunately, such conscious striving for originality serves no purpose; it merely increases the chaos. Moreover, we must seriously ask ourselves if this exaggerated individualism does not ultimately lead to a subjective approach or solipsism in the broadest sense. For ultimately, knowledge is that which moves from the subjective toward the objective and the suprapersonal, as Max Weber once formulated it.

If, however, the pursuit of knowledge is further incorporated into the world of placards and slogans, then this trend away from scholarship toward the purely personal will only be strengthened. In place of a logical development of ideas, we will have only spring and fall styles to be discarded after a short time by the professional avant-garde, like high-fashion clothing. This is not to speak against the "new," only against newness for its own sake, which consciously tries to place itself outside history. How proud some scholars are if they can stamp their intellectual products "brand-new." In their enthusiasm, however, they often fail to notice that their ideas have been debased to the status of wares, whose only worth resides in their marketability.

If the scholarly market continues to move in the direction it has taken in the last decades, many will find the ideas articulated in this book old-fashioned. For after so many audacious attempts in the sphere of methodology, we will not advocate narrowness, as seductive as such an approach might at first appear to be. The following chapters represent a conscious attack against methodological specialization; they advocate a historical approach that would oblige all interpreters of literature to a responsible recognition of the whole, or at least, to an integrated perspective, so that they will not disqualify themselves in advance amid the ever more differentiated points of view and the steady growth in scholarship. Instead of giving new answers, the old questions will be asked anew. For in the wake of intense methodological specialization, these have been passed over too quickly. There is still no real justification for the fact that the older historical approach, with its truly illustrious record, was summarily consigned to the junk heap some fifty years ago. What role is it that the historical plays in the realm of artistic experience? In this area, is there not always an interrelationship between personal response and the historically determined response? Are our own seemingly unique responses not tied to a specific process of acculturation without which we would not even be conscious of them? Does historical awareness stimulate our aesthetic imagination, or is it merely a blunting factor that moves us ever further away from authentic experience? Need it lead us to the much abused "relativity of values"? So many questions, so few answers.

These questions, however, are not meant to be facetious. We would not pose them if we did not feel that they had a certain relevance to the contemporary. After the dizzying array of methods proposed in the last decades, it finally appears that more and more voices are searching for new fixed points. In so doing, they are turning once again to historical factors. Still missing in the current literary scene is a more dispassionate approach that would not view methodological originality as a virtue in itself. Such a suggestion naturally raises some basic questions concerning the utility of our own work, which aims to give the cumbersome machinery of modern scholarship a more meaningful direction.

The fact that the study of literature is institutionally sanctioned in almost all civilized countries, and is thus in a privileged position, should not seduce us into ever increasing self-satisfaction. Where is there a real relationship between literary scholarship and politics? Do the devotees of literature really still believe that their study prepares them to be effective purveyors of ideology within their own social systems? Or are the disciplines of literature and art only carefully nurtured comfortable oases that provide shelter from a technocratic world? Escape has its place, but would it not be better if we left the escapist elements in the arts to dilettantes and casual readers? For the serious student, the capacity of literature to point to the future is its greatest strength.

This dilemma will no doubt continue to exist until a new approach to the nature of historical thinking in questions of art is found. To come to terms with this, we must accept the view that the world is not only subject to decay, but also capable of growth and change. Only when scholars return to that former faith in progress that gave rise to the humanities in the first place, will we be able to overcome the mood of pessimism that has colored our thinking in recent years. We are all fully aware of the many world tensions, crises, and problems that speak against this suggestion. However, without some such objective, without some small particle of hope that one postulates for oneself, every consideration of art and literature necessarily becomes an end-in-itself which diminishes the humanizing power of art. Let us overcome our fear of history, for only with a deepened historical awareness can we restore the universal dimension to the "humanities." The fact that this necessarily involves a number of boundary crossings into the realms of politics, sociology, and the general history of ideas will presumably frighten only those who have already ceased to look beyond the limits of their own discipline.

Seen from this angle, the following is actually an "aesthetic for progressives," which extends beyond purely literary scholarship in its demand for an "interpretive synthesis." By this, we do not have in mind a simple additive, eclectic approach that would lead to an arbitrary pluralism of methods. Quite the contrary. Instead of encouraging vague and sweeping generalizations, the term synthesis is intended to bring out the concrete and historical elements of this approach. With this in mind, we use the word synthesis in two different ways. First, it serves to highlight the abundance of those sociopolitical, economic, and cultural factors that every sound interpretation must take into account if it is to bring to the surface the universality of a work of art, as well as its historical situation. This approach would help to take literature and art out of the hands of those escapists who only wish to savor its aesthetic quality. Second, it attempts to activate a historical, dialectical approach, which advocates the study of the past in the present for the sake of the future, and discourages scholars from using a static view of history in order to bury themselves in the eternal past. Our concept of synthesis, therefore, points not only to the wealth of concrete material, but also to that dialectical, developmental process that most of all makes the study of literature worthwhile.

Furthermore, our approach demands that scholars be contemporaries, that they not only recognize the process of development, identify with it, and work toward its realization, but also help others to become aware of the forces of progress. Thus, the word synthesis is not limited to methodological considerations. If that were the case, then our entire enterprise would only be a theorizing farce. As serious scholars and true contemporaries we must make the effort to bring art into the broader social realm. Instead of remaining content with a mere revival of historical thinking, or a study of the past for its own sake, as if the pursuit of history were meaningful in and of itself, we must proceed with a more dynamic, dialectic orientation. Only a synthesis of literature and historical awareness can provide ideologically useful models, and involve scholars in the very process of development which so many have frequently tried to ignore by holding firmly to the values of the status quo.

Most of the examples cited and discussed in the body of this book are taken from the realm of German literary scholarship, which, from 1900 on, offers a rather wide spectrum of schools and approaches in an especially clear and unadulterated form. In contrast (and with the exception of certain branches of Freudianism, and the new feminist criticism which arose relatively recently in the United States and has not yet taken hold in Europe), Anglo-American criticism is less varied and, as a result, somewhat less dynamic. The greater diversity of German criticism is, in part, due to the many radical changes that took place in the history of that country from the turn of the century to the present. These changes are, of course, all reflected in the various approaches to literature: from abstract existentialism to political engagement, from *Geistesgeschichte* and the history of ideas to the most rigid aesthetic formalism—there is virtually no school that is *not* represented. In discussing the major approaches to literature in the Western world, German scholarship, therefore, provides particularly useful models which are paradigmatic for the various schools of criticism in other countries.

Since the principle determining this book is not completeness, but the inner consistency of the thoughts here mapped out, the work could as easily be called "aesthetics from a historical perspective," or better yet, "aesthetics for contemporaries"—in any case, for contemporaries as they *ought* to be. This catchphrase is not meant to be merely modish. In this volume, true contemporaneity implies a quasi-permanent attitude, present in every era, which has always given thinking people the courage to try to involve themselves in a productive relationship with their own present. That is to say, the title "contemporary" will not be bestowed upon those who place the greatest value on the prevailing *Zeitgeist* but only on those who confront the inner contradictions of their own epoch and try to give them new direction. Such a perspective, long accepted as progressive in the arena of politics, could also prove to be extremely useful in the study of the arts in every epoch. Let us not be the "apes of our time," as Kurt Tucholsky once wrote with contempt, but its engaged dialecticians. For this purpose we need, above all else, a sharpened socio-aesthetic awareness, which attempts to find the characteristics of the epoch in even the least significant forms of expression of the human intellect. If we can bring ourselves to accept this approach, then the step from theoretical formulation to practical application in our scholarly activity will not be so very great. And with such an orientation we would no longer have to react to our own age either by escape or conformity, but would be in a much better position to attempt to transform it, as small as the area of our influence might be.

PART I

The Pluralism of Methods

Since 1900

Chapter One

THE RISE AND FALL OF POSITIVISM

I

The idea that man is not at the mercy of supernatural forces, but is an autonomous being, capable of bettering his condition by taking his fate into his own hands, is by no means self-evident. Such views were entirely unknown before the Renaissance and took hold only in the eighteenth century. At this time, the realization that all human experience was part of the process of history was welcomed and viewed as an ordering principle that could give direction to what had previously been accepted as a meaningless, eternally-repeating cycle of events. The following gave impetus to this trend: Francis Bacon, Fontenelle's *Digression on the Ancients and Moderns* (1688), Vico's *New Science* (1725), Hume's *History of Great Britain* (1754–63), Voltaire's *Essay on General History* (1756), Gibbon's *History of the Decline and Fall of the Roman Empire* (1744–81), and the work of the French Encyclopedists. Through these writers, the world of things became the world of man; a dynamic world view replaced a static one; the world became world history.

These same ideas cropped up in Germany toward the end of the eighteenth century, where they gave way to the concept of an upward-moving spiral or a step-like construction of world history, which viewed even general ideas, such as art or the beautiful, not as absolutes, but in terms of historical development. "It is absolutely impossible for a philosophical theory of the beautiful to exist in the arts and sciences without the idea of history,"[1] said Herder. This historically oriented dynamic view of the world which he propounded, above all, in his *Reflections on the Philosophy of the History of Mankind* (1784–91), corresponds to Goethe's conception of the eternal entelechy of everything living, and to Schiller's idea that only history validates the modern poet who is unable to attain the artistic stature or sensual immediacy of the ancients, but who transcends them in the modernity of his ideas.[2] Shortly thereafter, in the early nineteenth century, Hegel postulated that every work of art belongs "to its time, its people, its place, and is dependent on specific historical as well as other conceptions and purposes."[3] In his eyes, art does not stand apart from, but is well integrated with the events of history and the *Weltgeist* (world spirit) which can only reach its final goal in man's realization of absolute freedom. For this reason, Hegel wrote in his *Lectures on the Philosophy of History*: "World history only shows how the mind gradually comes to consciousness and to desire truth; awareness dawns, finds cardinal points; in the end, it reaches complete consciousness." Where previously God had reigned, man now governs. In turn, this gave rise to a philosophy of history that claims that the leading ideas of a period are the result of its inner dialectics. According to Hegel, without a logical succession of thesis-antithesis-synthesis, history would only be a blind game of chance, forever keeping mankind from consciousness and thus from freedom.[4]

Out of these constellations of thought there developed in the early nineteenth century a belief in progress or the forward driving force of history. Underlying all scholarship was the assumption that the world was historical, and therefore subject to change, both in the domain of the material and the spiritual. The first movements in Germany to arrive at particularly radical conclusions based on this supposition were the young, or left, Hegelians* of the late 1830s and early 1840s. Because they were historical materialists, they insisted that all structures of society were determined by material or economic conditions of life, even in the realms of religion and politics, even where Christ, the church, and the divine right of kings were concerned. A good example of this strictly historical approach in German literary criticism is provided by Georg Gottfried Gervinus, who, in his introduction to the *History of the Poetic National Literature of the German People* (1835–42), explicitly stated that his work differed from all other handbooks of its kind primarily in that "it was nothing but history."[5] By this, Gervinus meant to say that he viewed all historical phenomena from an empirical rather than a metaphysical basis. Furthermore, in studying the cultural trends of a period, he consistently emphasized historical progress.[6]

It is easy to imagine that from the very beginning such an orientation would be regarded with suspicion by the powers-that-be. Thus, as early as the Age of Romanticism (around 1800), and then more strongly in the Restoration period (1815–1848) we note the development of a persistent countercurrent opposed to the belief in progress. In this direction, the conservatism of Leopold von Ranke, the noted Berlin historian, was particularly influential, for he held that we should not judge every age according to "what emerges from it," but should attempt to understand it according to its "own self." Ranke's famous dictum speaks to this point: "All generations of mankind have equal rights before God, and the historian must see them in this same light."[7] With this one sentence,

---

* A group of philosophers, writers, and political theorists who stressed the more progressive elements in Hegel's thinking by applying his abstract dialectics to the material world. They are also sometimes referred to as left Hegelians, in order to contrast them to the right Hegelians, who obdurately supported the status quo.

Ranke not only dismissed all of Hegel, but also introduced a total lack of perspective, and encouraged a historical relativism according to which all values were equally valid. From such a static viewpoint, everything in the past was considered an honorable relic to be treated with piety, merely because it was labeled "old."

In the study of the arts, this development meant an ever greater erosion of the belief in the forward-moving thrust of history and the faith in progress initiated by Hegel. However, even the conservatives of the Restoration period realized that historical thinking could no longer be dispensed with. Instead of rejecting it, they tried to undermine the political implications inherent in the idea of progress, and emphasized only facts and other mechanical aspects of history, such as cause and effect. In almost all the humanities, this resulted in a curious schizophrenia. On the one hand, historical thinking attained undreamed-of breadth and brought forth entirely new disciplines, such as the history of law, the history of religion, history of art, and history of literature. On the other hand, at the very same time, a breakdown occurred in the belief in progress, without which these disciplines would never have come into existence.

In Germany, the year 1848 is the decisive turning point. After the failure of the revolution in this year, scholars of all political persuasions tended more and more to assume positions of resigned relativism, in which they carefully avoided all ideological positions, and concerned themselves solely with surface facts. The method or school that developed from this is scholarly objectivity or historical positivism, based partly on the work of Auguste Comte, according to which the source of all human knowledge is the given, positive fact. Positivist scholars eschewed all value judgments and theory building, taking as their goal the "viewing of history as an unbroken chain of causes and effects," as Wilhelm Scherer, the leading German literary critic of the late nineteenth century, once formulated it.[8] Others, however, referred to the method derisively as the uninterrupted veneration of pure facts.

Although this movement may be interpreted as a reaction to Hegel's speculative theorizing about the laws governing historical development, which had been so important a factor in the early nineteenth century, it nonetheless resulted in a general lack of orientation. In sharp contrast to Hegel, positivist scholars were no longer interested in the whole, but only in the detail. By refusing to look beyond their own position in time, by focusing always on the particular, never the general, they lost sight of the broader historical connections.

But to do positivism justice, we should distinguish between its two different phases: the relatively more historical orientation after 1848, which had developed in dialectical opposition to the historical speculations of the Hegelians, and the pedantic minutia-peddling of the 1880s and 1890s. In its beginnings, positivism was defined as a method that examined every work of art with respect to its special place in history. Whether in painting, music, or literature, all aesthetic manifestations served as expressions of their time and were actually seen as part of a historical continuum that admitted of no fissures or gaps, in the Darwinian sense. "Everything is predetermined," was one of the favorite maxims of this period. Such a viewpoint was still tenable around 1850, and led to substantially more concrete results than did the work of many Hegelians who felt compelled to subordinate everything to a single overriding idea. In the course of time, however, positivism was ever more decidedly understood in purely factual terms. Instead of emphasizing the developmental factors, positivist scholars arrived at an objectivism of the inessential. By this process, the historical force was reduced to a merely formal element. It was precisely this movement toward the empirical, however necessary and salutary in some respects it was, that ultimately led to the triumph of absolute factuality. By a thoroughgoing exclusion of all political, social, and religious problems, *fact* was viewed as the final court of appeal in all scholarly disputes.

Seen from an ideological perspective, this kind of positivism, this "abhorrence of all speculative errors,"[9] was a faithful mirror image of the attitudes of the established German middle class of the second half of the century, which had given up the political idealism of 1848 and was contenting itself with its comfortable economic position. What now stood in the forefront were not bold conceptions, political awareness, or the will toward social reforms, but the diligent gathering of small and even tiny building blocks, which were used to construct an imposing edifice of pure factuality, equipped with everything but a central idea. The pursuit of the artistic, which necessarily tends toward the universal, was thus degraded from a means to an end, to a mere end in itself. Such overemphasis of the factual inevitably led the positivists to treat the individual work of art only as scholarly material and to subject it to a strictly detailed method that turned ever further away from the general toward the specific. For fear of omitting a single characteristic feature, the emphasis everywhere was on completeness of description, discovery of sources, and embedding the accumulated data in biographical information.

Because of this narrowing focus on the purely empiric in the later years of positivism, there is hardly a single representative of this movement who did not succumb to the dangers of the statistical, the lexicographic, or the irrelevant. While a critic such as Scherer around 1870 still maintained a broad perspective, most of his students espoused an empty biographical approach that depended on an uninterrupted series of documents and records that gave prominence to ancestors' birth certificates and publishers' sales accounts. To the degree that the original historical impulse was still recognizable at all, positivism in the 1880s and 1890s became a kind of basket-weaving of a merely formal, genetic kind. In this way, all that remained of the demand for a sociopolitical and cultural-historical anchoring of all artistic phenomena is Scherer's formula, "inherited, experienced, learned," which is reminiscent of Hippolyte Taine's slogan, "race, place, time," and which, at bottom, is similarly static because it lacks any concept of historical development.

As a result of this positivistic objectivism, for which only surface facts existed, purely mechanical methods of scholarship, oriented to the natural sciences, necessarily made deep inroads in the humanities. Thus around 1880, in many academic circles the mere collecting of facts was itself viewed as a scholarly achievement, while any interpretation of the heaps of amassed material was usually postponed to a later day. In this era the ideal of the scholar was the directionless, omniscient polyhistor, who lent his immense knowledge to only one carefully selected subject and, with a gesture of renunciation, limited himself to plugging those famous gaps in the towering edifice of learning. This resulted in a period of spadework, which gave rise, in all of the historically oriented disciplines, to a method in which intellectual syntheses or philosophical perceptions played only a subordinate role. As in botany or chemistry, every work of art was carefully dissected into its components in order to reduce even the aesthetic to a materially determined causal nexus resting on the principle that absolutely everything could be explained. Whether scholars in the humanities wished it or not, a scientific mode of thinking became prevalent, which was identical with the inductive method employed by all the empirical-experimental sciences.

This is evident in the positivists' attitude toward the sciences and technology and graphically illustrated by the following quotation from Scherer: "The same power that gave rise to the unprecedented blossoming of industry, that multiplied the comforts of life, in a word, that increased man's mastery over nature by a giant step—this same power also directs our spiritual life: it sweeps away dogmas, transforms scholarship, and places its stamp on poetry. The natural sciences enter as victors in the triumphal chariot to which we are all shackled."[10]

Ironically, it was out of this very acceptance of the natural sciences that the reaction against positivism arose. For while the positivists welcomed technology because of its promise of external comfort, at the same time they viewed it as an uncontrollable power that would increasingly enslave the free spirit. Instead of resolving their fears by attempting to understand technology and thus perhaps control it, the positivists sidestepped the issue entirely by indulging in the traditional veneration of the classics. This led to a peculiar simultaneity of the positivist mania for collecting and for holding idealistically elevated judgments of taste, which exalted the works of Goethe and Schiller. Such dualism can be explained only in terms of the rising enmity to progress felt by conservative scholars, the defenders of the status quo who were extremely satisfied with their condition after the unification of Germany in 1871.

Surprisingly, most positivists were not conscious of the contradictions in their own attitude. In the pleasure they derived from collecting facts, they were convinced that they were making a significant contribution to the development of a modern world view. Yet, whenever basic political or social questions were raised, the positivists immediately retreated into their academic shells. Then, too, almost everything modern in literature and philosophy was suspect to them, especially every kind of thinking that seemed to oppose the Bismarckian status quo. Therefore, the positivists were neither genuine speculative thinkers nor real materialists. Instead, they propounded an academic objectivism that no longer had any kind of philosophical or ideological goal. As a result, their work lacked all perspective.

II

Because of this inner discrepancy, positivism, at the turn of the century, came to be viewed as a specter of absolute mendacity. What had been presented as scholarly restraint was now openly denounced as mere trading in petty details. Favorite terms of abuse by the critics of positivism were "motif-nosing," "parallel-hunting," "petticoat sniffling," or "literary sansculottism." What was being attacked was scholarship undertaken for its own sake, scholarship that had lost all meaning and value because of its increased focusing on the detail. As a result, the achievements of positivist literary scholars, such as detailed biographies, the publication of source material and encyclopedias also fell into disrepute, but that is another story.

Around 1900 there arose a new generation of critics consisting mainly of neo-Hegelians and neo-Kantians, who were once again oriented toward theory and did not have much use for positivist scholarship. Instead of scrutinizing the ever-growing mountains of material, which had been used only as documentary evidence for biographies and cultural history, these critics showed a distinct aversion to all mechanical, statistical, or materialistic methods. The scholarly ideal of the turn of the century was not the completeness of the material but the boldness of the ideas. Therefore, the inductive method of the natural sciences was ever more strongly pushed out by the inclination to theorize. Behind the sedulous growth of source material, there suddenly emerged a philosophical striving toward a new unity, a striving more concerned with principles and ideologies than with isolated facts. The essentials, not the surface of things, became the goal of cognition, a goal that led back to basic philosophical categories, such as epoch, style, structure, wholeness, and dynamics.

The driving force behind this neoidealism came from the realm of philosophy. Without doubt, the most important stimulus came from the works of Nietzsche, whose influence on the intellectual scene from 1895 on, can hardly be exaggerated. Particularly influential was his second "unseasonal" speculation *Concerning the Use and Abuse of History for Life* (1874), in which antiquarian positivism is depicted as a blind passion for collecting, which, in its indefatigable amassing of material and facts, completely loses sight of its own purposes. Nietzsche denounced the positivists as historically inclined eunuchs, neutral objectivists, or hollow intellectuals, who even consume the dust of "bibliographic trivia" with morbid passion. His own inclination is entirely to "life," to that "dark, driving, insatiable, self-loving power" that cannot be analyzed rationally.[11] In this hotbed of antihistorical thinking there developed around 1900 the so-called *Lebensphilosophie* which emphasized emotion, inspiration, and intuition, as the main forces behind human action. This was propounded by Wilhelm Dilthey and, also in part, by Georg Simmel. Another impetus that helped establish the neoidealistic approach to the humanities was Heinrich Rickert's *The Limits of Conceptualization in the Natural Sciences* (1896–1902), in which the modern cultural sciences were for the first time differentiated from the natural sciences as being disciplines operating not on general laws but on a purely individualistic basis. A similar orientation to the products of the mind is found in the work of neo-Kantians, such as Hermann Cohen, and neo-Fichtians, such as Rudolph Eucken and Hugo Münsterberg, who in his *Philosophy of Values* (1908), emphasized the life-giving power of real scholarship.

The scholarly goal of this neoidealism, which became the dominant trend around 1900, was the free creative spirit in the Hegelian sense, which seemed to be independent of all materially determined causality. Efforts to develop concepts specifically applicable to the humanities, free of all inductive elements, were everywhere in evidence. The purely genetic approach of positivism, according to which every work of art is explainable only in terms of its biographical background, was replaced by a general revival of philosophical, ideological, or purely formal interpretations, which concerned themselves only with things arising from the spirit, independent of all empirically provable premises. But what in theory looked like freedom from all materialistic, positivistic anchoring, in practice turned out to be a movement away from the historical connection of all intellectual-artistic phenomena.

This neoidealistic approach stemmed largely from the fact that historical thinking was blamed for the pedantry of the 1880s and 1890s. The neoidealists failed to appreciate the fact that historical materialism had itself arisen as a corrective to the speculative constructions of some of the Young Hegelians of the 1830s. The historian Gervinus and the positivist Scherer were therefore suddenly thrown into one pot and tarred with the same brush of historical relativism, called "historicism"* in

---

* A philosophy of history that rejects absolute values and assumes that in order to study the past we must accept the standards of a given period and avoid the intrusion of our own point of view.

a purely negative sense. The neoidealists were in favor of transforming all historically oriented disciplines into genuine humanities once again, that is, of moving away from the positivistic-empirical approach of the late nineteenth century to a world of essences and ideas.

All revolutions swing from one extreme to another; as the materialistic conceptions of cause and effect were given up, the historical and social presuppositions of all artistic phenomena were also rejected. The result was an intellectual somersault, which, because of its purely speculative orientation, necessarily led nowhere. Because of the growing contempt for technology, for the natural sciences, and for the belief in progress, this neoidealism was destined from the start to fail to attain a true concept of totality. While in the idealistic period of the late eighteenth century, Goethe greeted the first successful balloon sent up by the Montgolfier Brothers as an event of earth-shaking significance because he immediately linked the phenomenon of flight with the progressive freeing of mankind, the neoidealist period around 1900 created a milieu that encouraged a striking devaluation of technology, which ultimately led to an openly arrogant flaunting of art and philosophy over the natural sciences. Neoidealist scholars accepted technology where it affected their own personal comfort, but excluded it completely from the arts, the humanities, and philosophy. While Goethe's discovery of the intermaxillary bone had advanced evolutionary theory, one could no longer expect such a contribution from a poet like Rilke. And an aesthete like Stefan George would surely have found it beneath his dignity to spend his time disproving the Newtonian theory of colors, a task that Goethe had set himself.

The most confusing thing about this development was the fact that the neoidealistic reaction to positivism did not come, as one might have expected, from the traditional powers of church and state, but from the so-called artistic and intellectual avant-garde. Whereas in the early nineteenth century it had been the conservatives who were the major opponents of all forward-looking ideologies, now the attack came from apparently progressive circles. And in so doing, they invoked such confusing ideological constellations as progressive reaction, or conservative revolution, which rested on Nietzsche's principle of "eternal return." Names such as Lagarde, Langbehn, and Chamberlain are representative of many others.[12] But unfortunately, it was not only the neoidealistic rebels or the poet-prophets who cultivated such conceptions. Large circles of educated citizens also treated technology and progress as negligible quantities, quantities they could well do without in the domain of the arts and humanities. And so, in spite of all the emphasis placed on developmental factors, the spirit of progress that had been so strong in the first phase of idealism before 1800 now appeared to have spent itself.

Stimulated by the neoidealists, a steadily growing interest in the theoretical bases of human knowledge is observable in many branches of learning around 1900. In addition to this philosophical neoidealism, many other attitudes emerged: vitalism, neoromanticism, Bergsonian intuitionism, and all the neoreligious, theosophical, or mythological concepts of the turn of the century that rested on the principle that man is not determined by external factors but is the creator of his own destiny. At first glance, this sounds quite progressive. However, in their striving for universality, the neoidealists completely lost sight of the overall historical integration of all spiritual and empiric phenomena, an integration that can only be attained by a thoroughly historical perspective. For this reason, the neoidealistic yearning for synthesis led away from wholeness and resulted in the extensive splintering of scholarly efforts.

The positivism of the late nineteenth century seems to have been a relatively closed system of learning, which, in spite of all its tendencies toward specialization, revealed a basically homogeneous structure, but the neoidealists' efforts at synthesis led to a hitherto-undreamed-of pluralism of approaches. No matter what his field of study, the positivist had the support of a generally accepted method. Even work on the most obscure subjects was valued as a useful addition to that much admired edifice of learning, because the principle of cultural-historical determinism still stood behind everything. Neoidealism, however, opened the way not only for every kind of abstraction and preciousness, but also dilettantish charlatanism. The new theories that now came to the surface were rarely measured against the facts. Most scholars at this time considered their ideas incontestable and so, in spite of some sweeping generalizations, they ended up with a completely subjective system of values. Only this can explain the paradoxical fact that, while even the pettiest, most specialized positivists moved toward a clearly definable goal, the neoidealistic attempts to create a philosophical synthesis around 1900 resulted in a confusion of countless subjective methods.

No doubt, this can be explained by a variety of reasons. Probably the most important is the fact that the established middle class had reached the limits of its power and tried to compensate for the decreasing possibilities of political expression by means of intellectual extravagance. This explains why such a need for ideologies occurred around 1900 and why the power of idealism to change the world was suddenly looked upon as the ultimate hope. This scholarly reorientation was undoubtedly also brought about by the increasing saturation with the mass of material collected by the positivists. But by itself, this would never have produced such a radical upheaval. The responsibility for this must be attributed to the rising egotism of the late Wilhelmenian* bourgeoisie, who suddenly began to view the positivists' scholarly objectivity, and the resignation that accompanied it, as intellectually inferior. However, because they lacked the necessary belief in progress, they themselves were unable to replace it with a similarly closed structure of learning. For ultimately, it is only the belief in progress that gives all intellectual efforts their much needed direction.

By 1900, however, the middle-class scholars had become entirely too refined, too fearful, and too skeptical to entertain

---

* A term designating the period between 1888 to 1914 in which Wilhelm II was the emperor of Germany. In sociocultural terms, it is the equivalent of high Victorian.

such a vulgar idea which all too clearly pointed to the left. And so, one kind of narrowness was merely exchanged for another; pure factuality for pure idealism, which, in spite of all attempts at wholeness, could result only in overspecialization. The logical consequence of this enthusiastically heralded revolution in scholarship was a methodological pluralism that, because of its antihistorical bias, splintered into groups and sub-groups that included idealism, psychology, sociology of literature, history of ideas, and pure formalism. The one thing they had in common was that they all viewed the positivists' method, especially its historical orientation, as antiquarian, thereby calling into question the historical method in general.

It is rather difficult to arrange these groups in a meaningful series, for they almost all developed at the same time, and later on, overlapped a good deal. The following survey of the major movements of German literary criticism since 1900 therefore makes no pretense at completeness or of chronological accuracy. Only the most important movements have been singled out, and these will only be discussed to the degree that they betray their specifically antihistorical, and thus, anti-universalistic nature. It is generally acknowledged that, in addition to these methodologically narrow methods, an extensively modified positivism and a mode of interpretation that leans toward literary history have continued to exist and have remained quite active to this very day. The following chapters therefore present a series of models, and those only in their most characteristic form. For this reason, the individual sections should not be taken for an exhaustive survey, but only as examples of particular ideologies. A complete history of the subject would have required several volumes. What is of interest here are methods as such, and most often these do not appear as typologically pure specimens. And in the realm of theory, everything exists only in ideal form. The same can be said of the following models, which, in spite of their connections to historical reality, are not meant to be anything other than conscious constructions.

Chapter Two

THE IMPACT OF *GEISTESGESCHICHTE*

"The history of the human intellect is the unending meta-morphosis of the eternal essence of mankind."

—Fritz Strich

I

Broadly speaking, *Geistesgeschichte** is an approach to the study of literature and the other arts which emphasizes the history of problems, ideas, and sentiments. Because a number of such studies appeared in the 1920s, most literary scholars assume that *Geistesgeschichte* first developed in these years. When *Geistesgeschichte* is viewed more closely, however, we see that it actually emerged at the turn of the century and is itself the source for most of the nonmaterialist approaches to literature that have developed since that time. *Geistesgeschichte* grows out of a long tradition of German philosophical idealism which, in all its variations, insists that *Geist* (i.e., the powers of mind, spirit, intellect or reason) constitutes the essence of reality. Above all, *Geistesgeschichte* was shaped by the work of Dilthey, whose impact on the development of literary scholarship in the twentieth century can hardly be exaggerated.

* See also pages 31 and 45 ff.

For Dilthey, every person, and thus every writer, has a completely singular way of approaching life and of coming to terms with it. For this reason, in matters concerning intellect and emotion, he completely rejected the rigid principle of cause and effect which had been the dominant approach taken by the positivists. In sharp contrast to these, Dilthey relied completely on subjective, intuitive impressions and relegated all rationally explainable phenomena to the periphery. As early as 1883, in his *Introduction to the Humanities*, Dilthey had taken issue with the overly scientific orientation of the positivists Auguste Comte and John Stuart Mill. Furthermore, he insisted that it was not possible to explain the creative manifestations of the human mind or spirit; according to him, these could only be intuitively recognized. Moving further in this direction, Dilthey increasingly associated *Geist* with intuition and instinct until, like the very idea of life itself, it could hardly be debated rationally or analyzed.

Thus from the beginning, the so-called *Geisteswissenschaft*—the study of the products of the mind—became a kind of science of the soul, steeped in Dilthey's philosophy, emphasizing intuition, largely unconcerned with cause and effect. To a great extent, this approach deprives both life and literature of any conceptual framework; furthermore, from such a perspective, the most one can hope to accomplish in the realm of literary scholarship is to grasp the work of art intuitively or to reexperience the imaginative impulse of its creator.

In keeping with this assumption, in the *Imaginative Power of the Poet* (1887), Dilthey simply equated literature with "that which the poet has experienced." In so doing, he was not thinking of any causal or biographical connections between poetry and experience, but of nonrational phenomena, such as those fleeting memories that often inundate us in dreams or when we are half-asleep. For Dilthey, it was such occurrences, and not our conscious experiences, that decisively motivate us. Furthermore, Dilthey believed it was exclusively the intensity of his feelings that made the poet a poet. In this way he viewed literature on a purely subjectivist basis as an organ for the deeper understanding of life.

This is demonstrated most clearly in Dilthey's essay, "Goethe and the Poetic Imagination," which appeared in 1906 in his book, *Experience and Poetry*. With apodictic certainty he placed the imagination of the poet at the very center of poetry. Here Dilthey viewed the poetic element as something incommensurable that flows from the unconscious, often taking the form of a liberating confession or a rapturous prophecy. No wonder, then, that he singled out imagination and the power of recall as the two factors most significant in the creation of poetry. According to Dilthey's theory, true poets create everything out of their own inner experience, while external reality serves only as a catalyst. Even those elements that enter into the poet's mind from the realm of history or the world of ideas exist only for the purpose of making the poet more responsive and giving him a deepened understanding of his own life experiences. Dilthey therefore considered every work of poetry as a living creation of a particular kind which makes its appeal directly to the human soul as artistically shaped experience. For this reason, he based his evaluation of poetry on the intensity of the life embodied in the work of art.

According to Dilthey, we are moved only when a work expresses a real-life experience and when, through it, we also gain insight into our own souls. Because he so emphasized the emotional response, Dilthey shifted not only the whole creative process but also the reception of individual works of art into the realm of intuition. From this perspective, the only function left to literary scholarship is the purely experiential act of discovering "the I in the Thou." Accordingly, Dilthey especially valued letters and autobiographical writings, for he was far less interested in artistic form than in the "eternally pulsing stream of life" which manifested itself in immediately articulated expression. For him, the measure of highest creativity was always the "inspired state of being deeply moved" by what he understood to be elemental life experiences. As a result, he came to the significant conclusion, which was to be of great consequence in the history of literary scholarship, that the poet, like the prophet or the saint, far surpasses the philosopher in understanding the world, since he does not confine himself to purely rational knowledge, but relies on intuition, enthusiasm, indeed all the sensual modes of experience, in order to establish an all-encompassing philosophy of life, which Dilthey termed *Lebensphilosophie.*

It is easy to overlook the consequences that arise from such an intuitive, nonrational approach to the concepts of the mind. Because of its emphasis on elemental life experiences and its essentially antiintellectual stance, Dilthey's *Lebensphilosophie* tended toward an agnosticism that often took on a pronounced mystical coloration. Since reason was considered inadequate to explain either "life" or the human spirit, both of which were looked upon as the final court of appeal, all objective reality was invalidated. The door was thus opened wide for subjective arbitrariness, which was entirely in keeping with the spirit of this approach: intuition was elevated and became the decisive organ of cognition (as is evident in the philosophies of Bergson and Husserl), while the painstakingly executed work of the positivists was devalued and came to be viewed as the plaything of philological mosaicmakers and biographical quibblers. Not surprisingly, Dilthey repeatedly spoke of the interpretation of art as something highly personal, resting on the ability to recreate and thus accessible only to an elite. Such an attitude well reflected the arrogant demands of the late Wilhelmenian bourgeoisie who, prior to World War I, rejected all materialistic determinations in order not to be disturbed in their loudly-proclaimed pretentious inwardness.

As obvious as these elitist tendencies in Dilthey's philosophy may be, it would nonetheless be one-sided to view him only from this angle. For like all serious scholars, he showed a clear line of development ranging over almost fifty years. While at first the idea of those broadly-conceived, all-encompassing biographies that predominated in the 1870s appeared to him to be the "most philosophical form of history," a gradual softening is to be observed in his writings of the late 1880s and the early 1890s, when he moved toward intuitive impressionism marked by an emphasis on intensely felt experience. In these years, he rejected all biographical positivistic factors, and the artist became the great genius whose work was to be interpreted according to the intuitions of the observer, listener, or reader. From this perspective, even form lost its firm contours and was perceived solely as an inner expression that lent its distinct personal character to every sentence and every line.

But at the turn of the century, in keeping with the general return to ideologies, Dilthey rejected the psychological solipsism of the impressionistic era and endorsed the widespread tendency toward the construction of categories and typologies. In his many writings of this period one senses his drive to order all human expressions, varied as they may be, into one grand systematic philosophy of culture. Like the romantics, Dilthey glimpsed the vision of a spiritual unity of all cultural, political, and religious phenomena, which he tried to integrate into a single unified system. Such words as epoch, cultural synthesis, and spiritual organization became more frequent in his writings. In contrast to all positivistic atomization, he wished to be sure that the principle of wholeness received its proper due.

What interested him therefore in 1900 were primarily the creative bases of the divergent world views that had emerged at various times. Like all the neoidealists of this era, he tried most resolutely to get beyond the subjective basis of his intuitive approach by means of a philosophical system that bordered on the metaphysical. But even in these years, Dilthey rarely wandered into the rarified air of pure speculation; his systems, explicitly associated with *Geistesgeschichte*, still betray an immense knowledge of history and are, moreover, imbued with the spectrum of impressionistic perception and the spiritual breadth of his philosophy.

For this reason, Dilthey provides a good example of the splendors as well as the dangers inherent in the approach based on *Geistesgeschichte*. Although Dilthey had a sharp eye for the broader connections between abstract ideas and historical realities, he nonetheless often succumbed to the temptation of abandoning the historical basis and venturing onto the thin ice of purely theoretical constructions. Thus, in the first decade of the twentieth century, the last years of his life, he tried to subject all artistic expression to a strict typology resting on three clearly differentiated world views: *materialism*, which views physical matter as the only reality and holds that everything in the universe can be explained in terms of physical laws; *objective idealism*, which accepts nature as ideal or spiritual, but existing independently of any subject; and *subjective idealism*, which holds that nature has no existence outside the perceiving mind and insists that true reality consists of mental images or ideas.

Actually, in keeping with the basically intuitive orientation from which he never freed himself entirely, Dilthey traced these three typologies back to the spiritual inclinations of the individual poets under consideration. As a result, his philosophical system was reduced to a question of temperament. Dilthey tried hard to present these three modes of poetic world perception as if they were of equal rank and exemplified each with such illustrious names as Goethe, Schiller, and Balzac. Nonetheless, his own sympathy was clearly with the first two, since the materialistic outlook seemed to him rather inferior in comparison to the individual psyche and its impulse toward the spiritual. Because he slighted historical and causal factors, his three world views give the impression of being rather weak philosophical abstractions lacking in substance. Moreover, because of Dilthey's inclination toward typologies, he viewed the process of history as a continuous battle between the three opposing world views, which showed no development or progress.

This ahistorical perspective is neither new nor ideal, and led Dilthey to take a pessimistic view of history. In his writings, the term *Geistesgeschichte* is seldom oriented toward the future and most often results in an agnostic, relativistic world view. While conceding to the *Geist* an absolutely determining role, he nonetheless so obscures its function that in the end he seems to view mind or spirit as a totally irrational force. Ultimately, this conception gives rise to a series of expressionistic, existential, or purely nationalistic approaches to literature. It is not difficult to see how little room was left for the historical.

II

When we speak of *Geistesgeschichte* today, we usually mean an autonomous mode of thought that operates in the realm of theoretical speculation and is not subject to empirical criteria, as is history or sociology. In support of this definition scholars usually point to the fact that it is primarily such words as "being," "essence," and "cultural dynamics" that predominate in the writings of those who used this approach. These terms betray a distinct tendency toward categorization, a proclivity that reflects both the strengths and weaknesses of this method. While generalizations can help to bring order into a period, in practice the typologies set up by the literary scholars using the methods of *Geistesgeschichte* were often so far removed from the concrete that the works being examined seemed to dissolve into abstractions. It is therefore not surprising that in the wake of Dilthey's theories, neither the purely formal approach nor the empirical enjoyed particular popularity. Most literary scholars of the 1920s were determined to discover those characteristics essential to a given period, work, or artist which, in all likelihood, they could as easily have gleaned from relevant philosophical, political or aesthetic documents.

Dilthey, who was the revered model of the literary scholars using this approach, was remarkably familiar with the details of history; however, a distinct dwindling of historical awareness and a tendency to disregard the abundance of historical material is observable in his followers. For this reason, while most of the treatises of this movement appear to be rather comprehensive, they actually ignore the material basis and noticeably restrict themselves to generalities. The concept of *Geist* employed by the representatives of *Geistesgeschichte* around 1920 was completely devoid of social and historical connections; it more closely resembled Kant's philosophy than the universality of Hegel.

In spite of slogans such as "principal substance," "power of being," and "world concept," which would seem to indicate a branching out into all the spheres of time and space, the writings of these scholars leave one with a peculiar feeling of emptiness. But with an orientation so hostile to material reality, it is difficult to avoid such conceptual reductions. Precisely because of this constant yearning for the ultimate, true "totality" is never achieved. For the more one attempts to embrace the world with abstract constructions, the more the world, in the sense of empirically graspable reality, slips away. Such attempts to transcend the historical by means of the spiritual can only in the rarest cases lead to a genuine philosophical penetration of a given material that could in any way claim to be universal. Almost always the word *Geist* is used to connote a mystic spirit associated with Dilthey's *Lebensphilosophie* rather than with the perceivable and rational.

Here are several examples: As early as 1914, Julius Petersen, a leading literary scholar of his time, leaning on Dilthey, insisted that in the interpretation of literature scholars should make substantially closer connections between "poetry and the philosophy of its creator."[1] The goal of unity seemed to him possible only under the guidance of philosophy. Therefore, in a major study of German romanticism, he called literary history a "progressive universal science," whose highest purpose should be the creation of a synthesizing concept of unity.[2]

Similar assertions are found in the work of Rudolf Unger, who was the first to use the phrase "history of problems" to describe this broad synthetic approach aiming at totality. He too based his thinking on Dilthey, but bringing in the discipline of intellectual history he tried to overcome Dilthey's emphasis on intuition by relying on what was verifiable. In this way, he hoped to move toward a "true phenomenology of the problems of life."[3] Using almost identical words, Emil

Ermatinger, in his book *The Literary Work of Art* (1921), favors an approach to literature that is "philosophically reflective," in which the literary scholar would attain a truly empathic understanding of the spirit of the work, instead of allowing himself to act as the "lackey of the material" which had been in complete control in the era of positivism.[4] In brusque refutation of the methods of history and the natural sciences, Ermatinger was concerned most of all with the process of artistic creation. At times, however, he was carried away and ended up with exaggerated formulations, which equated the artist's inner life with the sublime goals of some world soul or spirit.

We find similar assertions in the work of Fritz Strich who, in these same years, believed it was the highest task of literary scholarship "to grasp the eternal substance of mankind, which wanders timelessly through the ages."[5] Oskar Walzel also subscribed to the idea of totality when he asserted, "The work of art can only be experienced as a whole; it can never be grasped conceptually."[6] Some scholars insisted on a "history of the development of the human mind,"[7] which would receive its main impetus from the realms of philosophy and religion, while others designated the poetic as the "symbol of the deepest spirit" of an epoch, because it was only there that the "eternal" and the "eternally valid" manifested themselves.[8]

Such a "spiritualizing" of literary scholarship was bound to lead increasingly to a neglect of all empirical elements. Thus by 1920 the single work of art had retreated to the background, yielding to larger units, such as certain clusters of ideas or characteristics that linked epochs to one another. Most literary scholars were weary of positivistic details and were eager for greater tasks as, for instance, the study of whole epochs, or philosophical analyses of such elemental life experiences as love and death. In the enthusiasm for broader connections, specific facts and circumstances were rejected as a valid basis for interpretation.

As had been true in an earlier period of German idealism in the eighteenth century, art and culture were now viewed as pure emanations of the human spirit or of life itself, arising from the artist's deepest urge for self-expression. The biographical approach of the positivists was thus more and more shunted aside and replaced by the idea of curves of development which encompassed entire cultures and were conceived of as being entirely autonomous. In the framework of this approach, the word literature, when used by scholars, always meant something creative, self-generated, something that emanated from the artist's deepest spiritual impulse and thus would not allow itself to be explained by any historical, sociological, economic, political or, in the broadest sense, empirically verifiable factors.

Inevitably, this led to remarkable contradictions. On the one hand, the free decision of the great individual, who created only out of his own soul, was held up as the ideal. On the other hand, there was a growing inclination to think in terms of larger contexts, i.e., entire epochs, which led to a conspicuous accentuation of all suprapersonal elements. But this contradiction is easily resolved when we recognize that the same intention informs both tendencies. In the one as well as the other, scholars were trying to move away from empiricism, either by emphasizing the self-determination of the great single individual, or by interpreting culture as a suprapersonal emanation of the human spirit that follows the rhythm of some inexplicable universal law. For the former, the model was Friedrich Gundolf's *Goethe* (1917); the latter is best represented by Fritz Strich's *Classicism and Romanticism* (1922).

Thus, when literary scholars spoke of epochs in the frame of *Geistesgeschichte* in the 1920s, what they had in mind were descriptive labels rather than historical categories. These scholars primarily borrowed such concepts of style, developed by art history, as gothic, baroque, rococo, Biedermeier,* impressionism, or expressionism, which they then tried to apply to literature, thereby exemplifying what Walzel termed the

---

* A term designating the conservative in literature and art during the Restoration period in Germany (1815–48).

"mutual illumination of the arts." It almost seems as if Jean Paul were thinking of this epoch when, in 1800, he asserted in his *Aesthetic Primer*, "No creature loves to classify as much as man, particularly the German."[9] Most scholars of this school proceeded deductively and settled for the concept of epoch, or, on the basis of a few arbitrarily chosen examples, they tried to intuit the particular "spirit of the times." Even in those fields where scholars were overwhelmed by a mass of concrete detail, they proceeded to look for fundamental conceptions and believed that they had found the decisive general characteristic of a particular epoch when they could point to two or three examples.

The research in romanticism in the 1920s is particularly instructive, for the idea of the romantic was so broadly conceived and allowed itself to be applied in so many different areas that the term quickly became a meaningless label. But the situation was no better in the other spheres of investigation in literary history. Instead of first drawing upon as much material as possible and only then advancing to a particular conclusion concerning a given epoch, literary scholars were satisfied to work with purely abstract conceptions, which all too often turned out to be clichés. One need think only of such equations as baroque = unfettered subjectivism; classicism = perfection; romanticism = infinity; Biedermeier = resignation.

One of the most prominent representatives using this approach, Hermann August Korff, in his multivolume work, *The Spirit of Goethe's Age* (1923–40), viewed classicism simply as a synthesis of rationalism (Enlightenment) and irrationalism (Storm and Stress)* which occurred entirely in the realm of *Geist*. Thus, while Korff must be credited for his contribution in the area of textual interpretation, it should also be said that he totally ignored the historical dimension precisely because his vision was dominated by a completely abstract world view.

---

* The period known in German as *Sturm und Drang*, designating the revolutionary spirit in German literature of the 1770s and early 1780s. Its main proponents are the young Goethe, the young Schiller, Klinger, Lenz, and a host of lesser-known writers.

It is obvious that such restriction to the realm of ideas is as questionable as the positive overvaluation of facts. While in the one, material factors are determining, in the other, abstractions dominate.

III

One of the most problematic attempts to order the basic human impulse toward self-expression proved to be the approach of structural psychology in the early 1920s. The attempt to subject the aesthetic to a psychological typology was not in itself new, having had a series of impressive predecessors. Schiller had tried it with the naive and sentimental, Nietzsche with the Apollonian and Dionysian. What distinguishes the situation around 1920 is thus only the sheer number of the efforts and the audacity of the constructions.

The main impetus for this approach came from the psychology of character, of culture, and of nation. In this connection, Wilhelm Dilthey must again be mentioned first. Stimulated by his effort to distinguish between materialists and two kinds of idealists, a series of typologies were established: while some scholars perceived a basic duality between soul and spirit and such polarities as male-female and stasis-motion, others saw a division between "open" and "closed" forms of life and between positivists and metaphysicists.[10]

There were those who tried to classify all artists according to their physical postures; Ernst Kretschmer, for example, in *Body Structure and Character* (1921), differentiated between pyknics, leptosomes, and athletic types, which literary scholars interpreted as the distinction between realists, romanticists, and classicists. One psychologist drew up a five-part classification in which artists were divided into sensory, motor, imaginative, reflective, and emotional types. Eduard Wechssler's *Esprit and Geist* (1927), which bore the subtitle, "The Essence of the French and German," attempted to establish a psychology of national types. Relying on the old cliché, he portrayed the

French as nervous, irritable, sensual, effeminate and impressionable, while the Germans are described as sentimental, abstract, introspective and asocial. In the area of cultural morphology, we have Oswald Spengler's familiar *Decline of the West* (1918–22), in which he distinguishes between three basic types: the classical-Apollonian, Arab-magical, and western-Faustian, whose prime cultural symbols are, respectively, the body, the cave, and infinite space.

A similar tendency toward the creation of types is observable in the art history of these years. As early as 1908, Herman Nohl applied Dilthey's three-part division to painting and concluded that Velazquez was a realist, Rembrandt an objective idealist, and Michelangelo a subjective idealist. He further associated these divisions with a naive type infatuated with the sensual, an energetic type who moves directly toward his goal, and a sentimental type who uses only indirect means. From this, it becomes clear that Schiller also influenced this trend. In the attempt to do justice to form as well as content, artists were divided into those who emphasized form and those who emphasized color; painters and sculptors were separated into ideoplasts and physioplasts. Still others tried to define the contrast between classic-harmonic and gothic-expressive; in so doing, they made use of the art historian Heinrich Wölfflin's differentiation between renaissance and baroque. Gothic was defined as willful, expressive, ecstatic, in contrast to the classic eternal Greek spirit, which was supposedly well-balanced, serene, and bound to tradition. Others in this same group distinguished between oriental, gothic, and classical types, and on the basis of these divisions, tried to derive some universal principle which would encompass the entire artistic development of man.

In the realm of literary scholarship, this penchant for typologies is best exemplified by the work of Oskar Walzel who, after Dilthey, is one of the most important representatives of *Geistesgeschichte*. By setting up a triadic division, Walzel tried to reduce the profusion of the material to a few basic types. Like Dilthey's, his scheme differentiates between three basic world

views: the classical renaissance type who emphasized form;
the German gothic who was primarily concerned with the
contents; and the German organic type who, like Goethe, inclined toward a well-balanced synthesis of form and content.
Strich's well-known division between classic and romantic
rests upon a similar typology that combined Wölfflin's attention to form with Dilthey's emphasis on contents. The
extremes of this approach are best demonstrated by the hazy
abstractions of Herbert Cysarz who, in his *Literary History
as Geistesgeschichte* (1926), differentiates between spatial-ab-
stract and time-bound poets.

In addition to these pairs or triads, we also find in the
literary scholarship of these years a number of typologies
based on geography, nationality, or psychology of style, which
were held up as eternal types of the human spirit. Thus
scholars postulated a "man of the middle ages" a "baroque
man," an "expressionist" mind as if there really were eternally
recurring spiritual or psychological types that could transcend
their specific place in history and could thus be used in the
realm of structural psychology. This also applies to the stereo-
types of phylogeny, such as the image of the Prussian or the
Austrian, and especially the exaggerated racial types created
by Josef Nadler in his *Literary History of German Tribes and
Regions* (1912–18). Here we are dealing with types that even
in principle, let alone in reality, are so unreal that they necessarily lose their firm contours and ultimately become entirely
meaningless.

IV

One inevitable result of this tendency toward the creation of
types was the setting up of laws intended to encompass the
entire history of art and culture; these laws, it was believed,
recurred rhythmically in some organic sequence. As was true
for most of the studies in *Geistesgeschichte*, scholars leaned
on German idealism and drew their models primarily from the

work of Herder, Schiller, Hegel, and especially from Goethe's conception of the "epochs of the human spirit," which he described in a series of adjectives: theologically-sacred, humanized-universal, mechanistic, and finally, chaotic. Judgments that were still considered objective in Goethe's time moved, around 1900, into the realm of pure speculation; not even the wildest hypotheses were rejected in the effort to establish a new wholeness and to discover laws governing the human spirit. Scholars were careful, however, to remain entirely in the realm of the spirit and never to descend to the material level.

Once again, by far the most impressive example of this approach is offered by Dilthey, whose ideal constructions concerning the styles of art already showed the beginnings of an all-inclusive systematization which conceived of the growth and decline of cultures as biological phases of an organic development of mankind. What had been understood by Hegel as the universal history of the human spirit was here reduced to a *Geistesgeschichte* whose only goal was the abstract periodization of all artistic and intellectual phenomena. In these years, a similar shift from the study of concrete details to a search for eternal laws governing the whole history of culture is observable in all the humanities. The several different world views which, for Dilthey, still rested primarily on the individual artist's temperament, were ever more strongly systematized by his disciples.

Richard Hamann's *Impressionism in Life and Art* (1907), which clearly aims at cultural morphology, is a good example. Instead of concerning himself with the historical place of individual works, as was usual in the era of positivism, Hamann concentrates primarily on the study of entire cultures. He sees these as developing in organically predetermined cycles. For him, impressionism is a regularly recurring phase of development that can be seen in all aging cultures. The ultimate goal of his research is the establishing of an ordered "series of styles." The "philosophic pleasure of surveying," not the digging out of plentiful data, is Hamann's "ideal of scholarship";

it is his aim to forge a "formula for the entire history of mankind" that would give a broad perspective even to the merest detail. It is therefore not surprising that his last chapter ends with the terse demand, "More Hegel!"[11]

The following era is dominated by exaggerated expressionistic constructions. The most important work in this mode is Oswald Spengler's aforementioned *Decline of the West* which, in effect, is an eclectic summation of all the neoidealistic and expressionistic tendencies that had developed since the turn of the century. Spengler transforms the traditional division of antiquity, the middle ages, and the modern age, into a series of "morphological relations," which he tries to substantiate in terms of biology as well as *Geistesgeschichte*.[12] In this, his chief slogan is "organic," by which he means the inner growth continuum of a particular culture, which is not affected by material factors. Spengler so completely removed details from their historical context that all empirical data were easily assigned to the blurred categories of *Geistesgeschichte*. On the basis of the psychological types (Egyptian, Apollonian, magical, Faustian), Spengler postulates a regular succession within each of four cultures (Egyptian, Classical, Arabic, and Western), which all declined and became "insubstanital, trivial civilizations" after an initial period of blossoming. Spengler claims to have observed this phenomenon of growth and decline in cultures as diverse as the Egyptians at the time of the Hyksos, the Greeks in the Corinthian age, the Arabs under the Abbasides, and the West in the period of Biedermeier. In his analysis, the term gothic is always used to describe the beginnings, the term baroque, the endings of cultural cycles.

An example that best demonstrates the seductiveness of Spengler's thesis is Herbert Krauss's book, *The Laws of the Waves of History* (1929). As in Spengler's system, here too the continuous ups-and-downs of cultural momentum predominate. The resulting wavelike motion is interpreted, on the one hand, as "the rhythmic working out of biophysical powers," while on the other, it is based on the principles of "plastic-painterly" set up by the art historians Riegl and

Wölfflin. On the basis of these theories, Krauss comes to the conclusion that four waves course through every culture: the romantic wave, which is the primary impulse, then the main wave (realism), the mature wave (baroque), and last, a transitional wave. By this scheme Krauss means to suggest that this fluctuation is guided by a natural law reminiscent of the periodicity of the female sexual cycle.[13] Other scholars followed suit and equated Egyptian, Greek, and Western civilizations with symbolic, naturalistic, and idealistic tendencies. Each of these cultural organisms was granted a period of 2,100 years, which were predicted according to carefully plotted isochronal tables.[14] In contrast, yet others—more modestly—were satisfied with rhythmically recurring cycles of one hundred, two hundred, or three hundred years.

Art history's attempts at periodization proved to be as influential as the organizing principles of cultural morphology. In this area, scholars usually began with formal principles by means of which, like Wölfflin in his *Basic Principles of Art History* (1915), they tried to prove the existence of a continuously alternating succession of open and closed, plastic and painterly, multiple and singular styles, or primitive, archaic, and classical forms of expression. In this vein, others stressed the fluctuation between surface and depth, haptically and visually oriented periods, or successive and simultaneous spatial perceptions. The eminent art historian Erwin Panofsky distinguished between the "morphous" and the "amorphous."[15] Such theories were often extended into vast systems, and described in books that bore such titles as *The Sculptural and the Spatial as Basic Principles of the Artistic*.[16]

In these years, similar tendencies can be observed in musicology. Thus Hans Mersmann, in his essay "The History of Styles in Music," which appeared in 1921 in the *Yearbook of Peter's Music Library*, tries to subject the nine epochal styles in the history of Western music to a strict regular rhythm, which leaned on Wölfflin's pairs of categories. He concluded that the numbers 1 (Gregorian), 3 (Ars Nova), 5 (Renaissance), 7 (Viennese Classicism), and 9 (The Schönberg circle), largely use linear-closed form, while the numbers 2 (Meistersinger), 4 (Gothic polyphony), 6 (Baroque), and 8 (Romantic) tend more toward the open-pictorial.

In literary scholarship this tendency toward mathematical periodization did not have such crude results, although scholars did not wish to be outdone by Wölfflin or Spengler. Oskar Walzel, in *German Literature Since the Death of Goethe* (1918), viewed the single epochs of the nineteenth and early twentieth century as a series composed of objective idealism (the period of Goethe), materialism (literary realism), and finally, subjective idealism (expressionism), which largely correspond to the three kinds of world views suggested by Dilthey. In his creation of epochs, Fritz Strich also reaches back to Wölfflin. He speaks of "basic conceptual principles" that rest on the "eternal polarity" of classic and romantic styles leading to a conspicuous duration in flux.[17] By far the most sweeping attempt to create a thorough phraseology was Arthur Hübscher who viewed all of German literature as a continuous fluctuation of the polarity between mind and soul and their eventual "fusion into harmony." In considering the laws of periodization, Hübscher arrives at the following divisions: the early and late Middle Ages, the Baroque, Storm and Stress, Romanticism, and Expressionism are epochs characterized by antithesis, while the flowering of Middle High German, the Renaissance, Rationalism, Classicism, and Realism, are especially harmonious. The result is a carefully plotted wave line, similar to Spengler's or Krauss's.[18]

We may well smile at these efforts or dismiss them as antiquated. Either attitude, however, would be not only presumptuous but also false, for many of these insights are quite accurate. There is no doubt that cultures labeled archaic, classic, and baroque form a sequence that cannot readily be reversed, even if this development takes on very different coloration within individual cultures. The danger in these theories lies mainly in the fact that they are repeatedly taken out of their historical contexts and expanded into a universal principle intended to cover the whole history of culture. Within the framework of carefully defined limitations, it would at times be quite appropriate to work with curves of ripening or withering. But if one applies this classification to hundreds, even thousands of years, the whole undertaking immediately becomes absurd.

The reason scholars came up with such astounding theories should not be difficult to determine for anyone sensitive to ideologies: the theory of waves clearly served to mask the marked decline in the belief in progress and the dwindling of historical consciousness within *Geistesgeschichte*. For this reason, scholars accepted either the primacy of "the eternal recurrence of the same," or they made use of mutually exclusive alternatives that continuously swung from one extreme to another. What looks quite comic at first glance, on closer inspection turns out to be deeply ideological, thus exposing just how unidealistic this neoidealism associated with *Geistesgeschichte* really is. For in contrast to the idealism of Goethe's time, which *Geistesgeschichte* so often leans upon, all concepts of progress are here omitted, and so this approach turns to the agnostic and the pessimistic.

So long as scholars cannot find a genuine perspective, they will always succumb to laws of periodization which supplant the principle of a goal-oriented development of the human spirit with that of eternal circularity or an equally senseless shifting between two antithetical poles. For this reason the theory that postulates cultural peaks and valleys, whose early representatives of the 1920s are widely ridiculed, is, in fact, very much alive today. Within the last fifteen years, Gustav René Hocke, in his much-respected book, *The World as Labyrinth* (1959), once again divided the whole of western culture into a regularly fluctuating sequence of styles, classic and manneristic, that follow one another with precision. In his opinion, the former tends toward the natural, the concise and the harmonious, while the latter moves toward complexity, artificiality, and the chaotic. Throughout, Hocke makes amply clear that his sympathy and admiration are with the latter style. In this realm, we hear constantly of noble but skeptical indecision that only takes pleasure from what is in the broadest sense questionable, doubtful, and crisis-oriented. Thus some find the earliest traces of modern art in mannerism, follow it through romanticism, symbolism, art nouveau, and surrealism to the theater of the absurd.

Almost every study of the grotesque, the absurd, the macabre, or the satanic that has appeared since 1945 shows that behind this kind of periodization there lies a conscious ideological approval of antirealism. While in the Eastern bloc the emphasis is more on the periodic fluctuation between revolution and reaction, in the West the tendency, especially in "modern" circles, is to accept Hocke's position, according to which all realism gives way to mannerism, in order to help the abstruse, the complex, the tragi-comic and the deeply ambivalent come into its own.

Chapter Three

NATIONAL, VOLKISH,* AND RACIAL ASPECTS

The scholarship based on German *Geistesgeschichte* was seriously undermined by its strong nationalistic bias. While in theory, scholars using this approach viewed all products of the mind as manifestations of a universal human spirit, in practice, they held that these creative energies were most clearly evident in the domain of specifically German literature and art. In their attempts to go beyond the materialism of the late nineteenth century, scholars committed to *Geistesgeschichte* chose to concern themselves only with those elements which, as one historian so eloquently expressed it, "moved Godlike in the eternal and fecund innermost recesses at the heart of the universe."[1] This elevated language, meant to evoke the "Faustian yearning" of the German soul, shows that in the sphere of

* A hybrid word, derived from the German adjective *völkisch*, that is used by English-language historians. Literally, the word means only "of the people." In Germany, however, prior to the 1930s, the word had been used only by chauvinistic groups. With the advent of Nazism, this emotionally charged term became one of the most widely used words of the Third Reich, celebrating the purity, superiority, and glory of the German people.

Geistesgeschichte even Goethe and Schiller were interpreted in strictly nationalistic terms; literary scholars were increasingly attracted to those literary images that appealed solely to the emotions—the primitive "Earth Mothers" in Goethe's *Faust* or some equally inexplicable "transfigurations of the soul." Such emphasis leads one to question the very assumptions on which *Geistesgeschichte* was based. Whose soul was, in fact, under discussion? Almost always, the German one. No wonder then we find so little mention of humanism, cosmopolitanism, or any other broad perspectives in the writings of this school. Moreover, when any references to previously established period concepts, such as rationalism, do occur, they are almost always meant to be pejorative.

In place of these terms, scholars engaged in *Geistesgeschichte* preferred to use broad categories, such as "The Age of Goethe," or "The German Movement," which are considerably more impressive, though far more vague. As a result of this trend, classicism was ever more strongly associated with non-rational elements, so that ultimately not much of its rational stance remained. At the same time, the word *Geist* was so inflated and increasingly charged with national associations, it virtually came to represent a religious emanation of the Nordic-Germanic spirit. This helps to explain why the concept of *Geistesgeschichte* is in principle untranslatable, and why it has been incorporated as a foreignism into most other languages. Even its closest English equivalent, the phrase "history of ideas," entirely fails to capture the nonrational elements inherent in *Geistesgeschichte*. To trace the development of these nationalistic tendencies, it once again becomes necessary to examine the ideological sources of this approach.

The first symptoms of national emphasis are observable around 1900 when Dilthey's *Lebensphilosophie* was given a marked nationalistic interpretation. The driving force in this direction were the efforts of the bourgeoisie to rebuild from within the crumbling facade of the Wilhelmenian Empire. Rejecting the materialism of the 1880s and 1890s, scholars searched the past for characteristics that could be considered

Germanic "in essence." In this effort, they were drawn not only to philosophical idealism, but also to romanticism, a concept that had played only a subordinate role in the second half of the nineteenth century. It was not until the first decades of the twentieth century that the interest in German romanticism became prominent; its mystical orientation, it was believed, would effectively protect Germany and the "Germanic spirit" from the forces of "Western rationalism" and possible domination by foreign influences. Ultimately, romanticism came to be viewed as the most Germanic of all epochs.

In the realm of the literary scholarship of these years, studies of romanticism by scholars such as Ricarda Huch, Oskar Walzel, and Dilthey were especially influential. Romanticism was almost always associated with metaphysical longing, subjectivity, and a yearning for the Germanic past, which gave it a decidedly nationalistic slant. Formlessness, spirituality, and the search for a religious foundation for all cultural expressions were also considered especially Germanic, while the spirituality of all humankind was thought to manifest itself most clearly in the Nordic-Germanic tradition.

But in the 1920s, the focus shifted somewhat and the romantic yearning for the Germanic past gave way to national-*racial* elements. The new emphasis on race proved to be quite seductive and attracted not only opportunists, but also dedicated scholars into its orbit. In their enthusiasm for national-racial elements, even the latter were soon no longer able to distinguish "manifestations of the Germanic spirit" from simple chauvinism. For example, in 1925 Emil Ermatinger attacked the apolitical aspects of the aesthetic approach to literature and demanded that scholars once again stand in an "active relationship to the national spirit."[2] It seemed to him that modern literature was essentially deficient in spirit and commitment to the "contemporary nation as a whole" that had been very much alive in the Romantic period.[3] A similar pride in the "German movement" informs Paul Kluckhohn's study of the idea of love in German romanticism.[4] This same tendency is even more marked in the work of Rudolf Unger, who concluded

that the most important result of the "great German movement" was the "defeat of enlightenment."[5] In Unger's work,
the human spirit is almost exclusively identified with the
"Germanic."

This merging of national-racial elements with the universal
human spirit brought about a great degree of confusion. The
study of epochs was particularly affected, since the only factor
that now seemed to be in the least important in any work of
art was the eternal Germanic spirit. Oskar Hagen is representative of many others, when he called the "Germanic" a
basic psychic orientation, independent of any political, social,
or historical factors. Furthermore, Hagen associated the Germanic with the unlimited, the synthetic, the transcendental,
the organic, the individual, and the expressive, which, according to his theory, are characteristics present in periods as
diverse as the gothic, baroque, romantic, and expressionistic.[6]
Such ideas were especially prominent in the work of Herbert
Cysarz, who, in 1930, asserted that in the sphere of German
art, everything was so "antichronologically twisted in and
upon itself," it would be senseless to try to derive particular
epochs from it. According to Cysarz, literature was not the
"embodiment of a universal spirit," but the continual "rebirth
of the national spirit." For this reason, he referred to historical
data as "more or less falsified reports concerning mostly un-
reliable speculations of anonymous corporations," whose
epochal categories could only be of interest to "stamp col-
lectors."[7]

From such a perspective, ideas become completely interchangeable in time. Thus, in the late 1920s, one finds frequent
references to the continuity of the Germanic spirit which
was thought to be unaffected by the flow of history. This
attitude paved the way for the nationalization of all concepts
of epoch. But in order to retain some hold on concrete factors,
scholars tried to differentiate between epochs as being "more"
or "less" Germanic. As a result, those characteristics associated with the Renaissance, rationalism, classicism, or realism
were termed "foreign influences," estranging the Germanic

spirit from its "origins." On this basis, one scholar called the Renaissance a "misfortune for Germany";[8] Oswald Spengler also referred to this period disparagingly as an epoch "entirely without depth of ideas."[9] While most scholars rejected rationalism and classicism, they frequently quoted the writers of the Storm and Stress period, and especially the romantics. The exaggerated attention given to national elements and the prevailing aversion to anything that smacked of materialism led literary scholars to ignore the bourgeois realism of the nineteenth century, though some tried to make it respectable by dubbing it "poetic or idealistic realism." On the whole, scholars were interested only in those epochs which stressed romanticism, idealism, the baroque, formlessness, and the transcendental. In short, they favored those eras in which the Germanic spirit was not obscured by any foreign influence and could manifest its own highest potential.

The Gothic was one of the first periods to be affected by the rising emphasis of national elements. This particular era had already been glorified as a genuine expression of the true Germanic spirit in the days of the young Goethe and in the period of Romanticism. But while scholars at that time still maintained some historical perspective, those associated with *Geistesgeschichte* simply ignored the leading role of the French gothic, long recognized as important by art historians, and tried to define the gothic solely on the basis of an abstract idea of "Germanic essence," associated with a Nordic disposition, moving toward the expressive.[10] What had once been a clearly defined historical style was now viewed as a "spiritual intention," a "linear drive upward," or a "mystical transfiguration," comprehensible only from the perspective of *Geistesgeschichte*. Once again Spengler provides a good example, when, in his *Decline of the West* (1918–22), he offers the highly questionable formulation "Viking-Gothic."[11] This tendency becomes frankly pre-fascistic in the work of the art historian Hans Much, who singles out the racial nobility of the gothic yearning for transcendence as the genuine expression of the "higher Teutons."[12] In the field of literary scholarship, the concept of the gothic was influential only in rare cases. When it was used at all, it was meant to refer to the timeless emanation of the old Germanic spirit, which, it was believed, had never completely died out in spite of the negative influence of the Renaissance and Classicism.

The second important focus of this nationalistic approach was the Baroque. Here, literary scholarship was faced with untried territory and therefore tended to lean more on art history. A good example of *Geistesgeschichte* in the realm of the baroque is Wilhelm Hausenstein's *The Spirit of the Baroque* (1920), which identifies baroque elements, defined as "expression at all costs," in the work of Grünewald, Greco, Tintoretto, and Kokoschka.[13] Instead of keeping the historic baroque clearly in mind, Hausenstein simply equates the baroque with ecstatic expressionism, whose main features he identifies as the religious impulse toward the transcendental coupled with a fervent passion for God, culminating in a yearning for new cathedrals. Even Wölfflin, who initially seemed to have a strictly formal orientation, was caught up in the increasingly more emotional interpretation of the baroque, as is demonstrated by the following quotation from his *Basic Principles of Art History* (1915): "Italy always preferred the plane, while the Germanic North was instinctively oriented toward depth."[14] One art historian was so carried away that he spoke of a baroque Rembrandt as the Germanic counterbalance to the "dangers of the renaissance."[15]

Unfortunately, these wild pronouncements were eagerly taken up by literary scholars. Thus, Fritz Strich interpreted the baroque tendency toward the asyndetic piling up of words as *the* basic category of all Teutonic poetry, which later reappeared in German romanticism. For him, the inner form of a work of art is not static, but has an active Germanic quality that is always in the process of "becoming."[16] In similarly vague terms, the baroque was variously characterized as a "spontaneous outburst of deep Nordic feeling," "gothic permeated by the renaissance," "the configuration of feelings which constitute the Germanic,"[17] or "the expressive inten-

sification of the 'I.'"[18] Typical of this orientation is Willi
Flemming's *German Culture in the Period of the Baroque*
(1937), which places an even greater emphasis on the struggle
of the individual and, with what are decidedly fascistic over-
tones, describes baroque elements as "the art of our race."[19]
Even scholars who were considerably more moderate, now
saw in the literature of the seventeenth century the beginning
of that "great irrational" tendency which gave rise not only to
romanticism, but to the "unfettered individualism" of the
modern period.[20]

But of all the epochs, romanticism offered by far the most
fertile ground from which to extract a national identity. As
evidence, we have a comprehensive survey like Julius Petersen's
Defining the Essence of German Romanticism (1926), which
equates modern German literary scholarship with research in
the Romantic. Because Romanticism attempted to synthesize
art, culture, and scholarship, this period became the showpiece
of nationalized *Geistesgeschichte*. The philosophical orientation of *Geistesgeschichte* and its lack of interest in aesthetic
elements is well illustrated by Max Deutschbein's *The Essence
of Romanticism* (1921), in which he differentiates between
intuitive, voluntary, and productive romanticism, while scorn-
ing literary and historical factors.[21] The best example of this
approach is Fritz Strich's *German Classicism and Romanticism*
(1922); here Strich shifts Wölfflin's "basic principles" of art
history to the realm of spiritual prime phenomena or "elemental
experiences," and simply identifies romanticism with the "inner
driving force of German being," reflecting a specifically German distaste for everything rational and formal.[22] A few years
later, Romanticism was referred to as the period in which the
German spirit found its genuine artistic style;[23] it was also
extolled as "our most Nordic movement."[24]

The concept of romanticism thus lost its historical contours
and became equivalent to the Germanic spirit. In his book *A
Thousand Years of German Romanticism* (1924), Joseph
August Lux viewed the gothic, baroque, romantic, and expressionistic as equally important manifestations of the eternal

romantic mode in which the German spirit was most fully realized. In this way, the Germanic and the romantic were used virtually as synonyms. In time it became more and more modish to glorify the romantic as a symbol of the metaphysical, as the basic impulse behind a "Germanic rebirth"[25] associated with music and the irrational. As a result of this development, the research in romanticism of the early 1920s which had been oriented toward *Geistesgeschichte* was turned into a study of the Germanic, betraying a clear affinity for later fascistic tendencies. The actual high point of this trend occurred, of course, in the years after 1933, when, within the framework of so-called "Germanic studies," all the conceptions of *Geistesgeschichte* were subsumed by the idea of the Nordic. What had still been called romantic in 1925 was, after 1933, transformed into a nationalistic concept of totality, in which spirit is so intermingled with racial concepts of blood that it can hardly be discussed in rational terms.

II

In addition to these tendencies associated with *Geistesgeschichte*, other factors also contributed to the formation of a nationalistically oriented literary scholarship. One of the early adumbrations of this movement was the tribalistic approach, which developed as a parallel to interest in regionalism around 1900. This school de-emphasized historical development and placed greater emphasis on regionally determined ethnic constants, which in turn influenced artistic phenomena. This perspective originated with the work of Hippolyte Taine, who in the 1860s and 1870s singled out "milieu" (particularly race and geography) as the single most important factor in all cultures. Because the power of nationality seemed to him so overwhelming, he favored a static point of view emphasizing the organic connection of the writer to his milieu and rejecting all revolutionary tendencies, whereby he revealed the conservative nature of his theories. However, while Taine used positivist methods, the German milieu theorists at the turn of the century were mainly interested in glorifying the national essence, and so rejected Taine's rational, materialist approach. By a shift of emphasis, the milieu theory took on a distinctly national, regional, or tribal coloration; as a result, the French formula *race, moment, milieu* was replaced by the German slogan *Blut und Boden.**

The earliest document showing such national-racial tendencies was August Sauer's much-praised essay of 1907, "Literary History and Folklore." However, it was Sauer's disciple, Josef Nadler, who gained wide attention for this approach with his four volumes of *Literary History of Germanic Tribes and Regions* (1912–18). According to Nadler, there exists not merely a single Germanic spirit but a whole series of Germanic tribes. While Nadler's basic perception of regional differences is no doubt valid, it is almost impossible to define these concretely. In its emphasis on obscure detail, Nadler's literary history is positivistic, but his basic approach remains ahistorical and speculative. Thus, we see that as early as the first decade of the twentieth century there already was a movement that later easily shifted into "volkish" literary scholarship.

A similar tendency is at the heart of what is called "generation theory," a trend which reached its peak in the years between 1925 and 1933. It, too, combines a highly systematic, one might almost say sociological approach, with nonrational elements. In this field, scholars combined statistics with biologically determined national factors. What is of particular interest in this seemingly precise method are the "biological" components. The chief impulse in this direction came from Wilhelm Pinder's work on generation theory, in which he based himself on Nadler, among others, and characterized his own work as biological *Geistesgeschichte*. His most important idea was the hypothesis concerning the "noncontemporaneity of contemporaries," which he explained by the "systematic

---

* Literally, blood and soil. One of the central slogans of the Nazi party, stressing racial purity and closeness to the German soil.

grouping" of birth waves.[26] This aspect of his theory was extremely influential because it challenged the previously defined concepts of epochs, and at the same time pointed to the biological dynamism behind these birth waves.

Leaning on Pinder's wave theory, Julius Petersen also heralds the "series of generations" as the most important "rhythmic pattern of fate," which must be seen as something "ungraspable," as a "spontaneous act of nature."[27] From such a nonrational stance, it was easy to view generation theory from a nationalistic perspective. Thus, one theorist established the purely biological principle of "waves of youth" to correspond to his ideological preference for the youth groups known as the *Wandervögel*.[28] A similar move toward the nationalistic occurred when Günther Gründel singled out the racially inspired waves of youth as the true carriers of culture in whom the world of tomorrow realizes itself. Equally pre-fascistic is Broder Christiansen's differentiation of styles according to generations: D-style (day before yesterday, impressionism), Y-style (yesterday, expressionism), T-style (today, *neue Sachlichkeit**), and F-style (future, volkish).[29]

But, by themselves, none of the movements outlined above would have succeeded in creating a specifically "fascistic" literary scholarship, in spite of their increasingly nationalistic emphasis. What gave the final impetus was a scholarship obsessed by the idea of races, which no longer paid the slightest attention to historical or sociological factors. In this sphere, too, a variety of impulses can be seen as early as 1900.[30] Most influential was the work of Houston Stewart Chamberlain who quite openly fused the dreams of a Germanic noble race with national religious thinking and Nietzsche's will to power, until he created a dilettantish but highly convincing mixture of racial and imperialistic phrases, which singled out the Aryan stock as the decisive ferment of the entire cultural development of humankind. He replaced the concept of a

---

* A movement in the arts, originating in the early 1920s, stressing a new realism, characterized by simplicity, sobriety, and cool distance.

feudal nobility with a nobility of blood, which he then applied to all cultural phenomena. Chamberlain held that history, religion, culture, and the founding of nations were the work of Aryans, while he viewed all other groups as racial bastards responsible for the decline of culture.

On the basis of this theory of race, Chamberlain developed an ideology which claimed the Germanic people as the last legitimate branch of Aryans who had been called by God to rule the world in order to save humankind from complete bastardization. The process by which the Nordic race became the "chosen one" is amplified in his two books, *The Foundations of the Nineteenth Century* (1899) and *Aryan Ideology* (1905). In these, he fully subscribed to the myth of Germanic superiority; however, in spite of its metaphysical tinge, his writing amounted to no more than cheap sloganeering, giving renewed impetus to the old national cry, "Germany First!" Building on these theories, Chamberlain's followers sought a new Aryanism that heralded war as the arena for drawing on unspent racial strength. Out of this complex of ideas there developed an ideology which clearly prefigured fascism, in spite of the philosophical phrasing of its theorists.

Among the better known of Chamberlain's disciples was Willy Pastor, who, in *The World in the Time of Man* (1904), interpreted the entire history of the world as a battle between the Germanic sons of the sun against the dark, aimlessly vegetating cave dwellers of the south. Like Chamberlain, Pastor held that the sum total of all cultural accomplishments were Aryan achievements. He even tried to prove the existence of a superior Nordic caste within Chinese, Egyptian, and Assyrian cultures. According to him, whenever the Germanic master race was absorbed into another culture, the inevitable result is a "chaos of nations" and cultural decline. Scholars of this persuasion came up with rather wild hypotheses. One concluded that the Germanic race was entitled to dominate the world.[31] Another attributed the collapse of Greco-Roman culture to the "racial chaos" of late antiquity that was the inevitable consequence of the leveling of the caste structure.[32]

Yet another attributed all the "creative elements" in Italian art to the influence of the north.

As in Chamberlain's work, here too one finds the hypothesis that every decline of a "higher culture" was due to the "extinction of the blondes," and that only the influx of Germanic giants from the north saved Italy from the chaos which befell Roman culture.[33] Thus we see that a search for Aryanism was well under way as early as 1905. Michelangelo and Raphael were viewed as great-grandsons of the Langobards, the Spanish painters as descendants of the Visigoths. In his book, *Ascending Life* (1910), Willibald Hentschel claims that "in good German" Leonardo da Vinci should be called "Leonhard von Vincke."[34] In the same spirit Buddha and Osiris were given a Saxonian origin[35]; yes, even Christ himself was characterized as an illegitimate Germanic scion, in order to emphasize his divine Nordic decendancy.

As the powers of fascism grew ever stronger toward the end of the 1920s, a fully developed "racial aesthetic" came into existence. It is interesting to note that here one often comes across the names of scholars whose work had already appeared around 1900 or 1910. But while in these early years they had largely been outside the mainstream of serious scholarship, they now were revered as the ideological models of a movement that was becoming increasingly more popular. For example, a man like Ludwig Schemann who had started around 1900 as an unknown follower of the French racist Gobineau, in the years 1928 to 1931, suddenly came out with his major work, *Race in the Humanities*. Previously active regionalists enthusiastically associated themselves with national socialism, and attacked all modern art as racial degeneration.[36] Others posited a racial foundation for all cultural achievements, which, because it had no rational basis, could easily be expanded from the narrower realm of the "volkish" to the more broadly imperialistic.[37] Here we can see that basic tendency of fascism to distract scholarship from concrete facts and to becloud all cultural studies, so they could more easily be used in the service of national socialism.

For this reason, it would be foolish to speak of a really systematic national socialistic "literary scholarship" in the years 1933–1945. Because scholars relied so strongly on nonrational concepts in order to avoid dealing with historical factors, they were incapable of following any principle through to its logical conclusion. Therefore, the specifically "volkish" literary approach of the Nazi era always inclined to the eclectic. It attached itself indiscriminately to the studies of romanticism at the turn of the century, to expressionism, to the typologies of *Geistesgeschichte*, to the Aryan emphasis of races, to "volkish" existentialism, and to the study of regions and tribes. As a result, methodological confusion set in; all approaches based on concrete evidence retreated into the background, and no really new ideas developed in the very era that had been so proud of its revolutionary spirit. Scholars took existing theories and reinterpreted them from a "volkish" or racial perspective.

Good examples of such distortions are provided by the tribally oriented followers of Nadler, "volkish" existentialists like Pongs and Fricke, chauvinistic practitioners of *Geistesgeschichte* like Petersen and Korff, or nationalistic expressionists like Cysarz, whose intellectual development took place in the period around World War I. Even the academic journals of this school which appeared around 1933 and 1934 are not particularly original. Most of what they published was just gibberish, the essence of which was the idea of a new "science of life in a German-organic style," that opposed all "aesthetic-individualistic points of view."[38] Others spoke of a breakthrough to a "Germanic scholarship," in which "heroic idols" and a "strong will to power" would stand in the foreground.[39] In whatever they took up, they dreamed of activism, revolution, and fighting spirit, to which they attached a "biological mysticism of the national character."[40] With great pride, many even claimed to have "prepared in the spiritual realm" what now became reality in "political form."[41] Unfortunately, this was not mere lip service, but corresponded exactly to the facts.

In itself, this situation was bad enough. But how do such

phrases relate to literary methods and scholarship? If one can find any intellectual element in this "volkish" chaos, then it is the strong emphasis that is placed on "biological" components. This is evident in several approaches. By far the least pernicious was the so-called approach of "morphological literary scholarship" propagated by Horst Oppel and Günther Müller, which, in addition to its racist tendencies, still retained numerous ideas inherited from the period of Goethe. Thus, one hears of growth, blooming, and fading, understood by many in purely cyclical, cultural terms, while others used morphology to develop a political expansionist theory based on the principle of the "right of the young nations." Some of these morphologists even became tribe-conscious and set the healthy peasant "stock" of the German people against the degenerate big-city world which, they believed, had been weakened by "Western influences."

Their contempt for city life is reflected in the term "asphalt literature" which they applied to all writings about the city; in it, they felt, Jews and socialists were free to carry on as they pleased. In these morphological studies, references to German heroism abound; the Nibelungs' determination to face destruction rather than to sacrifice a single ounce of "volkish" conviction was applauded. Victory or death was the war cry. Most often, the demonic and the tragic were identified with the essence of the "Germanic." For this reason, the national-socialistic approach to literature becomes most clear when it concerns itself with "racial essence" and brings art into the realm of "blood." Ludwig Büttner's *Ideas for Biological Literary Criticism* (1939) offers a good example of this pseudo-scientific approach that rejects all historical explanation and recognizes only the racial essence of the Nordic as the highest criterion.[42] This conception, which cannot be defined either in psychological or ethnological terms, could be used to prove anything: it clearly mirrors the German people's determination to dominate the world. From this perspective, an ever increasing number of serious literary scholars considered it the "deepest instinct of the Nordic race" to storm "exultantly into the swords of the enemies."[43]

As one might expect, this apparent revolutionizing of German literary scholarship led to an artistic imperialism that tried to usurp everything of value for German art. Following Chamberlain, Germanic art is equated with heroism, organicism, irrationality, intuition, metaphysics, creativity, and aristocracy, while the art of nonGerman nations is denounced as uncivilized, decadent, or degenerate. In this way, after 1933, scholars arrived at a kind of Aryan-hunting that explained everything in terms of the Germanic and extolled the racial superiority of the German nation in the realm of literature and art. In the framework of the earlier *Geistesgeschichte*, German art was specifically associated with the inclination toward exaggerated expressionism, heroic will power, and a "volkishly"-tinged religious inwardness. Now the Germanic was equated with the desire to conquer the world, as reflected in Nordic *Wanderlust*, by which, it was believed, the German people demonstrated their cultural superiority as a creative master race.

In this connection, one could mention numerous scholars who adhered to established epochal concepts in discussing literature up to the middle of the nineteenth century, but were only interested in proving the superiority of the German race in the later periods.[44] Because these scholars were primarily interested in affirming the "German rebirth" and the "regeneration of the race," their work moves away from all scholarly conceptions and toward political imperialism. Instead of contributing to the "chronicling of history," they were interested only in what Herbert Cysarz once admiringly called the "eternal rebirth" of the "German spirit."[45] Ultimately, that "study of things German"[46] so popular in these years, was at once amorphous and imperialistic; therefore it would probably be best not to classify these works as literary scholarship at all, but to view them simply as examples of a "volkish" journalism that conformed all too willingly to the party line of the day.

Chapter Four

THE INFLUENCE OF PSYCHOANALYSIS

I

Not surprisingly, the psychoanalytic approach to literature also developed in the crucial years around 1900. While the roots of psychoanalysis go back to late nineteenth-century positivism, the discipline also bears the imprint of Dilthey's *Lebensphilosophie*. The psychoanalytic tendency to rely on the principle of cause and effect to explain all psychological phenomena is particularly positivistic. In examining the figure of the artist, literary scholars made use of psychoanalytic studies like Cesare Lombroso's *Madness and Genius* (1864) and Max Nordau's *Degeneration* (1892), which had radically challenged the idealized portrait of the artist established in the classical-romantic era. According to Lombroso and Nordau, artistic talent was the result of physical or emotional disequilibrium; even the most successful artists were neurotics, paranoids, or manic-depressives. By the 1880s, the concept of genius had been thoroughly debunked, and even the most "divine" inspiration was attributed to such factors as elevated pressure in the brain, mental aberration, or sexual perversion. In short, the artist was no longer an inspired "Olympian," but only a borderline case, a bohemian ruined by heredity or environment, a spiritual pretender.[1]

In keeping with these theories, a school of psychiatry that concerned itself primarily with erotic abnormalities arose in Germany. Its principles were based on Krafft-Ebing's *Psychopathia Sexualis* (1886); its chief advocate was Paul Möbius who produced a series of pathological studies of such outstanding figures as *Rousseau* (1889), and *Nietzsche* (1902). According to Möbius, neither reason nor emotional disposition were especially important to creativity. He viewed all human expression as a manifestation of unsatisfied libido, in which the subconscious is the determining factor. Clearly, this is the period in which decadence is held in high esteem and the myth of the "sick artist" takes hold in the imagination of the public. Is it possible to conceive of Rilke without his migraines? Oscar Wilde without homoeroticism? Hanno Buddenbrooks without his attraction to death? Because of the neoromantic predilection for dreams, phantasies, and the imagination, this movement proved to be extremely important to the development of psychoanalysis; symbolism and art nouveau, with their emphasis on nonrational elements, were similarly influential.

Although Dilthey's conception of the poetic was largely based on his theory of "life-forces," that is, on biologically determined elements, in contrast to the conceptions of psychiatrists like Möbius, he had no intention at all of debunking the artistic impulse. Through the lens of *Lebensphilosophie*, Dilthey viewed art as a spontaneous primal experience, related to spiritual as well as material factors. Nonetheless, he relied rather heavily on physiological elements, a tendency already observable in the work of Nietzsche, who remarked that it was always the "chaste stallions" who were the best "neighers." Ultimately, Dilthey's *Lebensphilosophie* led to a contradictory view of art, which, on the one hand, attributed to art a godlike power, but, on the other, devaluated its spirituality. In his essay on "Poetic Imagination and Madness" (1886), Dilthey linked the poetic imagination with neurotic daydreams, thus building on the old Platonic dictum, "There is no great genius without a touch of madness." Following Dilthey, others went even further and equated art with dreams, impulses, and suppressed erotic emotions, especially with the yearning to reproduce, which, if not granted, was fulfilled only by art.[2]

Such ideas lead directly into the writings of Freud, whose early work can only be understood in the context of this background. For while Freud polemicized against positivism and Dilthey's *Lebensphilosophie*, his own exalted interpretation of the aesthetic principle, which he viewed as an indispensable psychic phenomenon, makes sense only in the light of these earlier theories. Freud opposed any overly idealistic conceptions of art or the artist; nonetheless, he believed that artistic perfection always involved a spark of genius. He rejected the narrow-minded positivism that concerned itself only with principles of cause and effect, but was fascinated by the apparently inexhaustible ability of the human mind to sublimate the unfulfilled desires of life by means of the rich experiences of art. For this reason, Freud not only studied what art consciously expressed, but also searched for its hidden meaning, which, be believed, revealed the suppressed sexual urges of the artist. He begins positivistically by emphasizing the "imagined satisfaction" that the work offers to the creator and the receiver, both of whom are trying to compensate for their sexual deprivation by means of art.[3]

Freud first presents this theory in the essay, "The Poet and Daydreaming" (1907), in which he compares the artist to a child whose thoughts often shift from reality to phantasy; in Freud's view, the artist, like the child, takes both equally seriously. But while the child openly admits his curiosity and readily gives in to daydreams, the adult is no longer able to follow the pleasure principle unselfconsciously, and therefore releases phantasies only in created form, as "art." In contrast to the so-called "average person," who conforms to reality and is able to find satisfaction in life, the artist continually searches for the fulfillment that reality denies him. For this reason, Freud views all art as surrogate satisfaction, as conscious or unconscious "corrections to a frustrating reality." Freud relates these frustrated desires to the Oedipal conflict, which, he believes, cannot ever be erased from the unconscious. In this connection, Freud writes of the poet, "A strong real-life experience evokes the memory of an earlier one, usually associated with the poet's childhood, which gave rise to the poetic impulse in the first place; poetry allows the new experience as well as the old memory to come to the surface."[4]

By suggesting that poetry provides an escape mechanism for the poet as well as the reader, Freud sharply reduces the spiritual element in poetry, but nonetheless assigns art a relatively important place. Art becomes a kind of therapy in the face of an intolerable reality. According to Freud, only art allows those who are emotionally deprived (in which category he includes all civilized adults), to release their inhibitions and give their imagination free rein. He thus speaks of art as an indispensable blessing and a pleasurable reward which relieves tensions. From this perspective, the aesthetic realm becomes a frontier "between the reality that denies our wishes and the imagination that fulfills them . . . our frustrations disappear like clouds in the beautiful world of illusions."[5] Even destructive or aggressive impulses can, according to Freud, be sublimated and defused by means of art. For this reason, Freud called art a "mild anesthetic."[6]

On the whole, however, he was not overly optimistic about its effectiveness. While he preferred art to religion, in the final analysis he viewed art only as a pleasant diversion, an escape, an opiate. But since Freud saw no other hope, he believed that art was a comfort that answered at least some of our human needs, and to a degree, relieved our frustrations.[7] It thus seemed to Freud that academic work and artistic production were the most rewarding substitutes for the pleasure of the senses—far less dangerous and far more reliable. Furthermore, he recognized that such productivity was not only socially sanctioned, but often even rewarded by fame and fortune. On this basis, Freud suggested that it would be foolish *not* to restrict oneself to artistic or professional activity, a mode of life that Schopenhauer had already recommended many years before.

On the whole, Freud's conception of art remained fairly fluid, but in the years after 1900, when scholars were eager for ideologies, it was extended to its logical extreme and rigidly systematized. In his book *The Artist: Attempts at a Sexual Psychology* (1907), Otto Rank schematized Freudian thinking. For him, art was like the dream: simply an unconscious expression of suppressed sexuality, which entered a kind of "psychic compromise" with our consciousness. Rank equates the artist with the neurotic who throughout his life is fixated in a condition of infantile sexuality because of his early Oedipal ties to the mother.[8] In his voluminous study of the *Incest Motif in Poetry and Myth: Basic Principles of a Psychology of Poetic Creation* (1912), Rank attributed poetic power to an unresolved infantile conflict, thereby singling out incest as the basis of the aesthetic impulse. Rank repeatedly insists that there is no essential difference between the creation of poetry and the imaginary acting out of incestuous feelings, and he supports this assertion by listing hundreds, if not thousands, of examples. Literature is thus merely the end product of the unconscious suppression of incestuous impulses.

Rank asserts that in trying to free himself from guilt feelings, the poet ultimately retreats into the imagination and produces art. For the individual with a strong sex drive, art provides the only means of resolving the conflict between the restraints of culture and his own primitive urges. The real artist succeeds in holding at bay the powerful demands of his libido by escaping into the voluptuous phantasy of wish fulfillment.[9] Poetry is thereby defined by Rank in purely psychological terms that close off alternate modes of interpretation.

A similar one-sidedness governs Wilhelm Stekel's *Poetry and Neurosis* (1909), except that in his work it is not incest, but neurosis that is assumed to be the basic impulse underlying artistic creation. Stekel writes dogmatically, "All artistic creation stems from a single source: the unconscious; neurosis is the goddess who gives artists the talent to express their suffering." But in contrast to Nordau and Möbius, Stekel never views neurosis as degeneration. He, too, considers the poet spiritually abnormal, but he does not see him as mentally ill. The early Stekel, however, proves to be an orthodox Freudian in that he describes poets as eternal children who love to expose themselves by means of literary confession. Like Freud and all later psychoanalysts, Stekel is convinced that only the deepest personal conflicts "press the pen into the poet's hands," enabling him to sublimate his desires and thereby to free himself from his problems and complexes. For Stekel, then, the creation of poetry is a "healing process by means of self-analysis," which at first glance appears to be entirely private.

However, since Stekel usually links the individual neurosis to some "universal" problem common to everyone, he finds this view of the creative process particularly representative.[10] Because he insists on a single source of art, all material aspects, such as political, socio-economic, historical, religious, or general intellectual factors become completely irrelevant. The logical consequences of this approach can be seen in the work of Hanns Sachs, who, in collaboration with Otto Rank, considered aesthetic pleasure to be completely separated from the world of action. They deemed this particularly applicable in the case of tendentious works, where the reader is in danger of becoming overly engaged and thus obstructed from free flights of the imagination. They suggest that "only those who completely lose themselves in a work of art can feel its deepest effects, and for this reason it is absolutely essential to turn away from the goals of the present."[11]

In spite of the many modifications to which it was subject, this concept changed but little during the next ten years. In spite of all the emphasis given to the psychology of the individual, psychoanalytically oriented scholars inevitably end up with the same explanations of art: fear of castration, the Oedipus or Electra complex—that is, with a small, easily summarized set of motives, which transform even the most complex works of literature into variations of eternal sameness. According to these scholars, God is always a projection of the father, the young hero is usually identified with the spiritually confused Oedipus, and all natural phenomena, particularly if they involve caves and wells, point to the mother. Some even go further and see primitive sexual symbols in all convex or concave forms, as if there were only phallic or vaginal motifs against which even the constant censorship of the superego is powerless.

But this approach also has some advantages which should not be overlooked. Ultimately, psychoanalysis gave rise to a new view of the dynamics of human psychology. Through Freud we became aware of the constant battle in the human psyche between the id and the superego. Since Freud, human drives have played an increasingly central role in the interpretation of literature. The same can be said for Freud's theory of artistic sublimation, which provides the basis for his aesthetic perceptions. Freud's work was instrumental in supplanting the false idealism associated with the concepts of neoromanticism and *Geistesgeschichte*. Since the "imago" was formulated, who would still speak of the muse or divine inspiration?[12] The interpretations of Ernest Jones, Marie Bonaparte, Saul Rosenzweig, Geoffrey Gorer, Simon O. Lesser, K. R. Eissler, and not least, Freud himself, are representative of the stimulating conclusions offered by this approach. Unfortunately, however, even the best works using this method, such as Edmund Wilson's brilliant study, *The Wound and the Bow* (1941), always associate the artistic impulse with morbid or neurotic elements, which can only be explained by the infantile complexes of the particular writer under discussion.

Therefore, quite early in the development of the psychoanalytic approach to literature, a number of voices spoke out against this interpretive *tour de force*. Many found it simply absurd to search for Oedipal connections in every artist. Such criticism came primarily from the camps of the formalists, who quickly saw that indiscriminate reliance on biographical data ultimately jeopardized the very idea of poetic creativity itself. What room did the psychoanalytic approach leave for elements of form, genre, or linguistics? Did this method not violate the sanctity of the aesthetic elements? Formalist critics were particularly provoked by the fact that Freud viewed the formal aspects of a work of art only as an appetite-whetter. As a result, they associated Freudianism with positivism and rejected its overly scientific approach to the most sublime expressions of humankind. If poetry were only a "substitute satisfaction," they argued, one could just as well read clinical records. Even Walter Muschg, who sympathized with some aspects of the psychoanalytic approach, wrote in 1930: "Not the completed work, but the hidden how and why of its creation attracts Freud. The less perfect a work of literature is, the more it attracts him. . . . For this reason, it is fragments, or unsuccessful first drafts that he examines most closely. Whenever he sees unquestionable perfection in a work of art, he passes over it, as if it did not exist, because its artistic quality does not touch him deeply. Only the role of the unconscious fascinates him. . . . He is not interested in individual works of art, but in the creation of literature in general."[13]

For these reasons, most literary scholars rejected psychoanalysis, particularly in Germany, where, after 1933, Freudianism was denounced as "semitic filth." But even in Anglo-Saxon countries, which had originally been receptive to Freudianism, the formalistic attack on psychoanalysis grew much stronger in the 1940s and 1950s. In his 1953 essay "On Artistic Production," Frederick J. Hacker writes, concerning psychoanalytically oriented literary scholarship in the United States, "Our science has clarified everything concerning art but art itself."[14] From the viewpoint of "new criticism," psychoanalysis lacked respect and understanding for the formal aspects of literature, its linguistic structure, and particularly its "poetic" elements. Even some Freudian critics objected when literature was interpreted in purely psychological terms and no attention given to literary values or questions of aesthetics.

But Freudianism cannot properly be attacked by the simple question: what became of art as art? Rather, one should ask, what has happened to the material and historical factors which influence the production of art? To confine oneself to archaic, basic situations like the Oedipus complex simply does not do justice to the diversity and complexity of modern industrial society. We no longer live in primitive tribes, and even in the earliest phases of our childhood we are subjected to a variety of influences. Overemphasis of primal experiences presupposes mechanical repetition of human history, a position all scholars should certainly have abandoned as the result of our deepened understanding of history over the last two hundred years.

The ahistorical infantile Oedipus complex is not the only impulse in this world. There is also a history of the human mind in which even the concept of "neurosis" has its specific place. The same applies to Freud's theory of the social alienation of the artist, which accurately mirrors the cultural situation around 1900. All the poets Freud analyzes resemble his contemporaries at the turn of the century, the symbolists, neoromanticists, or art nouveau artists, who wished to flee reality and had taken as their motto "back to nature, back to utopian wish-fulfillment." For these same reasons Freud speaks of the "narcotic" function of art, which releases us from the restriction of harsh reality. But is this all that art can do? Can it not also relieve our suffering by making us more fully aware, awakening our zeal for life, calling us to action?

This, then, must be our point of departure if we are to criticize Freudianism. Because psychoanalytic scholarship is totally ahistorical, it does not advocate change, but only adaptation to the status quo. Freud himself was fully aware of this problem. In *Civilization and Its Discontents* (1930), he once spoke of art as an opiate, which "under some circumstances" is guilty of draining off "great sums of energy that could better be used to ameliorate the human condition." Nonetheless, he radically rejects the possibility of an ideal state. He is convinced that nature with its "unequal distribution of physical and mental attributes is very unjust."[15] Freud repeatedly recommends coming to terms with the unalterable, using the illusory world of art as a hypnotic intoxication. The one thing that particularly recommends art to Freud is its capacity to take us into the world of dreams and erotic phantasies. No wonder Brecht obliquely slapped at Freud in his attack on "culinary" art forms like the opera: "The illusions [of opera] have a socially significant function. The intoxication is indispensable; nothing can replace it. Nowhere, if not in the opera, does a human being have the opportunity to remain human."[16]

II

Considering the idealistic orientation of *Geistesgeschichte*, it is not at all surprising that in the 1920s this literary school responded to Freudianism with open scorn. However, *Geistesgeschichte* was receptive to the psychological approach of Carl Gustav Jung, whose work represents a kind of "science of the soul," emphasizing the creative, the spiritual, and the irrational. For this reason, it was Jung not Freud, who was invited to contribute the essay on "Psychology and Poetry," to Emil Ermatinger's *Philosophy of Literary Scholarship* (1930), by far the most impressive demonstration of the approach of *Geistesgeschichte*. In this essay, Jung rejects psychological determinism as the source of poetic creation in favor of the idea of an "inspirational vision" resting on "primal experiences." For him, poetry is not a secondary, channeled response reflecting contemporary historical forces, but a primary impulse, expressive of an "unknown being," that manifests itself in the images of myths. When discussing this prime source of creativity, Jung uses his concept of the "collective unconscious," which is the great reservoir of all archetypes and thus far surpasses the here and now. In order to avoid the banality of the present, the poet must always be a "seer" drawing his inspiration directly from the collective unconscious. Only in so doing can the poet's images be symbols based on archetypes. Thus Jung closes his essay programmatically, "The secret of creativity and the effectiveness of art lies in our reversion to the original state of the *participation mystique*."[17]

Some aspects of this theory are comparable to the work of Freud, particularly Jung's emphasis on the unconscious and primal experiences, except that Jung did not view sexuality as the only determining factor; his idea of the "collective unconscious" also includes purely mythical, religious, and even generic elements. For example, his primal experiences are based on a whole constellation of irrational impulses that surface concretely for the first time in prehistorical myths. Jung separates art quite sharply from scholarship. Instead of seeking rational meaning in art, we should rather be "captivated by its images, signs, and symbols," in order to maintain contact with the "living secret" of life. Jung's approach thus limits itself primarily to a single question: "To which impulse in the collective unconscious can the image developed in a given work of art be traced?" Jung usually relies on myths in order to answer this question; through these, he believes, not merely the individual, but the voice of all humankind speaks. According to his theory, the creation of literature involves the unconscious translation of the archetype into the language of the present, "whereby it becomes possible for each individual to be in touch once again with the deepest sources of life, which would otherwise remain buried."[18] While Freud wishes to lift the unconscious into the conscious so that the ego can assert itself where previously only the id had ruled, Jung advocates a rebirth of the spirit by submersion into the unconscious.

It is hardly surprising that Jung's theories found their way more quickly into literary scholarship. Freud's exclusive concern with the sexual was seen as a breach of academic etiquette, but Jung's spiritual "flights" in the primitive appealed especially to those scholars who had been oriented to *Geistesgeschichte* and to Dilthey's *Lebensphilosophie*. Through their writings, Jung's theories quickly spread to the entire western world. In Germany the works of Novalis, Tieck, and E.T.A. Hoffmann, were frequently subject to Jungian interpretation as were the poetic "sign pictures" of symbolism and expression-ism. Some scholars now portrayed the creative person as the "plaything of superhuman powers," who ultimately succumbs to the flood of voices and images streaming over him.[19]

But in the Germany of the 1930s this trend soon waned (in comparison with the Anglo-Saxon countries), for the Nazis rejected psychoanalysis as being "un-Germanic." Therefore, the most influential literary scholarship based on Jungian principles was carried out in England by Maud Bodkin. In her exploration of the *Archetypal Patterns in Poetry* (1934), we find no trace of the positivistic elements still accepted by most disciples of Freud; in her book all material factors are transformed into an indistinct chaos of images and voices. Like Jung, Bodkin traces the attraction of poetry to basic archetypical stimuli. She speaks of the great Earth Mother, of the archetypes of paradise, hell, or eternal rebirth without offering any specific examples. Some assertions are even more abstract. Thus, the archetypical "pattern" of tragedy is defined as the tension between "self-assertion" and "submission."[20] Such hazy ideas are applied even to works like *Oedipus* or *Hamlet*, for which a Freudian like Ernest Jones had had a significantly sharper, more concrete interpretation to offer.[21] For many Jungians, a simple "tuning in" is often enough for the understanding of literature.

Clearly, Bodkin does not subject the work of art to analysis by reason, but relies almost exclusively on emotional response. For her, the only purpose of poetry is to put us in touch once again with the primal rhythm of the universe. In fact, she suggests that this rhythm manifests itself largely in the continual alternation of introversion and extroversion, between internally and externally oriented libido. According to her theory, when the tension between the two poles threatens to become slack, only literature with its greater promise of experience and its power to awaken us psychologically can restore a proper balance. Literature thus becomes a true organon for the secrets of life, which brings us back to Dilthey. But Maud Bodkin goes one step further and associates this spirituality with the mythical, the supernatural, and the religious. No wonder then, she concludes her book with the assertion—there is no essential difference between "religious and poetic faith."[22]

A modification of this approach made its appearance in America in the 1940s and 1950s. Richard Chase's book, *The Quest for Myth* (1949), offers a good example since it traces all forms of aesthetic activity back to mythology. Chase states quite explicitly that, "Poetry is a primitive, a fundamental product of man's mind and wherever it has appeared it has striven against human bias and exclusiveness to transfigure itself into myth."[23] On this point, others expressed themselves with greater restraint. For example, in his 1957 essay "Archetype and Signature," Leslie Fiedler differentiated between individual and mythical elements, and suggested that the Jungian process of individuation could only be realized when the archetype was inseparably bound to the personal.[24] In that same year, Walter Abell propounded a "psycho-historical theory of culture," published as *The Collective Dream in Art*, in which the collective consciousness functions as the point of intersection between the historical and the mythical. Northrop Frye's *Anatomy of Criticism* (1957) reflects a similar approach, offering a "new" methodological reintegration under the guise of the archetype. However, in spite of his attention to formal and historical aspects, Frye's conception of artistic receptivity also rests primarily on the recognition of particular mythological structures in art. Frye so expands his view of art that it eventually includes the sum total of all archetypical images, gradually branching out from the primitive into the more highly specialized.

On the basis of such theories, Morris Philipson published an *Outline of Jungian Aesthetics* (1963) attempting to summarize and systematize this approach. In Jungian terms, and in contrast to Freud, the single work of literature is not interpreted as the expression of individual neurosis, but as an eternally recurring manifestation of the collective unconscious. But are these differences really so significant? In the final analysis,

Freud's Oedipus complex is also a "myth" or an "archetype." And, whereas Freud's insistence on sexual determination seems too narrow, Jung's myths are entirely too vague. Ultimately, the Jungians also disregard historical factors and thus reduce the seemingly "universal" applicability of myth criticism to a highly one-dimensional plane. Therefore, limiting oneself to certain archetypes is as misguided as continuously circling around the Oedipus complex. Both concepts have become fetishes, worshipped as mindlessly as the ideological constructions of "Western man" or existential "essence."

Far from opening a new path to primitive "sources," as its followers so frequently claim, these psychoanalytical concepts often obscure the realities of our technological society. The widespread predilection for cave and well motifs cannot be explained by the archetypal yearning for the prenatal condition. A truly "universal" approach to these motifs would try to set up a comprehensive topology of all archetypal images, instead of relying on a few eternals, and exploring the process of poetic creation solely in terms of unconscious impulses. The same is true of other sets of images and ideas. Even if one rejects the notion of romantic love associated with *Geistesgeschichte*, one must nonetheless recognize that the historical development of the conception of love cannot be interpreted only on the basis of archetypes. Moreover, when one begins with the archaic or mythic, one is likely to end up with an ahistorical "prehistory" of humankind, which fails to recognize socio-cultural differences or developments. For this reason, inveterate Jungians often wrench literature from its historical context and interpret it in terms of mythical situations. Whenever their historical knowledge is insufficient, Jungians quickly reach for an archetype. And if, in so doing, they remain nicely general, everything will surely fall into neat patterns.

Chapter Five

SOCIOLOGICAL AND MARXIST LITERARY SCHOLARSHIP

I

Curiously enough, the sociological approach, which posits a necessary relationship between art and social stratification, also begins to develop in the years around 1900. Of course, late eighteenth-century scholars had already recognized that art and culture stand in a dialectical relationship to state and society and cannot be imagined without them. The same can be said of the many literary histories written since the Restoration period (1815–1848) that purport to be "Histories of German National Literature." However, these works generally confine themselves almost exclusively to the exterior events of history: wars, peace treaties, movements for national unification, changes of dynasties, or failed revolutions, while socioeconomic factors play a subordinate role. On the other hand, France and England, under the influence of Auguste Comte in the middle of the nineteenth century, had already developed a sociology of art that did try to explain the function of art by synthesizing socio-cultural factors.

74

In Germany, such an approach is discernible only in the 1880s, when, in the wake of Naturalism, studies of the individual were rejected in favor of statistical studies based on mass psychology. Now German scholars seriously began to explore Comte's basic thesis positing the interdependence of all individuals in society. With the acceptance of this theory, sociology can finally be said to have "arrived" in Germany. One of the first books in this school was the pioneering study, *Community and Society* (1887), by Ferdinand Tönnies. Because it emphasized the collective, this work was perceived to be an open assault on the cult of the genius which flourished in the period of German unification. In these same years, Karl Lamprecht began his *German History* (1891–1909), which de-emphasized the individual and focused on the masses; thus the development of culture began to be viewed in terms of broadly-based mass movements, and not as the work of particular geniuses.

In the realm of literary scholarship, such tendencies are evident in Kuno Francke's *Social Forces in German Literature* (1896) and Samuel Lublinski's *Literature and Society in the Nineteenth Century* (1899–1900). Although the titles sound sociological, these books on closer inspection prove to be more oriented toward *Geistesgeschichte* and the history of ideas. To be sure, they are strictly historical, and only partially incorporate specifically sociological elements. However, in the face of the growing philosophical neoidealism of these years, it was quite daring for these authors even to suggest such limited sociological theories. Had Dilthey and others after him not explicitly asserted that because of its tendency to generalize, sociology belongs strictly to the realm of the natural sciences? And, according to Dilthey's standards, wasn't only the individual historical case worthy of attention? Therefore, after 1900, in response to the pressure applied by the neoidealists, most literary scholars and art historians quickly shifted from sociology to cultural morphology. In their efforts to establish general categories, they were satisfied to focus on certain phases of life or biological cycles that still allowed attention to the individual; the categories they set up, however, became so abstract that they can hardly be considered sociological criteria.

The sociological approach thus became dormant and only came to the fore again in the 1920s. But even in this era, scholars felt the pressure of *Geistesgeschichte*. It was therefore only small groups, or loners, who tried to expand the ideological orientation of Ferdinand Tönnies, Ernst Troeltsch, Max Weber, or Werner Sombart. One school consciously worked to create types, basing itself on Max Weber's theory according to which sociology attempts primarily to forge typologies and general laws of history in order to integrate the products of the mind with the mechanics of social history.[1] An example of this is Arnold Hirsch's essay, "Sociology and Literary History," in which he described sociology as a discipline standing somewhere between the natural and cultural sciences.[2] Hirsch had in mind the uncovering of certain ideal types, which, in contrast to the largely intuitive method of *Geistesgeschichte*, can be identified only with the help of detailed quantitative analysis. But the time was not yet ripe, even for such a venture which more closely resembles Dilthey's *Lebensphilosophie* than sociology.

With the triumph of *Geistesgeschichte*, the image of the poet had become so cultish, that any theory emphasizing the collective appeared almost sacrilegious to conservative German literary scholars. Only those who transposed this sociological typology into structural psychology and did not interpret social types in terms of classes, but in terms of emotional attitudes, met with any success. Anyone who insisted on the determining power of the class structure or emphasized the dialectical relationship between social basis and artistic superstructure was sure to be accused of left-wing leanings.

Those who were oriented to the study of influences or the history of taste faced less opposition, because politically they were on relatively neutral ground. While representatives of the status quo rejected any suggestion of a relationship between class affiliation and the artistic representation of reality, the opposite approach, namely, studying the influence of a particular work of art upon society, was considered quite legitimate even by those who were oriented toward *Geistesgeschichte*. This approach provoked considerably fewer allegations of onesidedness. Thus, a book like Levin L. Schücking's *Sociology of Literary Taste* (1923) won at least some favorable critical attention since its sociological investigation was confined to dealing with those who make cultural choices, such as publishers, producers, and critics.[3] According to Schücking, at any moment in history one can find many clearly differentiated "spirits of the time," whose judgments of taste are often diametrically opposed to one another. However, Schücking never explores the origins of these many *Zeitgeists* nor asks how their taste is formed; he consistently avoids interpreting art from a strict sociological perspective as the final product of the collective will of a given group. For this reason Schücking does not achieve a real sociology of literature, but remains in the realm of the study of taste.

Those theorists who concerned themselves with the socially determined origins of certain styles and movements were mainly involved in the study of generation theory. Here the major influence was Karl Mannheim. In contrast to others who were more biologically oriented, as we have seen in the chapter on racial and "volkish" elements,[4] he defined the generation as a "social layer of related individuals within a certain time period."[5] Naturally, so formal a conception remains rather vague and does not touch the actual background factors.

However, in 1933 even these tentative sociological studies were buried in the avalanche of "volkish" thinking. Not classes, but races were now the coin of the scholarly trade. As a result, the few impulses toward a sociologically oriented literary scholarship were quickly forgotten and could only be further developed outside of Germany. With the rise of fascism, Mannheim, Alewyn, Schücking, Auerbach, Hirsch, and many other sociological thinkers emigrated; their ideas were especially well received in France and the Anglo-Saxon countries, where there was no entrenched *Geistesgeschichte* to oppose them. Therefore, in these domains, much greater interest was afforded to the socio-literary approach than in Germany. One need only think of Ernst Kohn-Bramstedt's *Aristocracy and the Middle Class in Germany: Social Types in German Literature, 1830–1900* (1937), published in London and dedicated to Karl Mannheim, in which the German novel of the nineteenth century is seen from a sociological rather than an aesthetic perspective. The English counterparts to this would be such works as Walter H. Bruford's *Culture and Society in Classical Weimar* (1936) and his *Germany in the Eighteenth Century* (1939).

This situation changed little even after 1945. If anything, the West German aversion toward sociology in the context of literary scholarship gained even greater force under the influence of the cold war. Following an old tradition, one group of literary scholars focused on the specifically spiritual elements which they believed were present in all genuine literature. Others focused on the demonic, the existential, and the tragic. Thus, Walter Muschg writes, in his *Tragic Literary History* (1948): "Like the medical view of art, the sociological perspective sharpens the eye only for facts of the second rank and dulls it for the important things."[6] But most of the objections came from the new formalists whose methodological hallmark was textual analysis. According to them, sociological interpretation violated the absolute autonomy of all great works of art and dislocated the existing scale of values by emphasizing the trivial or the transient.[7]

In the face of so many negative reactions, the voices of approbation had a rather difficult time being heard at all. However, since the 1950s some softening has been observable. This assertion is supported by studies such as Hugo Kuhn's "Literary Scholarship and Sociology," which focuses on the crucial relationship between social reality and poetic fiction in the courtly poetry of the middle ages.[8] Elsewhere, Kuhn explicitly singles out the sociological dimension as the essential component in all questions of literary scholarship.[9] Others picked up the work of Schücking and concerned themselves primarily with the history of the influence of specific works and key ideas.[10] Hans Norbert Fügen defined the socio-literary method as a discipline which primarily concerns itself with "those social relationships that unite the writer as writer to his environment." He was therefore interested in such phenomena as bestseller lists, mass psychology, history of influences, statistics, writers' circles, kitsch, bohemian life, or questions of literary reputation, that is, factors that are socially determined, but not themselves centrally determining. Fügen also established a typology in which he tried to separate all literary artists into three types: those who conform to society, those who oppose it, and those who turn away from it.[11] Unfortunately, what we gain from such a classification is not immediately evident.

But even these timorous voices were barely heard. Only a few concrete sociological studies of literature appeared, especially in the area of Medieval German literature, where the terrain was somewhat less dangerous. But in general, the situation remained essentially unchanged till approximately 1965, and this, in spite of all the encouragement given to this approach by the writings of Walter Benjamin, Georg Lukács, Hans Mayer, and Theodor W. Adorno, which began to be more widely available in these years. Sociology was either consigned to the cultural periphery or discounted as a purely auxilliary discipline entirely outside the inner sanctum of literary study. As a result, even so substantial a work as Arnold Hauser's *The Social History of Art* (1953) had considerably fewer repercussions in West Germany than in the Anglo-Saxon countries. In the West Germany of the 1950s the word sociology still carried political implications and was immediately associated with Marxism. And this was an ideology which scholars in the West would much rather leave to the East German literary establishment. Let us, therefore, first turn to the East where, paradoxically, those very sociological studies that had seemed so daring in the West were either considered harmless or cited as examples of vulgar materialism.

II

In contrast to a strict sociological orientation, which views the class structure as the only possible basis of social analysis, Marxism goes one step further and sees even the class structure as the product of determining forces. According to Marxists, the class structure is not natural or god-given but grows out of the economic system of production that continuously brings forth new social stratifications. Therefore, the culture of all classes in every period is determined by underlying economic conditions. As a result, either consciously or unconsciously, all artistic productions are necessarily a product of the ideological superstructure. According to this perspective, nothing is autonomous. Everything is tied to everything else, and integrally related to the virtually unlimited number of determining factors within the dialectics of society.

Marx himself provided the foundation for this theory, as far as the economic system is concerned, in his *Capital* (1867–1894). In the realm of aesthetics, however, it took much longer for anyone to develop a truly Marxist perspective. What Marx and Engels said on the subject of literature and art is quite fragmentary and not easy to understand outside the specific historical circumstances in which it was written. Consequently, even the earliest attempts to create a Marxist aesthetic, which appeared in the late nineteenth century, are not tied to any specific system and have, since then, been subjected to continual correctives by the political organizations of the Marxist camps. For this reason, the history of Marxist aesthetics is also the history of the socialist and communist parties, a subject that can only briefly be touched upon here.

In Germany, Franz Mehring must be mentioned first; his anti-Prussian and antimilitary feelings had already come to the fore in the early 1870s.[12] He did not however turn to Marxism until the period of the "laws against Socialism" (1878–1890), when internal domestic contradictions became increasingly evident. With the rise of naturalism, literature itself became considerably more engaged. Supported by these currents, Mehring could dare to attack the whole of German literary scholarship associated with the reactionary Hohenzollerns by publishing his *Lessing Legend* in 1896. Unfortunately, in this endeavor he remained alone. For in these years, the social democrats had not yet developed their own cultural policy and were even hostile to naturalism. With the motto "knowledge is power," they offered their supporters a blanket endorsement of the bourgeois cultural tradition, which, in the realm of literature, usually meant a glorification of the German classics.

Even Mehring could not free himself entirely from this concept and gave surprisingly free rein to philosophical idealism. As Belinski before him, he frequently differentiated between art and social action, between the purely aesthetic and the purely political, instead of grasping the close interrelationship between these two spheres. He particularly prized the old Kantian assumption that art only concerned itself with the beautiful and that the main criterion of beauty is "disinterested pleasure."[13] Like the German idealists, Mehring believed that great art can develop only in tranquil epochs, while during periods of class struggle all literary phenomena necessarily become tendentious and, as a result, *un*artistic. He therefore envisioned a proletarian culture only in the future; for the present, he viewed the daily political battle as the most pressing issue. For this reason, the social democrats saw Schiller's *William Tell*, and not Hauptmann's *Weavers*, as the most "contemporary" drama. Only from Schiller's plays could one learn how to deal with tyrants, it was said in these circles.[14] It would, therefore, be wrong to speak of specifically social democratic aesthetics. In the sphere of politically oriented sociology in the years around 1900, we have few others besides Mehring; the essays of Clara Zetkin might perhaps be mentioned. Otherwise, a conciliatory revisionism flourished.

In order to trace the further development of Marxist aesthetics, we must look beyond Germany. The most important representative of this school at the turn of the century was the

Russian Georgyi Valentinovitch Plekhanov who, in contrast to Mehring, sharply criticized all idealistic aesthetic systems. Unlike the German social democrats, he viewed art more as a reflection of the basic socio-economic structure. But strange to say, he too could not completely free himself from the criterion of the beautiful. As a result, Plekhanov is against all tendentious art that makes use of political rhetoric and thus, in spite of his Marxist convictions, he attributes a degree of autonomy to artistic creation; this necessarily brought him into conflict with bolshevism.

When the Russian Revolution broke out in 1917, and when the first Spartacus group and then the Communist Party was founded in Germany, the situation in the area of cultural politics was still entirely fluid. Although the communists were quite ambivalent toward such modern movements as expressionism, cubism, dadaism, futurism, and Tatlinism, they at first supported all of these on purely tactical grounds. This ambivalence remained even when, in the course of the 1920s, developments like the *neue Sachlichkeit*, the cult of the proletariat, the theater of Piscator, and *Literatura fakta* appeared on the horizon. Seen from a cultural-political perspective, no decisions were made at that time, and the aesthetic problem was once again simply postponed. As a result, the Marxist philosophers and cultural politicians of this epoch, particularly Georg Lukács, Karl Korsch, and Ernst Bloch, are today generally viewed as heretics. One need think only of Bloch's *The Spirit of Utopia* (1918), which is entirely expressionistic. The same is true of Lukács's *Theory of the Novel* (1916), in which he takes a Hegelian approach and defines the novel as the product of "transcendental homelessness." While in this work Lukács still stands on relatively neutral political ground, his book *History and Class Consciousness* (1923) became a document of the so-called left-deviationists. Actually, all of these writings still remain within the realm of spiritual engagement and attempt to encompass all of reality with audacious conceptual constructions. Thus they frequently resemble a phenomenologically oriented expressionism. The same is true of the considerably more moderate social democratic writers of these years.

Marxist aesthetics became systematized only after 1932, when the Party in the Soviet Union began to label all modern movements as modernistic, formalistic, or bourgeois-decadent. Then the real clean-up started, and with it, the ideological hardening that was recorded in history as the era of Stalinism or the "Shdanov period." Cultural functionaries became suspicious of Western sociology, which they now equated with vulgar materialism and a highly questionable objective stance. In this struggle, the principle of absolute partisanship was victorious; they sacrificed even the writings of Plekhanov and the left-deviationist cult of the proletariat. In 1934, the phrase "socialist realism" was adopted by the Party as the goal of the new movement, and it quickly developed into a normative concept that viewed aesthetic expression mainly as a vehicle for party politics: only what the Party approved was realistic. Since so many left-wing European intellectuals took refuge from fascism in Moscow, the term "socialist realism" did not remain confined to the Soviet Union, but became the most important principle of communist aesthetics on a worldwide basis. As a result, almost all Marxist theoreticians of the 1930s and the early 1940s used the degree of realism in a work of art as the essential aesthetic criterion.

While Marx and Engels had been considerably more open-minded in their judgments of art, the Marxist ideologues of this period measured all cultural endeavors in terms of their political effectiveness. Most of them worked with the concept of the "two cultures," according to which the art of every period can be divided into two groups: that of the exploiters and that of the exploited. Thus, every work of art is seen as a document of the class struggle. The art of the exploited is realistic, that of the exploiters, formalistic. Unfortunately, the concept of the two cultures, already propagated by Lenin, became an integral part of "dialectical materialism" precisely at a time when party cultural politics were in a condition of extreme obduracy. According to the party line of the 1930s, art was thought of as a direct or indirect expression of a particular social class; that is, art was believed to illustrate socioeconomic processes that in themselves possessed neither aesthetic nor existential autonomy.

In this connection, the position of Georg Lukács is particularly interesting, since he fully complied with this line in the years of his exile in Moscow, consciously avoiding left-sectarianism which still tried to keep alive the proletarian avant-garde of the revolutionary writers' associations of the late 1920s, but not supporting the growing nationalism of the Stalinists. He, too, was an advocate of socialist realism. But when Lukács speaks of "great realists," he uses the works of critical realists like Balzac, Stendhal, Pushkin, Gogol, Scott, Keller or Tolstoi as a standard against which he measures the contemporary novels of socialist realism in the Soviet Union and finds the latter wanting. His more traditional stance is also reflected in his preference for works of late-bourgeois critical realists such as Thomas and Heinrich Mann and his admiration for the period of German Classicism.

In Western Europe and the United States, Marxist cultural politics developed along somewhat more independent lines. With the exception of a few diehard party hacks, left-wing theorists in these countries were less dogmatic and tended to allow greater freedom of literary expression. Aside from the model provided by the Soviet Union, which at that time was the only existing communist state, these Marxist fellow travelers were mainly influenced by the devastating effects of the depression of 1929, the rise of fascism in Europe, and the Spanish Civil War. In these years, particularly in the United States, a social criticism developed that tried to bring Marxist aesthetics into the American tradition and resulted in such works as Granville Hicks's *The Great Tradition* (1933), C. Day Lewis's *The Mind in Chains* (1937), and Bernard Smith's *Forces in American Criticism* (1939). Some literary historians even speak of this period as the "red decade in American criticism." In England, it was chiefly Christopher Caudwell who provided a Marxist aesthetic in his book *Illusion and*

Reality (1937). It is interesting to note that, like Lukács, Caudwell followed the lines of Hegelian thinking: he defined freedom in terms of "self-recognition," and he argued that humankind had first to go through a mystic and religious phase before it could turn to the aesthetic. While the positivists were interested only in objective reality and the idealists only in subjective reality, Caudwell tried to enter into the dialectic of these two domains. In any case, nowhere did he speak of socialist realism.

After 1945, Marxism was faced with an altogether new situation. Almost all of Eastern Europe and even China had become communist, a situation that led to the cold war. In such a situation, could the Soviet Union continue to be the only cultural political model for a Marxist aesthetic? Was it not likely that the existence of different communist states would necessarily lead to a gradual destalinization of aesthetic theory? The speed with which this did, in fact, occur, is demonstrated by the unusual success accorded to Lukács in the communist peoples' republics. For it was Lukács, and not one of the Soviet literary scholars, who was held up as the great advocate of a Marxist view of art. "We came of age only with the help of your teaching," wrote Johannes R. Becher enthusiastically in 1955. Lukács's books, written primarily during his exile in Moscow, now finally appeared in German, Hungarian, Polish, even in French and English, and thus reached a worldwide audience. The following volumes proved to be particularly influential for German literary history: *Goethe and his Time* (1947), *Thomas Mann* (1949), *German Realists of the Nineteenth Century* (1951), *The Destruction of Reason* (1953), and *The Historical Novel* (1955). These works mirror, even if in hidden form, the gradual dissolution of the Stalinist era.

Lukács's theory of the "partisanship of objectivity," like his theory of realism, leaves room for unorthodox interpretation. Nowhere did he hide the fact that his definition of realism implied a value judgment against the propagandistic works of socialist realism of the 1930s and 1940s, a position that brought him into conflict with his Hungarian compatriots as early as

1949. On the other hand, he never clarified just how broadly he conceived of realism. However, he did firmly adhere to the basic Marxist assumption that literature is a reflection of reality. For him, every work of art manifests " a power, dwelling within reality," which is anchored in the basic socio-economic structure.[15] According to his theory, this mirroring "of a reality independent of our consciousness"[16] is as far removed from naturalism, which only gives attention to absolute factuality, as from narrow formalism. What lies between these two extremes, he defines as realism, the chief goal of which is the depiction of typical characters in typical situations. Significantly, Lukács does not equate the typical with the average, but with the exemplary which embodies the social forces of change operating at any given moment in history. How strongly this conception of realism is influenced by works such as *Eugenie Grandet* or *Anna Karenina* is shown by Lukács's relatively harsh attitude toward Brechtian realism, which seemed to him to be too estranged from nature.

The impact of Lukács's theories upon Marxist aesthetics after 1945 can hardly be exaggerated. Until 1956, when Lukács finally discredited himself in orthodox circles by taking part in the Hungarian uprising, Eastern European literary scholarship, especially that of East Germany, might best be described as "one big school of Lukács." Aside from Lukács, there were only Ernst Bloch and his followers who represented a more liberal way of thinking, while the orthodox point of view was best represented by Paul Reimann's *Concerning the Realistic Conception of Art* (1949). Only after the twentieth party conference in 1956 did a greater diversity manifest itself as a result of the process of destalinization, which is still in effect today. Dogmatic dictums stood beside more open-minded theories, the Bitterfeld Conferences of 1959 and 1963 beside the writings of Hans Mayer. Some Marxist critics continued to toe the party line, while others supported the climate of political thaw. Thus, in 1959, there appeared in East Germany a book entitled *The Necessity of Art* by the Austrian Marxist Ernst Fischer; in it he frankly spoke out against socialist realism and all schematic oversimplifications of aesthetic theory which, he believed, did not do justice to the diversity of the modern industrial world. Ernst Fischer valued the literary complexity we find in the works of Kafka, Proust, or Joyce, and thought it could be useful in the creation of socialist art. Only a year later, however, the party sharply condemned all "third ways," representing a revisionary acceptance of peaceful coexistence.[17] Not surprisingly then, the voluminous 1962 study of *The Fundamentals of a Marxist-Leninist Aesthetic*, published by a Soviet collective of writers, omits the name of Lukács altogether; the volume concerns itself only with the propagation of socialist realism in its most rigorous formulation.

Since then, most of the East German theoreticians of culture find themselves engaged in a partisan quarrel, fighting against the strict interpretation of socialist realism on the one hand, against the formally oriented avant-garde of the West on the other. As in the 1920s, when Marxist scholars wavered indecisively between the cult of the proletariat and abstract constructivism, the quarrel is now once again fully in process. What shape this conflict will take, remains to be seen. However, one thing is already quite clear—scholars will not rely on the orthodox Shdanov line or on the two volumes of Lukács's *Aesthetics* (1963) which actually only bring together his previous views and do not offer anything new.

III

But since 1965 such disputes have ceased to be solely the concern of Eastern-bloc countries, and are discussed in the West with equal intensity. Here, however, because of the newness of the ideas and their hasty reception, the situation is even more confusing than in the German Democratic Republic. While in the East, Marxist aesthetics are being used to legitimize the existing political order, in the German Federal Republic these same aesthetics are used to further revolutionary causes.

The more conservative left-wing faction in West Germany

confines itself to the study of influence and reception. Good examples of this approach are: Hans Robert Jauss's *Literary History as Provocation for Literary Scholarship* (1967), Harald Weinrich's *Literary History of the Reader* (1967), and the essays of Karl Robert Mandelkow. Where previously socio-logically oriented scholars had divided the reading public into groups according to their taste, these scholars are primarily concerned with the "audience horizon of anticipation," which focuses on reader response. A more positive direction is taken by those who now study so-called "undervalued" literature, that is, works that had previously not been considered worthy of literary scholarship. Thus, a vast, multi-branched study of trivia and kitsch has developed which confines itself unthinkingly to so-called "lesser" works. In some respects, this field of scholarship represents a sociological maneuvering by means of which scholars appear to meet the demands of relevance without giving up their comfortable distinction between "higher" and "lower" literature. In the meantime, this body of material has been incorporated into the canon of German literary scholarship even by formalistic and conservative scholars eager to support a positivistic approach. For these studies do not threaten the aesthetic refuges of conservative scholars, because in the final analysis they only concern themselves with influence on *literature*, and not on *life*. As a result, and in spite of all its apparent social breadth, this branch of socio-literary criticism tends toward aesthetic narrowness.

Even the "critical theory"* of the Adorno school has already gained official status within German literary scholarship. What only recently appeared to be so threatening, today excites few, and even those, more on account of Adorno's style than his method. Adorno's acceptance in the West can be directly traced to his principle of the "negative dialectic," according

* This was developed in the Frankfurt school of sociology created by Adorno, Max Horkheimer, and Herbert Marcuse, based on a neo-Marxist view of culture, which also allows for a Freudian perspective as well as insights gleaned from the mass media.

to which one can still be progressive without giving one's ideas any particular ideological goals. No doubt, the adherents of the Adorno school see themselves confronted by a totally manipulated mass society and a vulgar cultural industry; it is perhaps for this reason that they have developed an idiosyncratic prejudice against all ideologies. Unfortunately, this often results in melancholy snobbery. Such an antisocial position, expressed in pseudo-Marxist terminology, necessarily leads to solipsism. However, the strict followers of the "critical theory" do not view this as a contradiction but as the ultimate legitimization of this "theory-less" theory. Although Brecht called the teachings of this school the worst brand of intellectualism, they too have taken their place among the officially accepted methods.

The Western literary establishment only becomes alarmed when left-wing scholars go beyond abstract theorizing and place the social element itself squarely in the center of literary study, thus raising the essential questions concerning the dialectics of basis and superstructure. Since 1967, a number of voices have been heard that go back either to the "classics" themselves, that is, to Marx and Engels, or else base their aesthetic concepts on Brecht and the later work of Walter Benjamin. These scholars no longer try to incorporate older literary scholarship but challenge it directly. As evidence, we can cite the recent debates in *Argument, Alternative, Metzler Texts*, and elsewhere, in which Michael Pehlke, Hans Wolf Jäger, Friedrich Knilli, Marie-Luise Gansberg, Paul Gerhard Völker, Helga Gallas, Hildegard Brenner, and other representatives of the "new left" criticize the traditional methods of German literary scholarship, and base their assumptions on materialistic conceptions of history. In contrast to the older bourgeois literary scholarship that chiefly concerned itself with typologies of form and ontological evaluation, they view every work of literature, and thereby also its creator, as an "ensemble of social forces" that can only be understood in terms of a dialectical interpretation of history.

By far the most daring step in this direction in the last few years was taken by Helmut Lethen, Friedrich Rothe, and Wilhelm Girnus, who, in a collective effort, attempted to institute a thoroughly Marxist-revolutionary literary scholarship. This is evident in their series *Materialistic Scholarship* (1971 ff.). Of course, as one might expect, in trying to define their own political and methodological position, they not only attack the older bourgeois scholarship but also the more liberal trends of the late 1960s. While strongly condemning the so-called petty-bourgeois intellectuals who waver between uptopianism and reformism (by which they mean the supporters of the "critical theory" as well as the authors of Enzensberger's *Kursbuch*), they advocate literary scholarship "in the service of the people." With such attacks they are trying to disassociate themselves from the kind of intellectual arrogance described by Herbert Marcuse, who viewed the rebellious students of the 1960s as the "new proletariat." These younger Marxist aestheticians are therefore particularly aggressive against those followers of Adorno who foolishly believe they can remain loyal to the needs of the proletariat by reading Kafka and Beckett.[18] While these Marxists admit that the "critical theory" affords considerable concrete insight into how culture is manipulated in a capitalistic industrial society, they nonetheless condemn its subjective emphasis which neglects the needs of the proletariat and caters to the isolated bourgeois ego. Furthermore, they assert that the "critical theory" consciously disavows the will to change by its false interpretation of the "dialectics of enlightenment." No less bitterly do they attack some of the literary scholars of the German Democratic Republic who support the "bourgeois" veneration of classicism and realism, and as a result, push the plebeian tradition into the background—and this, in spite of the Bitterfeld Conferences which urged the factory workers to take up the pen. Some of these ideas clearly display the exaggerated enthusiasm of the newly converted. Whether any fruitful theories will develop out of their objections, remains to be seen.

IV

For these reasons, a genuine Marxist aesthetic is still only an ideal in spite of Roger Garaudy, Lucian Goldmann, Leszek Kolakowski, Frederic Jameson, Robert Weimann, Helga Gallas, Ernst Fischer, and Helmut Lethen, whose writings provide the most hopeful efforts in this direction at the present time. But possibly the goal itself is illusory, since all truly dialectical thinking recognizes that every idea is but a temporary part of a historical chain of development. The question then arises: what does a method that can never realize itself concretely have to offer? First, there is its thoroughgoing historical emphasis that not only includes political events, but also tries to bring the socioeconomic basis of all intellectual and artistic expression into the study of art. Such a perspective is entirely legitimate and was unjustly neglected in those days when the world was still considered God's creation, and all notable events were viewed as the work of certain dominant personalities. But fortunately we have gone far beyond that. Today, one can hardly imagine anyone trying to reject a more or less materialistic world view. If such scholars still exist, then they are hopelessly behind the times. In general, Marxism is instrumental in providing scholars with a deepened awareness of the ideological backgrounds to literature and art. From this perspective, even the simplest poem favored by pure aesthetes takes on new dimensions, and is no longer merely peripheral but serves to reflect the current world situation; as Hegel expressed it, art stands once again in the center of the whole. In such a framework, art is assigned the task of transcending the particular and the individual; the aesthetic becomes the "most adequate form for the expression of humanity's self-consciousness." Only if art is assigned such a universal function, can it prove to be a significant factor operating "within the limits of the social and historical possibilities of its time."[19]

For this reason, many Marxists attack psychoanalysis, which, according to them, tries to avoid social change by celebrating human sexuality as a dominant force operating outside history. Similarly radical is the Marxists' rejection of the abstract, existential interpretation of art as representative of the general human condition. With equal vehemence, they oppose the pseudo-romantic glorification of the primitive, the archaic, and the instinctive; such emphasis, they feel, consciously serves to blur the ideology inherent in every work. The same Ernst Fischer therefore who supports Proust and Joyce, attacks the avant-garde in the West for its one-sided interest in the absurd, the grotesque, and the abstract, which he sees as a parallel to the rigid application of socialist realism in the East. He cites Ionesco's *Rhinoceros* as a particularly instructive example of the "*haute couture* of anti-humanism"; since the bizarre events described in the play are not motivated by an explicable ideology, the work functions as an apologia for the status quo.[20] For Fischer, as for Marx, only that which can be explained is really "real." For this reason, he believes it is the primary task of art to expose mystifications and clichés and to fight all nihilistic glorification of the asocial with the postulate of true freedom. Leaning on Caudwell and Lukács, Fischer believes that art has the capacity to free us from stifling forces, to help us change the world, which he perceives as developing and therefore as changeable. He asserts that genuine art should not hide real problems behind false myths, but should enlighten or awaken us, that is, should offer us a "foretaste" of a better world to come, as Ernst Bloch phrased it. Those who support this position argue that all great works of art point "beyond their time, are in union with the future, and legitimize the striving for a beautiful humanity."[21]

Two dangers are inherent in this dialectical conception of art, which tries to do justice both to the specific time period of the individual work and to its superhistorical significance. Some scholars go no further than the purely historical, or else, they only point to the dialectical curve of development; in either case, they do not live up to the demands of universality. Thus, even today, there are still Marxists who view art simply as the handmaiden of history, for whom literature serves merely as illustration. Such studies frequently bring to light the socio-economic tensions mirrored in a particular work of art: the concrete situation in the feudal society around 1200, the circumstances of the bourgeoisie around 1848. For such purposes, however, newspapers, pamphlets, official deeds, and other contemporary records could serve as well. Ultimately, all documents are relics of the past, and for this reason have some illustrative value. But is it the function of literary scholarship merely to teach us how things once were? That the past really is past? Of what use is the past, if it bears no connection to our own present? If art is only a dead reflection of the past, why then are we moved by it at all? The philosophical idealists around 1900 had already posed all of these questions in the face of the positivistic accumulation of facts. Broadly speaking, their answer was *Geistesgeschichte*, which confined itself to a highly selective, intuitive approach. If, indeed, Marxism can offer better answers to these questions, it ought not fall back upon the "radical historicity of art," which Lukács elevates to an absolute.[22] Such emphasis on history is thoroughly justified as a corrective to the formalistic approach, but fails in its purpose if it is made the end-all and be-all of literary scholarship.

The second danger of the Marxist view of art lies in its schematic application of the principle of dialectics. Largely at fault is Lenin's theory of the two cultures, according to which all humankind can be divided in two: the exploiters and the exploited, whose different forms of artistic expression always obey certain rigid rules. The resulting opposites are usually described by the labels "realism" and "formalism." According to some Marxists, the art of the declining classes is always decadent and formally mannered (which includes, of course, all modern Western literature), while the art of the rising classes is always progressive and realistic. Some theorists go even further and label all art which is humanistic and future-oriented as realistic. Thus, Paul Reimann characterizes the major writers of world literature, such as Cervantes, Shakespeare, and Molière simply as realists. Similarly he describes Goethe, Belinski, Heine, Chernyshevski, and Marx and Engels, as the founders of an aesthetics of realism.[23] According to this theory, there appear to be only two mutually exclusive styles in the entire development of art and literature: realism and formalism, a dreary separation into black and white. In contrast to those who emphasize the past and advocate a radical "historical objectivity," these theorists are entirely too entrenched in the present. As a result, their judgments are based on a preconceived view of history which gives rise to inappropriate judgments. For example, they fault writers of the nineteenth century for not finding their way to the working class; for withdrawing from society; for retreating from political engagement, and the like. These Marxist aestheticians seem less interested in the historically given than in squaring their literary judgments with the basic tenets of Marxist theory. Since Marx himself was an enthusiastic reader of Balzac and E.T.A. Hoffmann, he would no doubt merely have smiled at such efforts.

Chapter Six

LITERATURE IN THE SERVICE OF "BEING"

From the start it is important to recognize that in this chapter we will be speaking only of German existentialism, which must be clearly differentiated from the better-known French school of existentialism that arose after World War II and took an entirely different direction. In Germany, existential criticism of literature and art is generally traced back to Martin Heidegger's *Time and Being* (1927), in order to distinguish it from the earlier equally "philosophically" oriented *Geistesgeschichte*. To be sure, this distinction has some merits. Closer inspection, however, shows that these two approaches are more alike than different.

The practitioners of *Geistesgeschichte* in the early 1920s had already gone beyond Dilthey's psychological relativism and moved into the realm of "existence" and "being." They, too, spoke of "awakening," "serving metaphysics," and "existential commitment," which seemed to suggest some kind of non-directed engagement. This emphasis on activism developed because scholars equated the German spirit with the romantic notion of creativity, which now no longer stressed historical factors but myth or revelation. Ernst Troeltsch attributed this "activist contempt for history"[1] to the idealism of the postwar generation, which, under the influence of Nietzsche all wished to create values for the future, purely from within its own inner being. For this reason it makes no sense to attribute the "existential" components of this idealism solely to Heidegger. In fact, many of these ideas had already been in the air at the turn of the century. Thus the sources of *Geistesgeschichte* are the same as those of existentialism; it is often quite difficult to distinguish broad concepts like spirit and soul from life and existence. The approaches of *Geistesgeschichte* and existentialism both view art as a modality in itself, which cannot be expressed by any alternate mode of thought or feeling. The difference between the two schools is therefore at most one of degree and not of kind.

One might well ask, what specific factors associated with the movement we call existentialism set it apart from *Geistesgeschichte*? Is there only the semantic shift from the concept of "life" to that of "being"? Or does this shift in vocabulary reflect some conceptual development? While the disciples of Dilthey's *Geistesgeschichte* had a relatively good command of history and even used colorful details of a given period to vivify their *Lebensphilosophie*, the Heideggerians confine themselves entirely to abstract concepts like the great, the absolute, the essential, and the unsurpassable. Like Schopenhauer and Nietzsche, they are interested only in those geniuses whose clarion calls sound across the centuries. In taking this approach, some leaned on the work of Benedetto Croce, who, in his *Poetic and Nonpoetic* (1923), had extolled works of genius as the highest expression of artistic creation. According to Croce, tradition does not count, only individual great works, in which "pure spirit" or the "absolute" manifests itself. He rejects all time-bound literature as rhetoric, "applied" art, or worse yet, "nonliterature." Equally influential was the cult of the "great individual," as propounded by the adherents of the George circle, who viewed every poet as a self-sufficient monad, concerned only with his own essence. In the realm of literary studies, this resulted in some gross distortions. For example, in his *Goethe* (1916), Friedrich Gundolf concentrates almost exclusively on the "primal experiences" of his hero and tries to describe Goethe's phenomenological "being-in-itself," by ignoring all determining factors and connecting links. But the historical Goethe did value those very "cultural experiences" that Gundolf dismisses so disrespectfully; clearly, the real Goethe who lived around 1800, is of less interest to Gundolf than the "essential" Goethe. In order to emphasize the antihistorical tendency of his approach, Ernst Bertram, another member of the George group, went so far as to give his *Nietzsche* book (1918), the subtitle *An Attempt at a Mythology.* "What endures from the life of a great figure is not his biography, but his legend," he writes programmatically. Bertram describes his method as a process of mythologizing by means of which the particular artist is transformed into a guiding star.[2]

This brings us to the second distinguishing feature of this existential approach: its emphasis on the static, of that which has been "given" from time immemorial, that is, the "existential" in the broadest sense. In this approach one can discern a definite phenomenological pull toward the "thing-in-itself." The more these existentialists concentrate on the absolute, the more the real world slips from their grasp. As a result of this radical rejection of historical facts, which had first manifested itself in the work of Dilthey, we are left with abstract skeletal conceptions that attempt to characterize art as the expression of the "self" or of "being." In addition to Bergson's intuitionism and Husserl's phenomenology, expressionism, too, proved to be an important influence moving in the direction of Heidegger's concept of "being." As early as 1918 there was widespread talk of spiritual phenomena, whose essence could only be "illuminated," but not explained. Even such concepts as "being" and "existence" already played an important role in these years. Thus, in his *Foundations of Aesthetics* (1914–20), Emil Utitz insists that the prime purpose of the study of art is to unfold the many "layers of being."[3] His main concern here, as in Wilhelm Worringer's dissertation, *Abstraction and Empathy* (1928), is to transform the empirical world into the "spiritual," thus to arrive at certain prime ideas. For others, the artist is merely the "transmitter of primeval being," whose imagination stems from a phenomenological source.[4] In Ludwig Coellen's book *Concerning the Methods of Art History* (1924), art appears as the "final realization of the world idea in the sphere of sense perception," resting on the complete rebirth of "being" which is always in the process of "becoming."[5] Ernst Cassirer's *Philosophy of Symbolic Forms* (1923–29) is not quite so dense. But here, too, reality is only perceived as an existential abstraction. Like other expressionists, Cassirer does not see any mirroring of reality or mimesis in the symbols of art, but only in "intrinsic" reality, resting on the "pure expression" of the creative powers.[6] Roman Ingarden's *The Literary Work of Art* (1931) moves in a similar direction toward an ontological theory of the poetic that carries the idea of artistic uniqueness to its furthest extreme.

But it remained for Martin Heidegger to achieve a decisive success for this approach with his *Time and Being* (1927), although in this work aesthetic theories are given scant attention. Heidegger's enormous influence can best be explained by the fact that most of his ideas were already current and only needed an effective formulation to take hold in scholarly circles. After all Heidegger, like Ingarden, came from the school of Husserl, and in his early period had been influenced by a kind of phenomenological expressionism. Heidegger's major contribution to this movement was its jargon, a consciously mystifying vocabulary that repeatedly uses words like "existential," and "essential," in order to give the reader the impression of something basic, irrefutably absolute. In historical terms, we could define this phase of existentialism as late-expressionistic "science of being." In both, a strong activist element is at work: both herald the surging up of being, existential revelation, and the illumination of existence.

No wonder then, that shortly after 1933, in the sphere of "volkish" literary scholarship, one observes a definite turning toward Heidegger's speculations concerning existence. Heidegger's existentialism merged with the teachings of *Lebensphilosophie* and the nationalism of some of the George disciples, and was taken up by the Nazis as an elite fascist ideology, because in these years Heidegger enthusiastically supported all forms of activism. This is evident even in his little volume, *Hölderlin and the Essence of Poetry* (1937), in which he allows the "origins of being" to coincide with the "primal language of a people."[7] For his followers, the terms existence, essence, awakening, and national origins became virtually synonymous. These scholars were hardly able to distinguish between action and scholarship. In both areas they demanded the same "responsibility toward the essential." This existential approach is particularly apparent in the Kleist and Hölderlin scholarship of the late 1930s, which glorified the unbroken confidence in fate, Germanic toughness, and the irrational belief in the self. Hebbel and Grabbe scholarship also often tended toward this existential stringency, especially in its handling of the "tragic." By far the most instructive efforts in this vein are the works of Gerhard Fricke and Hermann Pongs, in which the existential is intimately connected to the "volkish" political.[8]

The theoretical foundation for this approach is offered principally by Hermann Pongs, Horst Oppel, and Johannes Pfeiffer. In *The Imagery of Poetry* (1935), Pongs defines the inner essence of all great literature as an "image-making ecstasy."[9] In contrast to a more rhetorical interpretation of poetic imagery, as one might expect from the title of his book, his study mainly emphasizes metaphors of emotion and instinct, which, according to Pongs, are not in the realm of *Bildung*, but exist entirely in the realm of the instinctual. Elsewhere Pongs charges literary scholarship with the task of illuminating the "existential power" of particular works of literature which ought always lead to a deepened understanding of the "whole."[10] Similarly, Horst Oppel pontificates, "Art dissolves the uniqueness of the individual by drawing him into the destiny of the whole."[11] Johannes Pfeiffer's assertion that literature is a blessing, a gift, a symbol of existence, in which the "human world reveals itself in all its depth of being" is clearly also based on Heidegger. Therefore, like all the other followers of Nietzsche and George, Pfeiffer establishes polar categories like the authentic and the inauthentic, the primary and nonprimary, shaped and unshaped, essential and inessential, in order to show how strongly the "essence of being" manifests itself in any given work of art.[12]

Following the general collapse in 1945, a *tabula rasa* resulted in the realm of German literary scholarship. But instead of taking the opportunity to reorient themselves, scholars either made superficial changes in the theories they had used before or else tried to avoid ideological commitment altogether. It is not surprising, therefore, that after 1945 there was a conspicuous blossoming of existentialism in all the humanities. Because scholars now simply wished to be rid of national components, Heidegger's writings offered an ideal philosophy for coping with the widespread mood of ideological disorientation. Nothing was simpler than to fill the existing vacuum with "being." Scholars were thus able to remain abstract, to meet the nihilism of these years half-way, and at the same time, to satisfy the old German inclination toward irrational turgidity.

Heidegger's treatise, "The Origin of the Work of Art," which appeared in 1949 in his collected essays, *On the Wrong Track*, was extremely influential. Heidegger here defines the true work of art as an instrument of revelation in which the "essential essence" reveals itself.[13] Thus, for Heidegger, art is like a "clearing" in the forest, a break in the confining everyday world of existence into the eternal openness of being. For this reason he burdens art with concepts like wholeness, fullness of being, or divine essence. In short, art is "truth," originating in the absolute, and for this reason art stands outside all cultural, political, religious, psychological, socio-economic, or in the broadest sense, historical factors. For Heidegger, real poets are only those who are seers or steadfastly pursue the "track of escaped gods who have fled into the darkness of the night of the world."[14] Many of Heidegger's observations bear a strange resemblance to Gottfried Benn's *Static Poems* (1948), in which nihilism also blends with abstract faith in being. In the one, as well as the other, all concrete, historically determined factors are dismissed with a series of derogatory epithets: "impersonal," "extraneous verbiage," "transitory," or "pathway to error." For Heidegger, concrete reality is superficial and illusory; behind it he posits a hidden layer of truth rooted in "being" that cannot be reached by rational means, but becomes manifest only in the magical world of the arts.

At this point it might be useful to compare these German theories with the existential literary scholarship of this same period in France, since it took quite a different turn there. Instead of retreating from social action in the wake of the Nazi occupation, French intellectuals (primarily Sartre, Camus, and Beauvoir—perhaps because of their work in the Resistance) emphasized the capacity of each individual to give meaning to the world by acts of social commitment. For this reason they stressed freedom and the need for creative action. In his influential essay of 1947, *What Is Literature?*, Sartre took up the relationship of art to society. He insisted that literature must be engaged with its own time, and he defined the act of writing as a form of commitment.[15] Though Heidegger's theories (from which Sartre derived some of his own ideas) have a similarly activist orientation, the two philosophers clearly stand on opposite sides of the barricades: while Heidegger accepted National Socialism in the early 1930s, Sartre became a Marxist following World War II.

But in Germany, existential literary scholars continued to extend Heidegger's key idea: that the essential function of art is "to bring to light the truth of existence," to provide a clearing in the workaday world that is largely overgrown with the "impersonal."[16] According to Heidegger's purely existential view of Hölderlin, art is given the task of creating the permanent. In general, those who use this approach view art as a prime power, incomprehensible to the masses, decipherable only by the blessed few. With such an elitist attitude, all methodology that is "learnable" naturally falls by the wayside. As in Dilthey's work, the self stands at the center, only now the accent shifts from "life" to that of "being." Thus Herbert von Einem asserted that the task of scholarship lies primarily in "perceiving 'being' in its primal origin."[17] Kurt Bauch described this process as the principle of existential "actualization."[18] Erich Ruprecht urged literary scholars to approach literature in Heideggerian terms "as a closed totality which can only be illuminated from within itself."[19] Encouragement in this direction also came from Emil Staiger and his school, who accepted the existential relationship to time as a basic poetic condition that has a voice in determining poetic expression. In his *Basic Principles of Poetics* (1946), he takes up Heidegger's "three ecstasies of the temporal," by means of which he tries to give the generic concepts of "lyric," "epic," and "dramatic" an entirely new meaning. One of Staiger's disciples carried this to extremes by attempting to define even the "novelistic" as a basic *a priori* human attitude.[20]

The result of these theories was exactly what Heidegger had wanted to avoid: "verbiage." The vocabulary of the existentialists became jargon. Especially in the literary interpretations which appeared between 1948 and 1955, one reads about "illumination of being," of the "existential miracle of poetry," "the existential bond to the Thou," "revelation through literature," and the "existential response." All literature became an incomprehensible "secret" that would only allow itself to be interpreted in parabolically encoded language. Where previously literary scholarship had required rational discourse, it now appeared as if only the existential response carried any weight. All empirical reality was thoughtlessly cast aside. "Literature includes no judgment concerning the reality that it is supposed to approximate; on the contrary, literature conjures an imaginative, self-contained reality beyond which it would be absurd to search," said Johannes Pfeiffer in 1956. Elsewhere he speaks of "returning things to their primal origins," and refers to poetry as an "ethical-metaphysical servant of being."[21] After such high-flown phrases, who would dare to speak simply of "literature" or scholarly objectivity?

Fortunately, however, signs in recent years seem to indicate that the "jargon of essentiality,"[22] as Adorno called it, is on the wane. Ultimately, scholars could not continue to rely on such terms as decision, mission, invocation, encounter, and relation. Even the "essential" becomes vacuous, if one is forced to partake of it in unadulterated form. The same applies to that fatal inclination toward the sacral, which prevailed in the circle around Heidegger. Who nowadays still believes in this immediacy of the creative act or in the god-given origin of the work of art? Who would suggest that art absolves us of all responsibility for the present? By far one of the most direct statements disavowing the existential approach to art was made by Arnold Gehlen, who asserted in 1964, "In Germany a theory that should really be disposed of is still in existence. It asserts that artistic expression is the result of inner compulsion, and only in this way is art created. This formulation once had a certain tactical value in the fight against academic pedantry, but as a program it was always insufficient because it was ego-tistical. Today, after we have passed the midpoint of the twentieth century, this theory is impossibly simple-minded. It puts the artist outside all meaningful concerns, for today, reason, science, and education have made deep inroads in all professions. That which fails to speak a clear, well-thought out language in the modern world, is altogether incapable of being communicated to the reader; and can art, of all things, be asked to make do with such a primitive theory about its genesis?"[23] The dominance of existentialism in the humanities thus remained an episode that eventually yielded to a more factually oriented formalism, known in literary history as the art of interpretation, new criticism, or formal analysis.

Chapter Seven

FORMALISTIC TRENDS

I

Even the method known as formalism or analysis of styles has its origins in the late nineteenth century, when it was offered as a much-needed corrective to the enormous influence of positivism. By means of a formal approach scholars hoped to get away from isolated biographical and historical facts and concern themselves once again with art for its own sake. In this direction, the exploration of form and style seemed to promise a new, autonomous approach.

In Germany, art history was the first discipline to adopt a formal orientation and it is not difficult to explain why it took the lead. While German literary scholarship had concerned itself rather narrowly with national movements at the turn of the century and often hovered close to chauvinism, art history maintained a more balanced international perspective and was thus in a better position to offer a more neutral approach. Second, stylistic analysis in art history involved the assigning of dates to works of art, but this factor played a relatively

minor role in literary study. However, this seeming methodological advantage also has its drawbacks, for it presupposes the
impossibility of our ever dealing adequately with the historical
background of the thousands of art works in existence today.
For this reason, art history eagerly accepts the principle of
the autonomy of art.

One of the best early representatives of formalism in art
history is Max Dessoir, who in his *Journal for Aesthetics and
General Art History* (1906 ff.) tried to reshape the positivist
art history of the late nineteenth century into a speculative
set of laws. To this end, Dessoir replaced concrete historical
factors with ideal categories like the "painterly *a priori*" or the
"sculptural." He proceeds entirely ahistorically; instead of
relating particular forms to particular epochs, he posits regularly recurring basic forms found in all artistic expression in
every period. But one searches his work in vain for some concrete examples of these forms. Perhaps for this reason Dessoir's
typology was soon eclipsed by a school which focused more
concretely on similarities of styles within a given epoch, and
gave serious consideration to the question of how styles come
into being.

Alois Riegl's *Problems of Style* (1893) represents one of the
first efforts in this direction. Riegl rejects the positivist assertion
that artistic form is in any way determined by material factors.
As a substitute, Riegl formulates the theory of "conscious
volition toward art," by means of which he hopes to reestablish
a more idealistic view of the creative process. In his opinion,
not the tool or the material but the "creative impulse" is the
determining factor in all creation of art; style is absolute and
cannot be understood in terms of cause and effect.[1] Riegl interprets even the geometric ornaments of prehistoric epochs,
which earlier art historians had associated with the techniques
of textile-making or basket-weaving,[2] as examples of pure
artistic "volition."[3] However, because such a glorification of
the creative impulse runs the risk of becoming completely
subjective, Riegl combines the "drive toward art" with a
regularly recurring sequence of "modes of representation,"

such as tactile and flat, classic and organic, optic and distant. Although Riegl's work was a significant contribution toward formal analysis before the turn of the century, his influence was rather limited, and his theories hardly known outside his own circle of students.

It was Wölfflin who gave the major impetus to the movement and finally gained wide acceptance for idealistic concepts of form. In the 1880s, Wölfflin had still been interested in sense psychology, but in the course of the 1890s he turned toward a strict formal-aesthetic orientation. Increasingly, Wölfflin came to view art history as a "history of visual perception," whose development was entirely autonomous. He therefore relinquished the historical perspective and derived his concepts of style from formal categories. His methodological reorientation is best illustrated by his *Classical Art* (1899), wherein the term "classical" signifies not only the art of Michelangelo, Leonardo, and Raphael, but also refers to some force outside history that follows its own inner laws and is unconcerned with changes in time. Thus, in addition to chapters on individual artists, *Classical Art* includes a section that mentions no names at all, but orders the material according to abstract concepts of form.[4]

In a later work, the influential *Basic Principles of Art History* (1915), which focuses on the distinction between renaissance and baroque, Wölfflin develops the principle of basic forms to its logical extreme and offers "style" as the single highest criterion in art. Biography becomes peripheral and is replaced by five basic categories: the change from linear to painterly, from flatness to depth, from closed to open form, from multiple unity to homogenized unity, and from absolute to relative clarity of representation. Wölfflin seemed to be aiming toward an "art history without names," by means of which he hoped to establish a systematic periodization encompassing the entire world of art. Such a goal left little room for specific styles or historical considerations, which then gave way to a new emphasis on forms of representation. According to Wölfflin, all artists are tied to particular "optical" possibilities which they cannot ever transcend.[5] However, he does not consider how these "modes of seeing" or "forms of representation" originate. Do they arise spontaneously from sheer human inventiveness? Or are they emanations of some world spirit? On this point, Wölfflin is silent. He ends his book with an apodictic assertion—form is an aesthetic absolute, unrelated to historical causality. The "how" and "why" of form seemed to him to be a secondary matter, of interest only to the cultural historian, not the art historian. Although Wölfflin received some harsh criticism even in his own day, especially from the positivists and the adherents of *Geistesgeschichte*, in the years to come he held firm to his basic principles and always bore the derogatory epithet, "formalist" as if it were a badge of honor. And perhaps he was right, for ultimately it was Wölfflin who paved the way for a formal orientation in all the arts, which at first appeared to be extremely fruitful. Had formalism not transcended the biographical detail? Had it not restored the aesthetic principle to its original status? Indeed, there were many scholars who hailed Wölfflin's formalism as the decisive breakthrough to a truly autonomous study of art, and proudly closed their essays with the inspiring motto: Art is my law.

II

Literary scholars were particularly eager to accept Wölfflin's "basic concepts," for in this field stylistic analysis was still entirely undeveloped. This helps to explain the naïveté with which they proceeded, as is perhaps best demonstrated by Oskar Walzel's *Mutual Illumination of the Arts* (1917), in which he tries to transpose Wölfflin's stylistic criteria from art history to the literature of the sixteenth and seventeenth centuries. For example, Walzel interprets Shakespeare simplistically as a "painterly-baroque" poet because of his "open" form. Arthur Hübscher takes a similarly naive approach when he tries to solve so complex a question as the difference between renaissance and baroque art by the formula "homogeneity instead of singularity."[6] In romance studies, Walzel's "mutual illumination of the arts" provided the basis for Theophil Spoerri's *Renaissance and Baroque in Ariosto and Tasso* (1922).

The attempt to apply Wölfflin's basic concepts to the study of classic and romantic was somewhat more successful. Once again, Spoerri was the first to free himself from all empirical data as in his 1918 essay on "The Essence of the Romantic," which establishes such pairs of concepts as confinement and resolution, organization and fusion, binding and loosening. Others contrasted stability and instability, rectilinearity and interwovenness, and extreme terseness and formlessness. By far the most comprehensive and best-known effort in this school is Fritz Strich's *German Classicism and Romanticism: Perfection and Infinity* (1922). Like Wölfflin, Strich attributes the history of style to an ever-recurring polarity of human expression and not to material factors. According to Strich, artistic expression stems from the two basic human impulses toward "perfection" and "infinity," which closely resemble Goethe's "prime phenomena" or Dilthey's "primal experiences."[7] For this reason, in spite of his reliance on Wölfflin, Strich was increasingly drawn toward the history of ideas, which largely ignores artistic form in favor of the spiritual or the ideal.

Nonetheless, Walzel and Strich were widely lauded as the founders of the school of formal analysis or stylistics. Scholars in all the arts began to speak of epochal styles not only in literature and painting, but in music as well. However, in spite of such enthusiasm, the "mutual illumination of the arts" led to few concrete results. Although the concept was widely adopted, it was usually applied only in the realm of motifs and ideas, for in the 1920s the influence of *Geistesgeschichte* was still so strong that an autonomous analysis of style could develop only on the periphery. In this respect, Walzel's *Form and Content* (1923) is an exception, for it presents Dilthey and Wölfflin as equally important models. But few others arrived at so well balanced a synthesis. In the realm of literary scholarship, Wölfflin's "basic principles" were soon given an

existential interpretation, which took critics ever further away
from the investigation of particular styles. While earlier studies
in the typology of styles, such as Richard Hamann's comprehensive treatment of *Impressionism in Life and Art* (1907),
were substantiated by an abundance of specific details, later
scholars working in this mode were easily satisfied with two or
three random examples. As a result, the principle of the "mutual
illumination of the arts," the study of epochs, and with them,
studies of forms and styles in general, fell into strong disrepute
from which they have never fully recovered.

III

In order to take hold, the formal approach needed yet another
stimulus. This impulse came from a more purely literary
realm. In Germany around 1925, there were some small circles
of literary scholars who were trying to counter the wild hypotheses of *Geistesgeschichte* with an exaggerated objectivity
that emphasized the importance of meter, rhyme, and genre. Instead of accepting an intuitive, phenomenological approach,
these critics stressed formal elements by which they hoped to
discover the inner laws of literary scholarship and thereby attain
a more objective view of literature. For this reason, these
groups frowned severely on interdisciplinary efforts and used
the term "boundary-crossing" as a pejorative label to dis-
credit *Geistesgeschichte*, cultural morphology, and national
romanticism, all of which were rejected as "extrinsic" approaches to literature. These groups were concerned with
style and genre, and thus they often referred to the "modesty"
that should confine the literary scholar to the boundaries of his
own discipline. As a result, their methodological efforts were
rather restrained in comparison to those of other scholars
using the formal approach before and after the mid-1920s.
The most important impulse toward formalism came from
studies in genre, which had been particularly neglected in the
previous decades. However, the genre approach of the 1920s is

quite conservative, since it stressed constants rather than changes in form. Instead of analyzing the interrelationships of particular genres in the historical framework of a single epoch, it leaned toward normative theories and rigorous formalism. Furthermore, these genre scholars were seldom able to see beyond their own cultural biases. For example, almost all these theorists around 1925 took an antimodern stance and repeatedly referred to Goethe's "natural forms of poetry," giving attention only to well-established genres such as the ballad, ode, or novella. No one in these circles would have bothered to explore the prehistory of the "epic theater" or forms like satire, parody, or popular ballads. These were not deemed worthy, not sufficiently traditional. The most significant studies in the history of genres between 1920 and 1940 were the surveys of Karl Viëtor, Günther Müller, Wolfgang Kayser, and Friedrich Beissner.[8] But on the whole, this approach could not be developed further at that time. "It was impossible to find colleagues who shared our enthusiasm," Viëtor wrote in 1952, concerning his *History of German Literature According to Genres*, which he had conceived as early as 1923.[9] In the 1920s it was the influence of *Geistesgeschichte*, after 1933 the "volkish" aspects, that worked against the acceptance of genre theory. Thus the formal approach began to be taken seriously only after 1945, when, as a result of the war, these other methodologies were declared bankrupt.

IV

The modish enthusiasm for the formal that swiftly followed the collapse of the Nazi regime must be seen as a kind of escapism. While some critics perpetuated *Geistesgeschichte* and others continued to take an outright chauvinistic, "volkish" approach well into the early 1940s, after 1945 all ideologies were viewed with suspicion and extreme caution. As a result, scholars turned to the aesthetic elements in art, and extraliterary factors more than ever receded into the background.

While even the most exaggerated studies in *Geistesgeschichte* in the 1920s had reflected some minor historical elements, scholars now swore allegiance to the work itself, and were interested only in textual exegesis. Art was to be viewed only as art and nothing else.

Numerous formulations to this effect could be cited. One of the earliest was Karl Viëtor, who in 1945 spoke of the "miracle of poetic form" as a phenomenon *sui generis*, entirely inaccessible by any extrinsic approach.[10] Horst Oppel in *Morphological Literary Scholarship* (1947) exhorted: "If you wish to discover what makes literature literature, stay as close as possible to literary form."[11] In 1948, Ernst Robert Curtius urged literary scholars to abandon the "all-destroying" method of *Geistesgeschichte* and return to the "autonomous structure of literature."[12] Walter Höllerer had a similar goal in mind when he asserted that literature was "neither a cultural-historical document nor a container for philosophical ideas."[13] Others propagated a literary scholarship that would confine itself to the "inner life of the autonomously experienced work," and concern itself only with aesthetic elements.[14] Not surprisingly, there was a proliferation of formal studies in a series of works bearing such titles as *Language and Literature* and *Literature as Art*.

However, in order for formal analysis to establish itself as the dominant approach, even these many individual studies would not have sufficed. For this to happen, a major theoretical study by an established scholar was needed. In this respect, one can hardly overestimate the impact of Wolfgang Kayser's *The Literary Work of Art* (1948), which concerned itself primarily with form and genre. Like other formalists, Kayser views the work of literature as a "self-contained structure" rather than a reflection of reality. He too insisted that literary criticism had to start all over again, and therefore ought to confine itself to those questions posed by the work of literature *as literature*, a position that meant a focus on the text itself.[15] Seven years later Emil Staiger supported this approach and expressed himself even more dogmatically: "If literary scholarship is to be renewed, it cannot rely on philosophical speculations or other questionable artifices, but must focus on a new close reading of texts," he writes in the *Art of Interpretation* (1955).[16] Like Kayser before him, Staiger does not expect criticism to explain, but to focus on those elements that best reflect the stylistic harmony of the work of art. It seemed to Staiger that a strict history of style would best reveal the essence of the "poetic" most directly. Therefore, with regret, he mourned the absence of a "Wölfflin of literary scholarship."[17] Staiger had hoped to provide a substitute for Wölfflin's *Basic Principles of Art* with his *Basic Principles of Poetics* (1946), but in this effort he failed because his focus was not sufficiently clear and he indiscriminately fused the formal elements with vague ontological conceptions.

But possibly not even the works of Staiger and Kayser together would have been sufficient to establish intrinsic analysis as *the* form of literary criticism in Germany, if, at the same time, this approach had not succeeded on an international scale. In the late 1940s and early 1950s, influence from abroad was considerable. The most important impetus came from the formalistic orientation of the comparatists, the theoretical formulations of T. S. Eliot, the English *Scrutiny* school associated with F. R. Leavis, the American "new criticism," French *explication de texte*, as well as Russian "formalism" which was not new, but had only recently been discovered abroad. Of these, the American new criticism of the early 1940s was the most influential, applauded in Germany because of its narrow, formal orientation, which scholars hoped would rescue literary criticism from the methodological confusion then so prevalent. While in the 1930s, following the great depression, many scholars in the United States had taken a sociological or even Marxist approach to literature, in the 1940s they were interested in literary perfection, and turned their attention to the principle of "organic unity," or the inner congruity of the individual parts of a work of art to the whole. Consciously rejecting historical and biographical details, the American new critics affirmed T. S. Eliot's view of the timelessness of all truly great works of art. In the United States, this formal approach represented a protest against several conflicting modes of literary criticism. On the one hand, it was an attack against positivist scholarship still operant in the 1930s, on the other, against the moralistic New Humanism of Paul Elmer More and Irving Babbit, which had itself been conceived in the first decades of the twentieth century as a protest against the material determinism of the positivists and naturalists, and against the cult of the individual associated with romanticism. New criticism was also viewed as a corrective to Freudianism and to the Marxist criticism of America's "Red decade." This may help to explain the vehemence of formalism in the United States, as well as its extreme antihistorical stance. Of course, the new criticism also had its forerunners. As early as 1910, Joel Spingarn in a Columbia University lecture had spoken of the need for a "new" criticism that would concern itself with the "how" of artistic expression. Equally influential was the work of the British semanticist I. A. Richards, who had been interested in the influence of language upon thought as early as 1910.

But the real breakthrough for new criticism came with the publication of Brooks's and Warren's anthology, *Understanding Poetry* (1939), in which the writers boldly asserted that "If poetry is worth teaching at all, it is worth teaching as poetry." They plainly considered all other approaches to literature outdated. Instead of analyzing a particular work primarily with respect to its contents, Brooks and Warren simply viewed a "poem as a poem."[18] Therefore, they preferred to work with concepts like image, symbol, structure, complexity, ambiguity, close reading, and textual analysis. It might be noted here that these critical tools were most fruitful when applied to the contemporary poetry of the period, and were, very likely, forged with this body of work in mind, especially as many of the theorists of the new criticism were themselves active poets. However, because these new critics rejected all historical perspective, they assumed that their method was the only valid one, appropriate to all poetry of every period; they placed the greatest value on that poetry which best lent itself to formal analysis. Cleanth Brooks and Robert Heilman eventually did produce *Understanding Drama* (1945), Brooks and Warren, *Understanding Fiction* (1948), but their exclusive interest in the technical aspects of literature led them to concern themselves primarily with poetry. Form is what interested the new critics, and in poetry, more than in any other genre, form *was* the meaning. In order to avoid the "intentional" fallacy, they eschewed discussion of contents and spoke mainly of autonomous structures of symbols and poetic wholes, which seem no less self-contained or "essential" than Heidegger's conception of poetry as "revealed being." Archibald MacLeish captured this mood well with his dictum: "A poem should not mean, but be."[19] Most new critics rejected the reality of the objective world as being irrelevant to literary criticism. Therefore, Brooks speaks of paradox; Allen Tate, of tension; John Crowe Ransom, of inner structure; and William Empson, of "seven types of ambiguity."

Curiously, many of these ideas had been anticipated by the Russian formalists between 1915 and 1930. But perhaps this is not so strange, for in the East as in the West, formal analysis represents a conscious reaction to a more politically engaged literary scholarship, a retreat into the realm of the aesthetic. The two most important groups in Russia were the Moscow school of linguistics and the St. Petersburg "Opajaz," to which such well-known scholars as Eichenbaum, Shklovski, Tynianov, and Jakobson belonged. This school had already turned sharply against biographically oriented positivism and instead argued for a formally oriented evolution of the aesthetic dimension, which is modified by historical events but not essentially determined by them. Under the influence of Wölfflin, Walzel, and Strich, the Russian formalists frequently speak of the pure "art of language" or the "self-sufficient word." They view the poet as a "maker," whose technique manifests itself primarily in the particular structure of words or in phonetic gestures. For this reason, their main interest is the literary quality of literature, which was known in the day of "l'art pour l'art" as "craftsmanship."[20] Similar tendencies can be seen in the work of the Polish integralists and the Prague school of linguistics, which developed only a short time later. They too devoted themselves almost exclusively to "discovering that which is peculiar to the literary material," as Boris Eichenbaum once described this purely formal approach.[21]

Therefore, it is hardly surprising that when René Wellek, who had been associated with the Prague linguistic circle, in 1939 met Austin Warren, one of the American new critics in the United States, they quickly discovered the similarities in their methodological orientation. Wellek's enormous influence on German literary scholarship after 1945 can easily be explained by the fact that he was able to draw not only on Anglo-American literature but also on the German literary tradition. Moreover, in contrast to many other new critics he was less radical, and even left some room for historical perspective. From among his numerous books and essays on method we will cite only his *Theory of Literature* (1949), written jointly with Austin Warren, which is easily his most influential work. In this book Wellek and Warren firmly spoke out against all "cause-governed methods," that is, against "extrinsic approaches" that make use of extraliterary factors. On this assumption, they assert that attention to factors like biography, sociology, psychology, or *Geistesgeschichte* leads the literary critic to neglect the formal aspects of the work of art. In their view, literary scholarship can only come into its own with an "intrinsic approach," concerning itself primarily with phenomena like form, language, style, genre, euphony, rhythm, metrics, metaphor, and symbol. Thus they write, most programmaticallly, "Literary study should be specifically literary."[22] Here too they join Cleanth Brooks and Kenneth Burke in considering the contents less interesting than the technical aspects of literature, its "making." As a result, they find no truly legitimate points of comparison between literature and life. For them, literature is simply "literature." To measure literature in terms of the real world, is to violate the aesthetic quality of art. Thus they speak of "fictional worlds" which operate according to their own inner logic. In their opinion, a work of literature can have no specific historical meaning since it changes with every reading, and is therefore continuously in process, at all times containing myriad future possibilities. For this reason, their literary theory does not recognize specific national or even linguistic differences as important, but always aims to keep the totality of world literature in mind. In this, they lean on T. S. Eliot, who once asserted that "the whole of the literature of Europe from Homer . . . has a simultaneous existence and composes a simultaneous order."[23]

In these years Wellek and Warren viewed the United States as the center of this new approach and were sure it would quickly supplant *Geistesgeschichte* and other antiquated historical methods that previously had given Germany the lead in literary criticism. Their scholarly model was the "teacher-critic" or "man of letters,"[24] who had such vast knowledge of literature that he could view all important works in terms of their global literary connections in time and in space. Since it is impossible for a single person to obtain such vast knowledge in the realm of history, they placed the emphasis primarily on a refined awareness of literary form. As a result, though their *Theory of Literature* rests on brilliant insights, it leads to a formalistic subjectivism.

V

The impact of these new critical theories on German literary scholarship can best be observed between 1950 and 1960. In these years, everyone praised "text-oriented structural analysis," which confined itself almost entirely to the formal-aesthetic qualities of the work of art. The entire focus of literary analysis was its technical artistry, not its mimetic qualities. For this reason, the aesthetic element was ever more strongly separated from all social and historical factors. As a result of this development, those "literary monuments" that had unmistakable social dimensions, were soon replaced by so-called "texts," in which only the formal structure was of interest. One could say that scholars developed a strong aversion to all "extraliterary" elements, which generally led to a narrow perspective, typically resulting in detailed, line-by-line analysis of a few individual poems. In addition, this method was particularly susceptible to dilettantism, since, in uncovering "layers of meaning" and the inner structure of a text, much was left to the ingenuity and private taste of the individual critic. The more exacting term "literary scholarship" was therefore replaced in these years by "literary criticism" or "literary description," both of which stressed the autonomy of art.

Closely connected to the question of interpretation is the extraordinary importance the formalists placed on questions of literary worth. Almost all the other approaches to literature —even *Geistesgeschichte*—had granted every individual work its specific place in the history of literature. Since earlier critics had wished primarily to comprehend literature, even lesser works had been suitable. The new critics, in contrast, concerned themselves solely with "masterpieces." Emil Staiger asserted that he was not interested in minor works but only in "works of genius."[25] Of course, this served to de-emphasize the historical ever more strongly. Clearly, if one wishes to "comprehend," one needs a comprehensive view of history. But interpretation or evaluation requires considerably less knowledge. Such emphasis on evaluation might have proved useful had their system taken even a few extraliterary elements into account. But unfortunately, all such factors seemed entirely too heterogeneous and too extrinsic for the new critics, who relied upon the "primacy of the aesthetic in the poetic work of art."[26] Such an extreme formal approach led to a peculiar double standard in German literary criticism. While literature of the "higher rank" was always considered to be absolutely autonomous,[27] for lesser, more "time-bound" works, the socio-historical approach was deemed suitable.

Broadly speaking, this strict confinement to the individual work can be traced back to the late 1930s. Staiger's earlier book, *Time as the Imaginative Power of the Poet* (1939), had concerned itself with the interpretation of only three poems. Such emphasis on individual interpretations, eschewing all larger connections, was also part of the "inner emigration" into which some scholars claim to have retreated in the Nazi period, as evidenced by Max Kommerell's *The Spirit and Letter of Poetry* (1939) and *Thoughts about Poetry* (1943). But this trend did not become dominant until after 1945. Only then did scholars speak of a hermeneutics of literature in Germany. Staiger correctly saw that this approach provided a method which concerned itself primarily with formal elements, "without looking to the right or the left, and especially not behind the work of literature."[28]

As explanation for this inward turning, one can point to several factors. First was the fact that after the war, scholars often could not lay their hands on more than a single text. In addition, because of the chaotic situation in the universities, they were often unable to find time either to study or produce larger works. Under such difficult conditions it was simply not possible to run seminars as they had previously been conducted, that is, on the basis of a philological and historical approach. But even more important than the external calamitous situation was the general timidity toward the historical element that had led so many scholars into a mistaken commitment to National Socialism. To most, the ideological impasse seemed so great that the sweep of history could no longer give meaning to the "whole." In addition, formal analysis seemed neutral and objective. Therefore, many scholars were quite satisfied with this methodological narrowness. In fact, those who tried to "cross the boundaries" of their disciplines were often ridiculed as dilettantes. In the individual work, literary scholars at last found the new security that they had been unable to discover in the larger social context. The methodological crisis in effect since 1900 seemed to be over, once and for all. The formalists were convinced that with the "art of interpretation" literary scholarship had finally come into its own, had been rescued from the shackles of alien disciplines. Now, the inner being of art seemed to stand in the center: the literary as literature, the poetic as poetry, were the favorite tautologies. Some scholars went so far as to thank literature for being what it is. In addition they were comforted by the fact that Anglo-American criticism was taking the very same "objective" direction, and thus a kind of international solidarity of literary scholars seemed to be taking shape.

Nonetheless, if one closely examines the supposed scholarly objectivity of the many interpretations published in these years, one is bound to be disappointed. At times, one has the impression that their approach is no less subjective than what some practitioners of *Geistesgeschichte* had offered. Although they theorize about the "art" of interpretation, and in spite of Brooks's warning against the "heresy of paraphrase," in practice they often end up with no more than a paraphrasing of the original. Staiger himself once admitted quite openly, that "the most subjective feelings serve as the basis of all scholarship! I cannot and will not deny it."[29] Dilthey had asserted much the same when he extolled empathy as the basis of all literary scholarship.

One should therefore seriously ask oneself just how "objective" this intrinsic approach really is. What is brought to the surface and how much is necessarily omitted in such confinement to individual masterpieces? Does one not end up with the old differentiation formulated by Croce, between the poetic and the non-poetic? In this connection, Horst Rüdiger once asked how German classicism would appear if criticism of it confined itself solely to a study of its poetry. From such a narrow perspective, Winckelmann would certainly have been almost entirely excluded; Klopstock, on the other hand, with his *Messiah*, his odes and dramas, would come off rather well. Little would be left of Herder but the poems and his efforts at drama. Two-thirds of Goethe's total output would have to be excluded. Rüdiger correctly asserts that "there are some literary historians who find the works of Plato, Cicero, Montaigne, Winckelmann, and Emerson to be a profound literary experience, that is, a genuine aesthetic experience, which Herder's poetry may perhaps fail to provide."[30] The perpetual insistence on the singularity and higher rank of imaginative literature must lead to pale aestheticism. After all, with such a rigid attitude we would no longer be permitted to study letters, diaries, memoirs, travel journals, or collections of essays. And even purely literary works that were not of the very first rank would be excluded from scholarship. This thinking leads to what Nietzsche, in aesthetic raptures, once called the "Olympus of illusion." If one must always keep the "miracle of form" in mind, the scholar's relationship to literature is apt to become quite sentimental. Thus, some interpretations of this period sound almost like religiously inspired exegesis.

But in the realm of this mode of formal interpretation, influenced mainly by Staiger, one could still distinguish the scholar's genuine passion for great poetry. How ideological this formalistic trend is, becomes evident particularly in the growing interest in hermetic poetry. One need only think of the conspicuous attention given to poets like the late Hölderlin, Baudelaire, Mallarmé, Trakl, Rilke, and Valéry, not to speak of the "language grids" or "verbal constructions" of recent poetry. As in new criticism, the lyric, by far the most subjective of all the genres, becomes the ideal of the modern, the purest, most absolute form, while prose, which is far more tied to content, is given a subordinate role in the realm of literature. Thus one recent volume in Germany to take this strict textual approach is called *Intrinsic Aesthetics* and is tellingly subtitled the *Lyric as Paradigm of the Modern* (1966).[31] The title is symptomatic of how strongly the formalists try to avoid all broad, universal connections and prefer to concentrate on the individual, the subjective, and at the same time the most formal elements. In this sphere, they continuously focus on the ambiguous and shun the objective. Thus it is not surprising to find a concept like "lyric obscurity" among the most important slogans of this school.

This school of hermeneutics tends to celebrate pessimism and assiduously avoids all theories of imitation or mimesis, by means of which a more positive view of reality might be offered. Therefore, in addition to the modish interest in lyric poetry, several peripheral modes of literary expression have come to the fore in recent years. One need only think of the rising preference for the manneristic, the grotesque, the absurd, the distorted, the tragicomic, the symbolic, or the surrealistic, which are widely interpreted as prefigurations of the "modern," and valued as such. As a result of such an orientation, concrete historical factors have increasingly been replaced by attention to elements associated with periods of decadence. These critics continue to assert that the world of art and the world of reality are two entirely separate realms. According to them, works of art exist only for themselves and say nothing about their surrounding reality. These pronouncements closely resemble Oscar Wilde's aesthetic doctrine, which he had formulated as early as the 1890s, that "art never expresses anything other than itself." Nietzsche had supported this idealism which tends to the formalistic, with the aphorism, "There are no facts, only interpretations."[32] Gottfried Benn had put it this way, "Art for its own sake, that means a kind of art that needs no supplement from the perspective of morality or sociology."[33]

For this school, then, the autonomy of the work of art virtually becomes a fetish. The images, symbols, and forms of art are assumed to be perfect and permanent, in contrast to the "real" world in which everything is imperfect and doomed to fade. The cult of form thus looks to art with yearning or nostalgia, as a lulling escape. However, this antirealistic orientation also has its ideological aspects, in that it serves to keep the artist safely divorced from the realm of politics. We can find a number of theorists who are ready to condemn even the slightest attention to realistic elements in a work of art as proof of historical or sociological thinking. The most moderate, in this respect, is René Wellek, who once asserted, "The theory of realism is ultimately bad aesthetics because all art is 'making' and is a world in itself of illusion and symbolic forms."[34] In general, for this school, the word does not reflect any objective reality, but is understood primarily as a formal sign. What matters is the subjective, solipsistic connotation of language, which can vary greatly from poet to poet. This seemingly objective analysis of language results in a complex, ambiguous theory of semantics, that, like the art of interpretation, becomes a kind of guesswork. The ideological conceptions of this school increasingly adapt themselves to a more symbolic or phenomenological approach, deriving from Husserl's *Ideas Toward a Pure Phenomenology and Phenomenological Philosophy* (1913), Cassirer's *Philosophy of Symbolic Form* (1923–29), Ingarden's *The Literary Work of Art* (1929), and Susanne Langer's *Philosophy in A New Key* (1942). In these, attention to formal elements coincides with an existential world view that could only be expressed by symbols or myths, and must be differentiated from Sartre's left-wing, action-oriented existentialism. As a result, these semantic formalists profess a phenomenological agnosticism that views literature in terms of a hopeless "plurisignification" or semantic speculation.[35] Thus in her *Problems of Art* (1951), Susanne Langer says of the literary sign, "It does not stand for something else, nor refer to anything that exists apart from it."[36]

Having entirely forfeited the usual function of language as communication, these formal theorists are left with abstract linguistic images and symbolic structures. They seldom speak of specifically human elements in the framework of these autonomous categories. Where do concepts like the tragic, guilt, or expiation fit in? Their place has been taken by such terms as craft, technique, information value, and particle of narration—that is, by formal patterns that apparently have little to do with the meaning of literature. In this connection, Max Bense once tried to develop a "technological aesthetic" in which he asserted that the principle of progress in art rests entirely on formal innovation. In his opinion, the "development" of art only uncovers the aesthetic qualities present in certain materials. Art thus boils down to sheer technique.[37] In this way the pursuit of literature ultimately becomes the pursuit of texts, whose "information value" can best be tested by means of semiotics, statistics, cybernetics, and computer science. And at this juncture the antirealistic orientation of formalism reaches its lowest point. Here, form and content are completely separated; absolute mathematical objectivity corresponds to absolute dissociation from ideology, resulting in empty abstractions. Good examples of this are provided by some of the recent "linguistic" efforts at interpretation, in which even the dramas of Schiller, Brecht, and Büchner or the frightening nightmares of Kafka are reduced to mere diagrams of entropy.

It seems doubtful that such static analysis, oriented to information theory, offers the *only* alternative to the historical approach which the formalists have rejected. In terms of information, virtually nothing is gained. As has happened before in literary studies, scholars are trying to reshape the humanities so they will fit into the "age of technology" and the natural sciences. But in so doing, they not only betray literary scholarship but also technology, which could offer significantly more useful results. In recent years, with the rise of more engaged approaches, particularly in West Germany, this extreme formalism has lost much of its power to attract; in fact, with the possible exception of structuralism, which must be viewed as a vestige and not as a new beginning, all formal approaches are in the process of retreat.

Chapter Eight

THE *DERNIER CRI* OF STRUCTURALISM

Toward the end of the 1960s, when the various formalistic trends in German literary studies seemed to have played themselves out, the approach known as structuralism was imported from France and immediately taken up by diehard aesthetes and those older formalists who had not yet retreated into the "great silence." We might well ask what this method had to offer and why it was greeted with such enthusiasm in Germany. But before we attempt to answer these questions, let us make clear that structuralism is not really a single method, but a label used to describe a number of related critical approaches associated with a variety of disciplines besides literature—anthropology, psychoanalysis, linguistics, philosophy. The number of names currently associated with this movement in France, where it has virtually replaced all other methods, is staggering. For this reason it is difficult to tell with any confidence who besides the established "greats" (Claude Lévi-Strauss, Roland Barthes) will be recorded in literary history as having been the most influential.[1] But in spite of this diversity within the structuralist mode, these scholars do share some ideas, particularly their faith in structures and systems as an effective means of explaining entire civilizations, languages, literary texts, as well as the workings of the human psyche. In addition, most of these critics frequently fuse an analytic with a synthetic approach and assert that every individual element in a given structure, literary or otherwise, must be seen in terms of the entire work, or all the works of a given author, or even more broadly, in terms of all the institutions of a particular civilization. Furthermore, almost all the critics working under the banner of structuralism either explicitly or implicitly oppose the developmental conception of history, which assumes that humankind is perfectable; as substitute they offer a subjective, static, pessimistic world view.

In this respect, the violent quarrel between Roland Barthes and Raymond Picard, which broke out in 1963, following the publication of Barthes's *On Racine*, is interesting and illuminating, since it brings to the fore one of Barthes's central tenets, now accepted by many other structuralists, that a work of literature is an independent system of meaning, undecipherable and inaccessible by any objective means. For Barthes, all criticism is subjective, and literary history, nonexistent; he only obliges the critic to announce his subjective approach and be consistent in its application. Picard, on the other hand, is closer to the old formalism in his insistence that language holds the key to the objective elements of a text. He considers the critic responsible for bringing to light the original meaning that the words of a text had for the artist. While Barthes was clearly influenced by the anthropological studies of Claude Lévi-Strauss, Picard shows affinities both to America new criticism, Russian formalism, and structural linguistics.

We thus see that what may loosely be called the structuralist approach provided those very elements that many scholars in Germany had sorely missed in the sociological studies of reception and influence offered by the followers of Lukács and Adorno in the 1960s. To be specific, structuralism is ahistorical, formal, and in spite of Barthes's avowed subjectivity, it appeared to provide an objective scientific method that conveniently provided independence from all ideological concerns and political divisions.[2] This certainly helps to explain why even so well-known an existential formalist as Beda Alleman views structuralism as a thoroughly acceptable method. He praised it for concentrating on the "literary qualities of the text" and for raising itself far above the "insipid methodological eclecticism" of historically oriented interpretations.[3] Therefore, it appears that the structural approach, which seemed so new and avantgarde in Germany, was really the last gasp of the old guard.

But some of the younger German scholars also took French structuralism to heart and viewed themselves as the "engaged" champions of this thoroughly unengaged method. They were dazzled by two aspects of the new theory: first, by the fact that it came from France and was thus not only chic, but politically neutral. Second, it promised exactness and was based on broader conceptions that seemed to transcend the private interpretation of literature, which had prevailed during the previous two decades when existentialism, formalism, and subjective psychology were the dominant critical modes in Germany. For these reasons many scholars welcomed structuralism for what seemed to be its objectivity and its suprapersonal, sociological, collective, and at times frankly Marxistic perspective.[4]

However, in terms of ideology, it is rather easy to unmask both of these apparent advantages. To be sure, structuralism undeniably comes from France.[5] But is this in itself cause to rejoice? And by unthinkingly accepting the foreignness of this theory as a positive factor in itself, are we not slipping back into the old clichés of national psychology, which value everything French as interesting, ignoring historical causality and the ideological roots of all doctrines? Many young Germans mistakenly associated structuralism with that long, impressive line of French critical thinking that extends from Voltaire to Sartre. Such a view is simply not accurate. Closer scrutiny shows that structuralism came to the fore in the years of Gaullism, around 1960, and is the product of that same resignation and political inactivity reflected in the static world view of the *nouveau roman* in those same years. Indeed, many aspects of structuralism can be traced to the political disorientation of those intellectuals who felt hopelessly alienated in Gaullist France, could not summon up the spirit to take an adversary position, and thus retreated into the study of myths and primitive cultures.

It is, therefore, no accident that the seminal work of this movement was Claude Lévi-Strauss's *The Savage Mind* (1962). This book was extremely successful in Paris. In its wake, many intellectuals quickly abandoned the Sartrean mode of existential engagement that had been dominant in France since 1945, and a period of luxurious *tristesse* set in. Thus from 1962 on we can speak of several schools of structuralism. In the sphere of literary criticism, it was such books as the previously mentioned *On Racine* (1963) and Michel Foucault's *The Order of Things* (1966) that built on Lévi-Strauss's theories and tried to apply the structuralist system of symbols to the world of literature, using the same signs and symbols that ethnologists had gathered from the behavior of primitive tribes. At first glance, this seems to represent a shift away from the private quality of existential literary criticism and a move toward a total view of artistic expression, following the general laws of human behavior. But this seeming universality is deceptive. For whoever insists on the timelessness of all political, social, or aesthetic structures, and speaks only of topoi, archetypes, and synchronistic regularities does not believe in progress. Barthes makes himself perfectly clear on this point. For him, literature is only apparently socially effective; in the large it can have no effect on life. It is not surprising to find that most structuralists dimiss Sartre's engagement as ridiculous or ineffectual. Why should anyone who can luxuriate in a variety of cultures and time periods be satisfied with a mere diachronic, time-bound mode of thinking?

The second supposed advantage of structuralism, that is, its scholarly exactitude, which promises complete scientific objectivity, can be viewed from the same perspective. From the standpoint of scholarship, this methodological claim rests on the famous differentiation between language as a suprapersonal system (*langue*) and private speech (*parole*), which the Swiss linguist Ferdinand de Saussure, the acknowledged father of semiotics, had already tried to set up as an ahistorical set of rules for the development of language as early as 1910. Lévi-Strauss is especially dependent on philology, which functions synchronically, and he openly acknowledges it as the starting point of his own theory. But in addition to linguistics, a whole series of seemingly scientifically oriented disciplines in the social and natural sciences have also been influential: ethnology, the study of myths (Mircea Eliade, Georges Dumezil), the concept of the "collective unconscious" (Carl Gustav Jung), Gestalt psychology, psychoanalysis, the new Freudianism of Jacques Lacan, Russian formalism, the Prague school of linguistics, philosophy (Foucault) comparative theology, phenomenology, mathematics, and even the more positivistically oriented aspects of sociology.

What unites these efforts is their search for usable structural models, and from these derive certain universal rules. Under the influence of Lévi-Strauss they usually choose the prehistory of man as the field for their scientific inquiries, that is, these critics study the thought processes of the primitive and the only partially developed, as they manifest themselves in myths, legends, and other prehistorical documents, in order to uncover the basic structures of our current nations, literatures, governments, legal systems, and those institutions which they consider to be unalterable. They search everywhere for archetypes, for blueprints of the eternal, fixed systems of symbols or predetermined forms that stand outside of historical development and human individuation. In their research the structuralists particularly like to descend to the collective unconscious, to the "mothers" of Goethe's *Faust*, to barely conceivable primitive powers. The fact that, in the wake of such researches, bourgeois individual psychology is broadly neglected and the emphasis falls more on the circumstances which determine man, is in general quite a good thing. But why do the structuralists stick only to the preconscious, the ahistorical, and the primitive? Again and again they show interest primarily in the structures that determine man and give less attention to those that man himself has created. And ultimately, it is only the latter that are really significant, for only in them does the actual dialectical process of history and human behavior really begin. Everything else is mere study of curiosities in the realm of man's prehistory, accessible only through archeology. Thus, Sartre was not far from the mark when he called structuralism a "logical scandal."[6]

The results of such a method, that is, those which are most prominent, often appear to be rather thin. The great majority of structuralist studies make prodigious claims, which they are not able to fulfill and offer little that is concrete. They are most instructive when they limit their research to primitive societies. However, in applying certain principles across the centuries, most structuralists end up with meaningless circles or with the only too familiar "eternal return of the same," in which a trivialized Nietzsche or, even worse, the cultural morphology of a Spengler is discernible. Though they go about it with considerably more subtlety, a greater variety of perspectives and a more confusing vocabulary than the author of the *Decline of the West*, nonetheless, in their theories they seldom advance beyond the limits of his intellectual horizon.

In the realm of literary scholarship, this discrepancy between the claims and the results is even more alarming. Using an approach which employs highly complex mythological or linguistic procedures, they arrive at conclusions that anyone with sound common sense or a rudimentary knowledge of history could equally well reach. But at least the structuralists remain in the sphere of the exact (as senseless as such exactitude may be in the realm of the humanities). Structuralism is far worse when it wanders into the essayistic and offers private phantasies as typological structures. Thus some German structurally oriented literary scholars have recently tried to divide the German novelists of the nineteenth century into "orderly" writers (Stifter, Storm, Raabe), and "wild ones"

(Gutzkow, Spielhagen, Fontane). If there is one structural category that is inappropriate for Fontane, it is certainly that he was one of the "wild" ones.

In summation, one could say that while structuralism did offer some formalists a view of broader connections, as an approach, it is nonetheless based on methods that have already been in existence for a long time and are in themselves as formalistic as those they were intended to replace. Its resigned pessimism has long been part of the vocabulary of all scholarly theories that build on Nietzsche and Spengler and are hopelessly entangled in themselves, in order to give their own lack of perspective a touch of profundity. Whenever aimless, ahistorical thinking makes its appearance, this kind of pessimism necessarily sets in. Such melancholy is the inevitable result of unengaged thinking. Aesthetes are as familiar with it as the Heideggerians, as the tragically doomed Nietzschians, as well as those with a musty intrinsic orientation, who try to hide their subjective bias and their fear of becoming declassé behind a massive enmity to progress.

For this reason, in a 1971 interview in the *Spiegel*, which faithfully mirrors the malaise of this approach, Lévi-Strauss asserted that all intellectual engagement is senseless from the very start, and he proudly called structuralism a method without any "practical results."[7] A similar attitude underlies Roland Barthes's book, *On Racine* (1963), in which he implicitly devalues all utopias and all progressive ideologies and views man as irredeemably fixed from time immemorial, living in unalterable circumstances. All that remains, for Barthes too, is *tristesse*. In this way, the structuralists are perpetrating the same kind of deception carried out by shamans and peddled daily by the mass media. For ultimately, like the puppeteers who manipulate and monopolize the mass media, they too view concrete circumstances as something mythic. Whether willingly or against their own wishes, they thus serve the very masters they blame in their writings for the regrettable corruption of the original state of nature. But this apparent contradiction is actually a structural characteristic of this ideology, which, in spite of all theoretical statements to the contrary, is primarily interested in maintaining the status quo. No wonder then, that structuralism has received such a favorable press in recent years. And it is this very attitude that plays into the hands of those in power, to whom every pessimistic utterance represents a further stabilization of their own position. Man seen as irredeemable, circumstances as unalterable, regulated as if from eternity—this pessimism is one of the most potent weapons used by the profit-worshipping establishment. In the final analysis, structuralism is an ideology according to which the entire world is prestructured (read "managed"), in which all people are suppressed according to primal laws (read "instruments of power"). In such a world man is only an object and no longer a moving force of historical processes. Here, not the individual but the apparatus of power reigns. One could conjecture that the enormous popularity of structuralist methods in certain branches of the American academy (especially comparative literature, French, English, and linguistics) represents a retreat from an unpalatable political reality and matches the current mood of despair and disillusionment. Only if they overcome this apathy, will scholars be ready to take a more hopeful direction in their literary scholarship.

PART II

Possibilities of a New Synthesis

Chapter One

THE DILEMMA OF OVERSPECIALIZATION

"Truth is the whole. The whole, however, is only complete by virtue of its development. Of the Absolute it can be said, that only at the end, is it what it really is."

— Georg Wilhelm Friedrich Hegel

I

After surveying the major approaches to literature and art of the past hundred years, one necessarily feels a degree of constraint. So much intelligence and imagination, and yet such narrowness and so many methodological dead ends. It is impossible to overlook the errors, omissions, and distortions of the various approaches. Nevertheless, one must be careful not to view these schools merely as a series of ignominious defeats. For no matter what the basis of the individual method—be it positivism, *Geistesgeschichte*, sociology, cultural morphology, the history of problems and ideas, psychoanalysis, Marxism, new criticism, formalism, or structuralism—all can lay claim to a modicum of truth, especially if they do not insist upon legislating their method. Nonetheless, such acknowledgment should in no way be taken as approval of an arbitrary eclecticism. Thus, Herbert Cysarz is wrong when he asserts, "No method is in itself better or worse; on the contrary, at any given moment one method is always the most fruitful; to apply the right method to the right object at the right time is the real secret of literary scholarship."[1] If this were correct, it would be perfectly sufficient to interpret a phonetic poem on a strictly formal basis, a novel of incest on a purely psycho-analytic one, a work like *Fathers and Sons* according to gen-eration theory, and poems about death according to the history of ideas. Yet even these few examples show that an eclectic approach is not broad, but narrow. In the final analysis, even the shortest poem about death has also its biographical, social, stylistic, and psychoanalytical aspects which are ignored if we base our interpretation solely on the "history of ideas." The same principle holds for every work of art.

For this reason an eclectic approach is not the answer to the dilemma of methodological pluralism. What each of the schools we have examined lacks, is not the subjective skill to apply the right method to the right object at the right time, but a new universal perspective that would place the small, concrete de-tail as well as the most subtle interpretation into a meaningful total context. In the years when Herder and Hegel turned their attention to aesthetic theory, such breadth was still taken for granted. Even in the era around 1850, the historians and early positivists still stressed the human dimension of cultural expression. Only in the period of late positivism in the 1880s and 1890s did scholars gradually lose faith in the socially progressive function of history, and the study of art and literature became an end in itself.

The new idealism around 1900 did little to halt this trend since all too frequently it lost itself in the realm of pure speculation. As a result, reality and philosophy, which always ought to stand in a dialectical relationship to one another, be-came increasingly estranged, until finally they separated com-pletely. The consequence of such separation can be seen today in the inability of theorists to communicate with pragmatists, even if they do manage to sit peacefully together at congresses and symposia. Thus the universalism that once prevailed in the humanities is increasingly superseded by the modern tendency toward specialization; the widespread celebration of the "scientific" encourages literary scholars to feel guilty if they do not confine their endeavors within narrow, carefully circumscribed limits. Even structuralism, with its apparent breadth, is of no help in this situation, since it is equally subjective and ahistorical, and because of its emphasis on structures, equally formalistic and overspecialized.

The root causes of this methodological narrowing were the focus of the first part of this book. Perhaps the most important reason lies in the simple fact that it is no longer possible for any one person to master the totality of the known with which one is confronted in one's subject. Even the most arduous effort to encompass everything in a single field would prove futile, for one would have to master not only the material already in existence, but also the new that is being steadily produced in ever greater quantities from year to year. In fact, it is quite impossible to keep up with everything, even if one attempted to do this only superficially. And as a methodological possibility, the merely dilettantish has long since been passé. Furthermore, the scholar in the humanities is continuously haunted by the "scientific" demands that his work meet the criteria of exactness required by the natural sciences, which encourage him to take an ever narrower approach. In addition, our substantially sharpened methods propel us ever more strongly from the macrocosmic into the microcosmic. In order to be scientific today, one is virtually forced to remain within one's own area and to avoid any methodological crossing over. Few would deny that this state of affairs presents a real dilemma which cannot easily be disposed of, even with the most convincing arguments, although usually scholars are inclined to push their doubts aside.

On the other hand, the second reason for this specialization, that is, the conscious rejection of history, is quite another matter. This is not the result of methodological constraint inherent in the research, but an ideological decision, resulting from the disintegration of the belief in progress. So long as scholars viewed the development of culture and art as a meaningful series of stages, details could easily be placed within a larger framework, and fit into the context of historical causality. As this belief lost hold, was even questioned as a postulate, the historical element was cast aside and no longer held any attraction to the scholar. For ultimately, historically oriented scholarship makes sense only if it can maintain a certain universal direction, at least as its basis.

If the scholar feels himself "above" history or questions it in principle, then he is likely to retreat into cynicism, resignation, or simple abstraction. But when history is taken seriously, it is always the "natural enemy of isolation," as Gervinus once formulated it.[2] Therefore, we ought not to dispense all too precipitately with the postulate of universalism, which emphasizes the developmental processes of humankind; without it, any historically based study of the arts is unthinkable. However, if one does reject history, then it is certainly unfair to blame this decision on the scientific method or the vastness of the material at hand. Let us keep in mind that overspecialization always reenforces the status quo and intellectual stagnation. If this occurs, we will have reached a scholarly situation that can only be characterized as ideological despair, unless we wish to suggest that only a complete loss of direction allows us to attain the ideal of "objectivity." Yet which of us would be willing to make such an admission?

II

One thing is particularly striking, that is, how willingly we have surrendered to the trend toward specialization. Instead of coming to grips with the dangers inherent in this development, we all too often make a virtue of necessity and accept the modern division of labor as absolutely necessary; as a result, we no longer feel competent in areas that lie outside our domain. Nowadays most scholars blandly accept their isolation in the academy, where they communicate only with immediate colleagues in a jargon that is comprehensible only to initiates. In comparison to the influence wielded by earlier scholars like Gervinus, Grimm, or Scherer, who still viewed themselves as "spokesmen of the nation," today's scholars in the humanities, even the most famous, appear to be mere specialists whose researches stir only the groves of academe, and sometimes not even these. Moreover, those who do dare to question the current situation, are immediately dismissed by many as "alien to the discipline." As a result, the single most important question in the humanities—the question, "How to proceed?"—plays only a relatively minor role.

In far too many disciplines scholars seem to be quite satisfied with the rise in specialization, with the retreat into the esoteric. In fact, pride in specialization seems to be growing. One might well ask whether any structuralist scholars actually take the trouble to translate their secret jargon into ordinary language when they address a wider audience? Our answer would have to be a resounding No. This is particularly ominous since the specialists are the trend-setters in almost all areas of our continuously diversifying technocratic society. Since they place greater value on rattling the tools of their trade than communicating, the field becomes even narrower.

In contrast, scholars who actually cross over the borders, are dismissed as dilettantes and greeted only with patronizing smiles, in spite of the fact that those who would deride them, themselves no longer possess a firm methodological foundation and merely take shelter behind a facade of formal scholarship. Most often this scholarly narrowness grows out of the conviction that genuine objectivity cannot be attained. Scholars therefore restrict their sphere of investigation and in order to attain any results at all they overload their terms with an enormous amount of ballast. Although they have long since abandoned the concept of an edifice of learning, scholars are, in effect, still collecting building blocks, just as they did in the era of positivism.

It is not difficult to predict the consequences of these efforts. Even the study of the arts, perhaps the most universal of all human endeavors, is in danger of degenerating into a mere end unto itself. In the same way that abstract art appeals principally to the painter himself, so the scholar in the humanities is in danger of speaking only to other scholars in his field. Eventually, art is discussed chiefly in terms of autonomy and intrinsic value, as if art had been produced in order to be tested for its formal harmony by specially trained professionals. With all of this emphasis on aesthetic factors, which does have its positive side, the work of art as such becomes increasingly unimportant. For if art no longer sees itself as an integrating constituent of the "whole," then we cannot expect the whole to take any interest in art.

In the framework of today's society, the humanities hold only a very marginal position.[3] At times they seem to have sunk to the level of mere navel-gazing, an activity that best thrives in a windless border zone.[4] The fault lies primarily with the formalistic, intrinsic approach that so many accept as the ultimate answer to the existing methodological confusion. But it is precisely the formal approach, focusing on technical aspects, that makes the study of literature unimportant for humanity in general. Who outside the academy, is interested primarily in form, structure, and genre? This is not to speak against the significance of these dimensions, but the part should never be mistaken for the whole.

Certainly there are other elements in art that are of far greater interest to us. If we have not succumbed to the aesthetic approach, *all* aspects appeal to us. For example, who would be willing to sacrifice the contents of a novel for language quality and structure? Who would relinquish the many dimensions, including political engagement, personal involvement, unconscious gratification, historical perspective, sociological perceptions, psychological nuances, even the simple fact of "how it ends"? And are these many aspects not themselves intimately connected with the form of the work? We know that many formalists would not grant us even this point. Why must it be that as soon as the word "plot" is mentioned in some circles, one is asked with undisguised contempt, "You mean the contents? I thought we were discussing literature." Hegel was still naive enough in this respect to admit that for him the purpose of art lay in "arousing and quickening *all* our dormant passions, emotions, and inclinations, in impregnating the heart and permitting the mature or immature person to feel all that the human spirit can endure, experience, and beget in its innermost and secret recesses." In this, Hegel included everything "that has the power to stir the human heart to its very depth, in all its myriad possibilities and dimensions, and everything else that the human spirit can offer to the emotions and the vision for the enjoyment of the spiritual and the lofty, the sublimity of the noble, the eternal, and the true, and also to make the misfortune and the misery, the frightful and the heinous, comprehensible." Hegel even goes on to say that "in its innermost, the human heart should share everything monstrous and terrifying, as well as all delights and all supreme happiness," and finally, that "the fantasy should abandon itself to the games of the imagination and indulge in the seductive magic of sensuously exciting perceptions and sensations."[5]

Let us not be abashed by such a statement and let us not demand less than we are entitled to. Literature is not a "pure" art that can exist independently like a beautifully formed object or a harmonious structure of sound. To limit the study of literature to formal elements would be no final "coming of age" for the art, as is often claimed by self-proclaimed modern or avant-garde groups. Quite the contrary, that would be a violation of its real nature. If strict formal analysis of paintings or musical compositions leaves us relatively unsatisfied, how much more inadequate is the purely formal analysis of literature, which by the very nature of its medium, language, is so closely bound to all aspects of the everyday world that it requires a forced process of abstraction to interpret it only as an aesthetic structure.

Ultimately, aesthetic perfection is only a theoretical possibility; in its concrete manifestations art is never free of imperfections. Let us not fool ourselves about what attracts us to art—not its formal unity or external perfection, but the inner fullness and evocative power of its contents. Often, the most superficial, derivative, and insignificant work of art is formally perfect, while the complex is rarely without some aesthetic flaws. This is not to suggest that minor forms can never touch us. Given the right moment, even the simple word "Spring" can fill us with enthusiasm or drive us to despair. But in the final analysis, works like *Don Quixote*, *Wilhelm Meister*, *Crime and Punishment*, or *The Trial* speak to us on many more levels than the most perfect poem. And in so doing, they set into motion all those elements of which Hegel spoke with such eloquence.

III

For this reason, it is absolutely essential that we preserve the postulate of universalism in the study of literature, in spite of the ever-increasing number of facts available to us, the claims of exactness of the natural sciences, and the rising emphasis on specialization. While this raises a large demand, which in practice can only be realized minimally, we submit that without some such postulate the scholar necessarily disqualifies himself from research. For if one wishes to be taken seriously (and who would not wish it?), one is practically forced to study literature from an "as if" perspective. All other perspectives are mere dead ends which may offer us idyllic refuges but can never help us find a meaningful connection to the "whole."

The real dilemma besetting the contemporary study of art and literature is not that we do not possess a valid method, but rather that its only possible realization contains a contradiction in terms. On the one hand, the demand for totality can never be realized, even by the most well-read genius whose brain functions like that of a computer. On the other hand, if the student of literature wishes to remain true to the discipline, if he wishes to place the smallest detail within a universal framework, he cannot help aiming at the ideal of completeness. Toward this end, in order not to lose sight of the apparently endless connections between literary scholarship and cultural history and sociology, he must constantly overstep the boundaries. The same holds true for all of the other historically oriented disciplines. Perhaps this is the time that the concept of "interpretive synthesis" first takes on genuine significance, if only in a purely quantitative sense. For the historical element is bound to a certain factual fullness, without which it always remains somewhat abstract. Since no one can know everything, a good interpreter of the monuments of art should at least try to keep an eye on everything, thereby constantly broadening the horizon of his knowledge in all directions. Certainly even that is only an "as if" proposition; without it, however, one cannot be either a true scholar or a good interpreter of literature.

All kinds of objections have been raised against such an assertion. It is argued that a preoccupation with the universal elements of the historical, cultural factors blunts the specifically aesthetic experience and for this reason is basically antiaesthetic. The advocates of this position view historical awareness and personal response as two entirely separate phenomena. Friedrich Gundolf once tried to formulate the contrast schematically as the antithesis between "cultural" and "primal" experiences.[6] From such a perspective one may well ask: Of what use is the postulate of universal knowledge, if only primal experiences enable us to be touched by art? What then does knowledge of the historical, psychological, political, or social add to our appreciation of art? Are these not purely external elements which serve only to impede our aesthetic response? But it is precisely this mode of existential appreciation that brings out the major fallacy of all intuitive methods. If we examine our primal responses more closely, it soon becomes clear that these experiences only become known to us after we have become "tuned in" to such feelings in the course of our education. They are not *a priori* categories of "givens," but are closely connected to our knowledge of history, which permits us to comprehend basic concepts like "love" or the "demonic," in the first place.

Precisely in this area one can all too easily fall back on the old romantic theory which insists that the essence of art, its

Holy of Holies, can be apprehended only by means of a mystical initiation. But in reality, between intuitive response and acculturation there exists so sharp a dialectic that it is impossible to conceive of one without the other. It is thus an undeniable fact that even the greatest works of art, such as the frescoes of the Sistine Chapel, Bach's *Well Tempered Clavichord* or Goethe's *Faust*, will not only not "touch" an uncultured person, that is, someone unconditioned in the historical sense, but, even worse, will merely elicit a mocking sneer. And have we scholars ourselves not had the experience, after reading more deeply in a particular epoch or the works of a particular author, of having everything suddenly become much more alive, of having history, which had thus far remained silent, begin to speak with a hundred tongues? While the ordinary person's interest in history often extends no further back than the times of his grandparents, for one who is historically aware, knowledge expands boundlessly. To dismiss this enlarged experience as mere cultural enrichment would be downright blasphemous.

One could more easily turn the tables and trace primal experiences back to cultural experiences: as for example, if a student after reading Bachofen, Nietzsche or Klages is suddenly seized by "cosmogonic eros" and condemns all bookworms as decadents or one-sided rationalists. Where such faith in primal experiences may lead, can best be seen in the work of the crypto-fascistic advocates of Dilthey's *Lebensphilosophie* and the followers of Nietzsche around 1900 who swore allegiance to a new "primitiveness," and on the basis of such an orientation were necessarily sucked into the maelstrom of regressive thinking. Let us therefore turn to a positive valuation of history. The broad range of historical knowledge need not signify a rise in antiquarianism, as Nietzsche feared in his *Thoughts out of Season*, but can bring with it tolerance and greater sensitivity to the range of human experience. In fact, the two are intimately connected, while all existential theories which bind us to particular "primal phenomena," lead us to dogmatic, one-sided, reactionary thinking.

No universal approach to art can do without recognizing the inner dialectic between acculturation and personal experience, form and content, the private and the historical. Obviously such a strong claim cannot be accepted at face value; it must prove itself methodologically effective and demonstrate that it does indeed lead to wholeness. Let us first hear from those who have already spoken out in this vein. In this way, we can bring what at first glance may look like a purely private demand for "interpretive synthesis" into the realm of the historically justified.

Chapter Two

THE VOICES OF
METHODOLOGICAL REINTEGRATION

While a great many scholars accept the formal approach without question, a number of theorists have since the 1960s tried to counteract the trend toward overspecialization by presenting possible models for a new integration. In addition to those who advocate a simple eclectic approach that applies the "right method to the right object at the right time," one also finds several schools that proceed somewhat more systematically. One large group urges greater historical awareness; of course, this emphasis on history has been in existence since 1900 and has never completely died out. In the 1920s, the last of the positivists supported such a historical orientation; now it is those oriented to sociology or literary history who reject phenomenological, existential, formal, or structural approaches.

In the years after 1945 such voices were still very isolated. In 1950 Fritz Martini first spoke rather cautiously of a return to "historical reality."[1] Two years later Friedrich Sengle was already more critical of the "rigorous cutting of the threads that run from the work in all directions," leading to "hothouse interpretations." He even went so far as to challenge those who scorned the historical to have the courage to abandon "this perilous field once and for all and to pursue philosophy or theology."[2] Since then scholars have gradually become more outspoken, especially as the opposition became increasingly more obdurate and one-sided. In 1952, Erik Lunding warned of the dangers inherent in "elevating formal analysis to an absolute."[3] In that same year, Heinz Otto Burger (who shortly before had come out in favor of the art of interpretation)[4] wrote in his *Annals of German Literature*: "Only the appeal to history, the work in historical perspective, can guarantee any unity to the study of literature."[5]

In contrast to those who concerned themselves exclusively with the intrinsic structure of single works of art, these scholars were in favor of an inner balance between the whole and the part, personal response and historical interpretation. That they were not alone in this, is proved by such essays as: "The Study of Literature as Interpretation and History" (1954) by Erich Trunz;[6] "Interpretation and Cognition" (1957) by Clemens Heselhaus;[7] "Poetry and Interpretation" (1958) by Hugo Friedrich;[8] "Toward the Unity of Literary History and Criticism" (1960) by Friedrich Sengle;[9] "The Problem of Style Changes" (1961) by Emil Staiger;[10] "*Geistesgeschichte* or Interpretation?" (1963) by Benno von Wiese;[11] "Between Interpretation and *Geistesgeschichte*" (1963) by Horst Rüdiger.[12]

On the whole, all these critics speak against strict analysis of form and urge integration of historical awareness with sensitive interpretation. In 1959 Peter Demetz wrote, with undisguised aversion to what he called "interpretive cloud-cuckoo-lands above fog banks of existential philosophy. . . . Signs seem to indicate that the antihistorical spasms of Western literary scholarship are giving way to a new tolerance."[13] Indeed, in 1963 Benno von Wiese—in sharp contrast to Wolfgang Kayser—placed literary history at the heart of literary scholarship. Such an opinion was hardly thinkable in 1950. Elsewhere he was even more explicit, "Too strong a separation from the disciplines of history must, in fact, lead to empty formalism."[14] Even Staiger wrote in a quite conciliatory manner, "Interpretation is interested in the creative power of the intellect; historical investigation of styles concerns itself with the inheritance, and with the process whereby this inheritance is integrated. The two methods do not interfere with one another. Together they struggle toward an understanding of the being and becoming of literature."[15] Even Wellek once again became considerably more tolerant of the historical element in the 1960s and asserted, "History cannot absorb or replace theory, while theory should not even dream of absorbing history."[16] Walter Muschg went even one step further, when he called "interpretation" a flight into the "ahistorical" and "meaningless," because it preferred to concern itself with the "canonical greats" and only discovered in them "that which was already known to us."[17] In similarly strong tones, Karl Otto Conrady rejected the formalist attempt to narrow literary history down to a simple "formal analysis of literature" and urged instead that every literary scholar "is, or always should be, not only an aesthete, but also a historian."[18]

Thus far it all sounds quite convincing. But is there really a new program beneath this conciliatory tone, or is this far-reaching readiness for reconciliation only the expression of an absolute lack of perspective that is ready to try anything in the name of liberal anarchy? Not that we have anything against liberalism; by no means, but of how much use is such a perspective? Is this not merely lax self-satisfaction? A democratic "Be nice to one another"? Agnosticism? Admission of ignorance? For when we examine these attitudes closely, most of them disappoint us in spite of their generosity. Is not this new emphasis on history or new "universalism" generally understood to be a validation of *all* literary perspectives? Frequently it is not the totality of human experience, but the totality of "texts" that is meant. For many of these scholars, it is still the aesthetic pleasure and not the value of understanding a particular work that gets first place. So long as this is not changed, literary study will remain an art of appreciation, trying to seduce its students into a predominantly aesthetic enjoyment of individual works of literature.

For this reason, and in spite of all the lip service paid to it, the historical is assigned only a peripheral role even by these liberals. Instead of viewing history as a base around which all other aspects could be ordered, they frequently treat it as an interesting accessory to which they are not committed. Thus, Hans-Egon Hass writes in his essay, "Literature and History," "A historical perspective is absolutely essential, if we are to disengage the general human elements from their inescapably historical particularity."[19] At first such a position is quite appealing and the attention to "general human elements" quite seductive, albeit deceptive. For such an attitude leads us to accept Goethe's dictum, that even geniuses do not transcend their own time in all respects.

From this perspective, it would simply be the task of the literary scholar to divest them of their timebound elements. In short, although the historical dimension is now given more attention by many, it is still viewed largely as a legacy, a biographical accessory, or mere commentary. While scholars now no longer speak like Kayser, in terms of an "inner" and "outer temple court" to describe the relationship between the aesthetic interior and the historical periphery, in practice a similar dichotomy often remains.

II

Historically conscious and more determined scholars were therefore not satisfied with such liberal compromises. In the final analysis, if we are content to keep the historical element merely as the background to the formal approach, then we will have achieved nothing more than a thinly disguised new idealism, in which empirical facts play only a subordinate role. For this reason Friedrich Sengle, in his essay, "Problems and Tasks in the Writing of Current Literary History," not only urged a reconciliation of interpretation and historical thinking but demanded an integration of methods that would counteract the false "claims to totality of the phenomenological, that is, the ahistorical method," even if it meant that on this account scholars were forced to encroach upon so-called "neighboring disciplines."[20] Using similar language, Erik Lunding pleaded for a stronger "polyinterpretability."[21] Walter Muschg called for "universal standards" in order to get away from the aesthetic narrowness of the purely "literary approach."[22] Others adopted the broad perspective of the comparatists and held up the interdisciplinary mode of research as the model for a regenerated study of literature.

In the mid-fifties similar voices began to be heard in the United States. Here too scholars were trying to counteract the narrow interpretation of single works with an eclectic combination of two or three methods. Thus, Kenneth Burke, one of the leading new critics, aimed at a gradual integration of sociological, psychoanalytical, and purely linguistic factors. In general, concepts like "multiple interpretation," "multiple parallelism," and "multiple causation" are once again playing an important role. For example, the art historian Walter Abell urges the combination of "depth history" with "depth psychology," in order to advance a genuine "psychosocial materialist synthesis."[23] Leslie Fiedler closed his attack against the narrow approach of orthodox Freudians and Jungians with the laconic call, "Only connect!"[24] Even a psychoanalyst such as Frederick J. Hacker writes, "The new approach will have to be an integrative and holistic one." For him, too, every perception is "neither a purely psychological nor technical nor sociological problem, but an intersection of all these areas."[25] Northrop Frye, in his *Anatomy of Criticism* (1957), goes even further when he tries to combine the symbolic, the historical, the archetypal, and the rhetorical. Still, while tearing down the barriers between methods, he relies heavily upon the archetype and its connection to all literary motifs, and thereby ends up with an expanded Jungianism. But on the whole, what Holman said about "more recent trends" is also valid here: "Among the tendencies, perhaps the most obvious has been the establishment of friendly relations and a degree of mutual respect among the various schools which in the thirties had the air of armed camps. The lessening of the intensity of the critical antagonism has resulted in a kind of cross-fertilization."[26]

However, in most cases the purpose of this cross-fertilization is passed over in silence. Thus we see that this trend, with some notable exceptions, frequently leads to an eclecticism that, in spite of its good intentions, rarely ventures into the truly universal. For example, the insights of psychoanalysis were combined with those of Marxism; political revolution was explained as the convergence of sociological factors with long repressed inhibitions. In this analogy, the superego corresponds to the ruling class, which constantly resists being overrun by the proletariat, that is, the subconscious. Others who have concerned themselves with the relationship between socio-pathological occurrences and ideological complexes, such as fascism, have come to similar conclusions. However, if we really wish to move toward a more comprehensive approach, considering the number of methods available to us, we ought not restrict ourselves to only two factors.

Ultimately, if we are really moved by a work of art, even its most popular element—for example, the myth complex so often drawn upon as the basis for a universal perspective—is only one element among many. True totality or wholeness would look quite different. Did not Ernst Troeltsch as long ago as the 1920s write, "All more precise analysis shows that every individual can only be understood from the perspective of a larger totality, that of family, generation, class, nation, historical circumstances, the total intellectual situation, and finally, all human connections; similarly, the real objects of historical scholarship have become not so much biographical singularities but rather collective singularities, such as peoples, states, classes, castes, cultural epochs, religious communities, and constellations of events, such as wars, revolutions, etc."[27] And even that is not all that falls into the domain of the supra-personal. For in the last fifty years we have added so many perspectives to our scholarship that methodological one-sidedness is obviously out of the question.

But some will object that such a totality of all scholarly methods is a utopian vision from the very start. They will ask: How can a single individual possibly manage to keep up? While in theory it might be possible, how does it operate in practice? Troeltsch would have responded to such resigned voices with the following: "Only a collective effort can solve these problems, which at all times presupposes rigorous factual knowledge of one's own discipline, and with it mutual cooperation and exchange. For this reason I have given up the more elegant monologue style used by my colleagues, and have carried out my work in continuous dialogue with those working on similar subjects."[28]

Repeatedly, we come across the suggestion of methodological reintegration and the idea of teamwork among the more historically oriented scholars. An essay by Helmut Kreuzer is exemplary; he observes, "Ideally, in every area of research, one person would combine the capacities of a cultural historian, an appreciator of the arts, a mathematical linguist, and an aesthetic theoretician. It seems to me that the subject under consideration, that is, literature itself, makes the pluralism of questions and directions, and all that goes with it, both necessary and legitimate. However, this in no way suggests approval of a disconnected hodgepodge of methods stemming from an unfounded theoryless methodological eclecticism. The processes of literary scholarship must always have the power to exercise reciprocal correctives."[29] Muschg also asserts that "teamwork" has become indispensable in the realm of literary history. One hears similar assertions in the United States, where discussions, conferences, and conventions have long played an important role.[30] Thus Stanley Edgar Hyman, who comes closest to the ideal of total analysis, regards the symposium as the most suitable working basis for doing justice to the "multiplicity of readings and meanings" in modern literrray scholarship.[31]

So far, so good. But which scholars are really ready to undertake such "teamwork"? Would this not mean submitting to the institute system associated with the natural sciences? What would happen to the personal touch? The private ambition?—many will ask with indignation. We believe that because these are essentially matters of vanity, they are ultimately unimportant. Whoever is not ready to do without his personal style, perhaps even his name, in writing books and articles, is still fixed on the essayistic. From a scholarly point of view, only *one* question is meaningful, and that is, "With what should such a team actually concern itself?" Once again, only with masterpieces to be interpreted by means of complex textual analysis? If this approach were used, the entire effort would result only in series of definitive compendia of interpretations, which take everything except the historical dynamics of the individual work into consideration—for these are accessible only from the vantage point of century or epoch. And to that end we need a concept of history based on ideology.

Therefore, such a joint effort would make sense only if we were clear about its purpose from the very start, and the whole project thereby given direction. For when teamwork is not applied in a meaningful way, even the most serious attempt at completeness is a meaningless act. And in the event that the emphasis were still on predominantly aesthetic questions, such teamwork would serve absolutely no purpose at all. Why should one devote so much effort to so circumscribed a problem? To set the scholarly collective a worthwhile task, quite different perspectives must be opened. It is absurd to speak of "appreciation" and "connoisseurship," when art itself no longer has any telos. Of what use is an ever more refined comprehension of art, when painting and poetry no longer fulfill any political, social, psychological, or historical functions and must remain content with a marginal position? Teamwork carried out under such conditions would never serve the cause of a new universalism. It is surely not enough merely to integrate the various aspects of scholarship with one another; we must go further and place the creation of art, as well as its interpretation, into a meaningful relationship with our basic social and psychological experiences.

III

The preceding paragraphs should have made clear that this new synthesis cannot be found either in the sphere of the purely aesthetic or the strictly scientific. For this reason, we as students of literature must stop trying to impress the natural scientists with our technical vocabulary, statistics, computerizations, and formal analyses. In these matters we cannot compete. If the humanities are to continue to make meaningful contributions to the modern world, they must not go on mimicking the natural sciences. In contrast to the technical experimentation of the sciences, the humanities concern themselves with the history of the ever-changing human spirit and with those factors that determine this change. Their promise thus lies elsewhere. Let us accept the fact that the humanities can never even begin to approximate the precision of the natural sciences, nor should they want to. What the humanities require of us is keen awareness of history and the ability to come up with new answers to the old questions.

From this perspective, the humanities resemble the phoenix, which untiringly regenerates itself out of its own ashes. The image is apt; for ultimately, everything connected to the living spirit must continuously renew itself. In this domain, there are no certainties, no formulas or statistics. All we can count on is the human potential for growth and development to keep us from stagnating or falling behind our own times. And for this purpose, a mere surface restoration of historical elements will not suffice. If we are serious in wishing to achieve a progressive orientation, we must surely appeal to the concept of the "whole." And to this end an "interpretive synthesis" is needed—one that would not be satisfied with a superficial integration of methods, but would try to enter into the dialectical rhythm of history and bring to the surface all its social implications.

If the historical orientation suggested above is not simply to serve as an oasis for empirically-minded scholars who seek to retreat into aesthetically more charming epochs, we must proceed from the postulate of progress, be it ever so cautious and tentative. For the study of history itself can become as neutral as aesthetic formalism or structuralism. The historian can also ignore universal connections, especially if he focuses only on facts and so-called objective appreciation of the works, writers, or epochs under consideration. A historical orientation therefore becomes meaningful only if the scholar understands the dialectical process of history, if he acknowledges that the world is in constant flux and thus capable of change. A genuine historical perspective is bound to come to terms with basic epochal structures and their individual variations, even for the smallest and seemingly least important problems. Only after we have determined the historical context of each work, are we at all qualified to pass scholarly judgment. If, however, scholars try to evade this historical perspective, they will inevitably reject the claims of universality of all truly great works of art that reflect not only the consciousness of their creators but their entire epoch as well.

From this point of view all historical orientation, even in literary scholarship, leads to the formation of step-like, graduated stages of development that do not necessarily move in exactly the same direction, though it is difficult to deny that they nonetheless exhibit some inner logic or progression. Once we accept this point of view, we recognize that even seemingly isolated masterpieces are part of an epochal frame of reference which gives the single work meaning beyond its individual particularity. Every era that strives to attain a universal consciousness of history, therefore, also concerns itself intensively with the classification of epochs. Thus Ernst Troeltsch argues that the "real philosophical element" of every truly "universal history" is hidden in periodization.[32] To him, the study of history seems meaningful only when the smallest detail is examined with respect to its place in the whole, a goal we can never attain without a thorough knowledge of the epochal structure of any given time segment. In the realm of literary scholarship Max Wehrli reached a similar conclusion, "The primary task of literary history is the division into epochs and the recognition of epochal styles."[33]

Within such time syntheses, hitherto unsuspected possibilities for research, suitable for a team as well as the individual scholar, easily present themselves. The study of epochs offers the literary scholar striving toward interpretative wholeness one of the best opportunities to penetrate art in depth, doing justice to the formal-aesthetic elements as well as those pertaining to the philosophy of history. Broadly speaking, the epochal approach is one of the few which offers us the possibility of bringing about a synthesis of interpretation and historical awareness. Moreover, it offers a methodological advantage in that it not only deepens our enjoyment of art, but also makes us conscious of the successive stages of the human spirit. For in seeking to discover the style determinant of a given period, the literary scholar is, from the beginning, compelled to confront aesthetic elements with historical factors. This dual perspective is extremely valuable to the literary scholar, who ought not to be interested solely in the factual or what in an ominous sense is considered lasting, but also in the dialectical processes of history that bring to light the significant factors of a given period. Perhaps the best statement of this seemingly modest, yet highly ambitious proposal is offered by Karl Lamprecht's study, *The Recent Past* (1912), in which he asserts, "This book does not have a static character but a developmental one, and for this reason is not interested in anything and everything about our time, not even in everything that is significant but only in those factors which decisively influenced the recent process of development."[34]

Well and good, some will say, but does Lamprecht's suggestion for study of epochs really exclude the subjective element entirely? Who will guarantee us that such syntheses will not also be based on mere intuition? Of course, such objections can always be raised in all of the "humane" disciplines, even in the seemingly more solid areas of editing or lexicography. If we allow ourselves the false expectation of achieving scientific exactitude in the humanities, we might as well give up at once. Let us rather accept the fact that what appears to be the weakness of our discipline, is also its greatest strength: that it deals with human experience, which is always individual, yet follows a suprapersonal development that can be classified according to certain periods. We would do well to side with Ernst Troeltsch also on this point; for he sees the constant redefinition of individual periods as the only possibility of penetrating into the historical fabric. Troeltsch claims that without objective periodization, all historical thinking would be senseless from the very start.[35] Such a hypothesis, still firmly rooted in the historical optimism of the nineteenth century, was bound to meet with harsh resistance from the existentialists and formalists. Let us first consider their objections to the much-debated concept of epoch and then turn our attention to the even more problematic "dialectics of culture."

Chapter Three

THE "EPOCHAL" AS A NEW COLLECTIVE CONCEPT

I

Concepts of style are debated only in those epochs that no longer have a clear style of their own.[1] This opinion was widespread around 1750, when a number of competing styles were vying for artistic supremacy. In German literary history these are generally classified as sentimentalism, enlightenment, storm and stress, and early classicism. Although some of these descriptive terms had already been in use in the eighteenth century, it was long before they could be separated from older, ahistorical categories, such as the beautiful and the sublime, conceptual and pictorial, high and low, Dutch and Italian. It took a number of influences to sharpen what were initially rather vague concepts. In fact, one could say it took the full force of eighteenth- and nineteenth-century historical knowledge. In this process, Herder's dynamic view of history, the Weimar classicists' penchant for classifying, the romantic yearning for the past, and Hegel's tripartite constructions, all had a part. Thus, the idea of epochal styles must be seen as

part of the development of the modern world view which continually strives to create new principles of organization.

To understand this process, we must go back in time and
trace its development from the beginning. Up to and including
the Baroque period, world history was viewed as a static
division between good and evil. In the early years of the Enlightenment, it gradually came to be interpreted as a dynamic
process showing a logical progression. After this had been
established as a basic principle of philosophy and history,
around 1800 it was taken up by other branches of knowledge
and applied to concrete events. To be sure, this took a long
time, for it was opposed by the entire machinery of the *ancien
régime*, which viewed the idea of historical development with
fear and suspicion, since it brought to mind the specter of the
French Revolution. Consequently, for a number of years, the
process of classifying the arts according to specific historical
concepts did not move beyond abstract systematization. The
result was a strange juxtaposition of historical and ideal conceptions.

Until the 1790s, literary scholars ignored developmental
factors and concentrated on establishing normative conceptions
of genre based on traditional aesthetic principles, which allowed
them to view Aristophanes and Goethe as representatives of
the same genre. With almost mathematical precision, scholars
subordinated specific examples to preconceived norms. The
more closely one examines the writings of the late eighteenth
century, the clearer it becomes that the Enlightenment in Germany stopped midway: since historical thinking could find
no foothold, scholars retreated into philosophical idealism. In
order for a more liberal attitude to take hold, political circumstances would have had to be quite different. Not even the
quarrel between the ancients and the moderns, which occupied
scholars in these years almost exclusively, led to historical self-
awareness. The historian Garve comes closest to such consciousness in that he always differentiates between the old and
the new from a sociological point of view, but Schiller, in his
tract "Concerning Naive and Sentimental Poetry" (1795–96)

remains preoccupied with ideal abstractions. The same ambivalence characterizes Goethe's distinction between classic and romantic, or Humboldt's concept of masculine and feminine art, both of which reveal an embryonic historical perspective, but have not completely overcome the tendency toward abstract theorizing.

Historical awareness begins to spread only in the wake of romanticism and through the work of Hegel, where ideal static conceptions suddenly give way to a dialectical succession of stages. It was Hegel's breakthrough to historical thinking that enabled scholars to conceptualize in terms of time gradations or epochs. Thus it was Hegel who brought about the Copernican revolution in the humanities. While eighteenth-century philosophers had dreamed of such a revolution, they themselves had been unable to carry it out. Its effect in literary studies was immediate and decisive: scholars abandoned all other approaches and established the method that has been understood as "literary history" ever since. While previously they had worked only with types and genres, they now began to think in terms of broad cultural connections. Thus, in addition to literary factors, the philosophical, historical, political, social, and economic conditions of every epoch were also taken into account, which considerably widened the scholarly horizon. This is particularly evident in the work of the Young Germans* and the left-Hegelians, as, for example, in Heinrich Laube's *History of German Literature* (1839), which gives equal attention to philosophy, literature, and historiography. This approach takes Hegel's dictum, "Every philosophy is its time, recorded in words," and extends it into the realm of artistic expression.

For example, in those years, the term "romantic school" did not refer only to poetry, as it came to later on, but included the whole spectrum of cultural factors and took for granted

---

* A school of progressive writers and political activists strongly influenced by the July Revolution of 1830 in France. In 1835 the adherents were suppressed by the government. Among them were Heinrich Heine, Ludwig Börne, Karl Ferdinand Gutzkow, and Heinrich Laube.

the interconnectedness of the individual parts to one another and to the whole. In time, the tendency to fill the Hegelian frame with concrete facts grew increasingly stronger. This is particularly evident around 1850 in the methods developed by the historians Leopold von Ranke and Jakob Burckhardt, which represent the first, and perhaps most significant attempts to fuse a broad, universal view of history with the specialist's narrow perspective. In literary criticism, men like Gervinus and Hettner successfully combined the urge to collect with political engagement and the objectivity of Young Germany, and arrived at some convincing epochal concepts. The historical orientation of this generation of literary scholars is well illustrated by the chapter titles of their works. Thus, Hettner divides his *History of German Literature in the Eighteenth Century* (1862–70) into sections like "From the Westphalian Peace to the Accession of Frederick the Great," "The Age of Frederick the Great," and "The Classical Period." Later aesthetes disapproved of this historical orientation, which they took to be a sin against the holy spirit of literary criticism.

Therefore, the more unified perspective gradually disintegrated in the era of Bismarck. We must remember that the failure of the Revolution of 1848 resulted in a considerably narrowed perspective in the realm of literary history. Though scholars held fast to the idea of historical research, they renounced all universal connections and, as a result, moved in two different directions: some focused unreservedly on national elements, while others adopted an equally unrestrained relativism, which came to be known as "positivism" in the history of science. Many scholars were political reactionaries whose flag-waving patriotism completely drowned out the more democratic, humanistic impulse of mid-century. Some supporters of Bismarck even viewed classicism and romanticism as mere preliminary stages for the glorious years of 1870 and 1871. Unfortunately, this point of view was rather widespread, even among prominent literary scholars. For example, in his *History of German Literature* (1890) Julian Schmidt divides the nineteenth century into "Under Foreign Rule," "The Restoration,"

"The Era of Literary Opposition," "The Parliamentary Era," "The Period of Unification." Needless to say, this nationalistic view did not encourage scholars to give much attention to the historical connections between epochs. Nor did the work of the positivists leave much room for such considerations, for they increasingly concentrated on collecting biographical data.

Not surprisingly, these distortions of the historical method provoked sharp responses, particularly at the turn of the century, when scholars compared the overspecialization associated with positivism to their goal of a new totality. Strange to say, many viewed this new orientation as a return to the idealism of the philosophy of history, and associated it with movements like neo-Fichtianism and neo-Hegelianism. In reality, however, this new idealism proved to be a remarkably formal affair. While scholars used terms like styles, epochs, and national essences, they continued to be preoccupied with theoretical abstractions. As a result, all of cultural history was seen as a series of artistically autonomous "styles" which at first glance seems to promise a return to historical facts and periodization. A second look, however, shows that this very movement, which tried hard to separate itself from positivism on the one hand and aesthetic impressionism on the other, nonetheless closely resembles the "art-for-art's-sake" orientation it had rejected. The reason is simple. In this context, the study of literature does not include the totality of all social, political, and economic aspects of life, but limits itself to those specific cultural elements which were believed to "determine style." Such a narrow perspective cannot possibly be viewed as historical. Furthermore, such a conception of style totally ignores the "whole" and concentrates only on aesthetic principles. But, in order to understand any style completely, we must also bring in the material basis of a given epoch.

The most striking example of this kind of style analysis is Wölfflin's *Basic Principles of Art History* (1915) in which the determinants are derived from pictorial "visual forms." Here Wölfflin sets out to define the aesthetic essence, "style in and of itself." Thus to Wölfflin, the baroque is merely a spatial style with a preference for depth effects. He totally ignores all other factors, such as the courtly mode of life, princely absolutism, and the counterreformational zeal for conversion. This limited focus gives rise to its own kind of formalism, as exemplified by Fritz Strich's *German Classicism and Romanticism* (1922) which, as we have seen, sets up vague antitheses like "perfection and infinity" without taking the concrete historical situation around 1800 into account.

Enthusiasm for styles rose markedly just after the turn of the century, when the whole history of art was divided into neatly calculated stages arranged according to preconceived notions of form, as if aesthetic development were composed of *a priori* categories which bore no relationship to empirical determinants. Most scholars believed that the creation of new styles was entirely in the hands of the avant-garde and bore no relationship to any other factors. Around 1900, as a result of the rapid social and economic development of the period, artistic styles began to follow one another with dizzying speed. Art nouveau appeared at a time when styles were managed commercially, when competition was so keen that publishing houses, periodicals, art dealers and even concert managers often manufactured styles outright. The publisher Diederichs pushed neoromanticism; the journal *Der Kunstwart*, regional art; Cassierer, impressionism. Thus art became a mere commodity; style an industrial trademark. As a result, works that did not easily fit any recognized style were in danger of being excluded altogether. One need only think of Kafka and expressionism. As a further result, many artists adopted the external trappings of a particular style and paid little attention to the content of their work. They no longer seemed to care about quality; only the packaging had become important.

This stylemania reached its peak at the time of World War I, in the years of cubism, futurism, and expressionism, when aesthetic theory leaned toward phenomenology and tried to interpret even the most complex periods according to a few intuited conceptions. Terms like Greek, classical, gothic, baroque, oriental, or primitive were bandied about. In the early

1920s, a number of different approaches converged: Dilthey's *Lebensphilosophie*, Breysig's step-construction of world history, Wölfflin's basic principles, the neoromantic discovery of the gothic and the romantic, Riegl's style-volition, Herman Nohl's typical styles, Walzel's mutual illumination, the expressionists' fascination with simultaneity, Spengler's cultural morphology, and the widespread enthusiasm for establishing polarities. By far the most important characteristic of this convergence of movements, known as the first phase of *Geistesgeschichte*, was its urge to establish ideal conceptions, cleansed of all empirical data. These scholars wished to devote themselves to the pursuit of "pure" knowledge and hoped to spiritualize the heaps of material amassed by the late nineteenth-century positivists. For this purpose, the study of epochs was eminently suitable, since it enabled scholars to reduce even the broadest time span to a single major conception. Once this had been established, it was easy to interpret all the elements of a particular epoch from a single perspective and thus create the illusion of order.

In setting up epochs, most literary scholars considered it unwise to borrow categories from the realms of politics, sociology, or economics, since these were still too closely connected to empirical elements. Instead, they preferred to use the autonomous concepts of style established by Riegl and Wölfflin. In the literary scholarship of these years we find numerous references to styles deriving from structural psychology, cultural morphology, and most of all from art history. Literary scholars hoped that in working with such classifications as romanesque, gothic, renaissance, mannerism, baroque, rococo, classicism, empire, Biedermeier, impressionism, art nouveau, expressionism, and *neue Sachlichkeit*, they would bring an element of order into the chaos of *Geistesgeschichte*.

This borrowing of epochs from art history proved to be particularly useful for lesser styles that did not easily fit into the prevailing polarities such as Greek and gothic. A good example of the usefulness of the new division into smaller segments is offered by research into rococo. The term derives from art history, where it had long been established as a neutral designation and had helped to establish convincing epochal structures. In literary history, it first appears as a chapter heading in the work of Julius Wiegand.[2] Two years later, Herbert Cysarz devoted two chapters to it, after which it came to be generally accepted.

But in spite of these positive results, we must also examine the defects of this approach. All too often, scholars merely took over the concepts of art history and applied them unthinkingly to works of literature on a purely intuitive basis, without even bothering to check out the equivalence. Naturally this presented some problems, especially when the formal categories of art history were combined with the abstract principles of *Geistesgeschichte*. In order to summarize the style and world view of a particular epoch, scholars created artificial constructs like the idea of medieval or baroque Man. But, because they themselves did not fully understand the historical aspects of these periods, they took these concepts of style to be basic modes of thinking recurring cyclically in time.

Such concepts as gothic, classic, romantic, and baroque were particularly abused and were in serious danger of losing their meaning altogether. Spengler speaks of the Arabian-gothic in Spain and Viking-gothic in the interior of the Magdeburg cathedral; the art historian Dehio mentions the "classicist" Holbein and the "romantic" Grünewald; in addition, Dehio favored mixed terms such as proto-baroque, baroque-gothic, and rococo-gothic. Walzel spoke of classic and baroque gothic. In the sphere of literature, Novalis served as a gothic-romantic, Kleist as a baroque-romantic. Thus, most style categories were totally robbed of their specific reference. Although these concepts had originally developed from the study of history, they were now treated completely ahistorically. The result was a series of clichéd labels based on questionable analogies leading to inconsistent conclusions. On the one hand, scholars insisted that styles were interchangeable and easily transposed in time;

on the other, they prized originality. Above all, they were confident that once art and artists had been properly labeled, their work was done.

II

Such excesses could only lead to sharp reversals. Especially in the academy, scholars rejected epochal styles altogether without even considering whether or not they had anything at all to offer. Thus from 1930 on, a curious paradox occurred: while the professors stringently avoided stylistic labels, these spread like wildfire in the "lower" spheres—that is, in newspapers, textbooks, antique shops, second-hand bookstores, and tourist agencies, which transformed even the most complex artistic phenomena into commercially viable superficialities. What skepticism against his own discipline must the art historian develop when, while spending a summer in Italy, he repeatedly observes the same phenomenon: buses stop in front of a church, exhausted tourists no sooner alight than they are dragged down the aisles or into the cloister; there they are informed that this element is early gothic, that one late romanesque; that here a renaissance prince is buried, there a tombstone displays early-baroque characteristics. Particularly well-informed guides even use terms like mannerism, Burgundian flamboyant style, or high-baroque sensualism, so that the layman becomes dizzy with "isms." One wonders why this happens and what those in search of culture really gain when a work of art or an entire church is given an abstract label that must ultimately sound like a value judgment. Is not the tourist inevitably given the impression that "gothic" is good by virtue of being "gothic"? Or is this merely another example of how scholarship becomes trivialized and reduced to a few convenient formulas? Can one possibly gain historical perspective by learning to recognize the typical as typical?

One thing is certain. Because of this phenomenon, a deep split has occurred, and the distance between popular summarizations and scholarly distinctions has grown ever greater. For this reason, already in the late 1920s, scholars attempted to turn literary criticism into a "literary scholarship" based on its own method and vocabulary, in order to separate it from the journalistic popularizations of *Geistesgeschichte*, which were rapidly gaining ground. In this sharp reaction against the superficial study of "isms," "Spengleritis" as it was called at the time, one can discern four distinct movements.

After 1930, there was the trend toward the national which elevated the Germanic in itself as the highest measure of style recognizable in all epochs. Many were firmly convinced that even the modern "national popular movement" developed organically from the past. The historical element, therefore, was not considered something that had been sloughed off, like a dead thing that could arbitrarily be dissected and classified, but was viewed as a constant source of rebirth.[3] Usually the gothic, the baroque, and the romantic formed the bases for such theories. These formless, transcendental, and exaggeratedly individualistic structures were considered the most German of all German styles, while epochs like the renaissance, classicism, and realism were associated with the empirical and, therefore, disposed of as being "un-German." Scholars were particularly partial to the idea of the romantic, which was divided into so many phases—proto, early, high, late, and neo—that some did not hesitate to speak of the "eternal romantic" of the German spirit.

A second trend relied on the catchphrase "German individualism." Here, only the great individual, the hermit, or the eccentric, was viewed as truly Germanic. Scholars pointed, above all, to the "misunderstood" greats, to Kleist, Hölderlin, Hebbel, Grabbe, or Nietzsche, as if German literature were entirely a literature of exceptional cases. In this way, they developed an aversion for group consciousness and conventions of style and lauded the typical "Germanic" turning within, to lyricism, romanticism, and music, as an essential quality of the national character. Because they failed to examine the underlying political implications of this turning within, they all too often made a virtue of necessity and overlooked its problematic aspects. For the roots of this conspicuous individualism are found in German small-town life, in the retreat to provinciality and intellectual narrowness, in the lack of a literary center. What would French literature be without Paris? English, without London? The fact that Germany developed few literary groups is hardly something to be proud of. Quite the contrary. For this provincialism represents a lack of sociability, the absence of a self-conscious bourgeoisie, and a deficiency of political awareness in German literature.

One searches in vain for a social or time-bound perspective. This is not to speak against the individual "greats"; we must remember, however, that it is not they who create literature, at least not literature on a large scale. For this purpose we would need at least ten Fontanes. What the geniuses, even extremely significant ones like Kleist, Büchner, and Hebbel, achieved within their circumscribed individuality, was seldom sufficiently intelligible to exercise a genuinely wide influence. Compared to world powers like Balzac or Tolstoy, even Stifter or Raabe seem to be minor. For this reason, German literature, and not only that of the nineteenth century, remains relatively unknown to the world at large. The enlightment and storm and stress already show the failure of group consciousness. And even Goethe's impressive attempt to establish an abstract-humanistic society in the small town of Weimar was destined to fail from the start. Thus, in spite of Schiller, Hölderlin, Jean Paul, and Kleist, "German classicism" remained a "one-man show." In fact, many view Goethe as the very symbol of modern "individualism."

An equally strong aversion to the dominant stylemania developed in the camp of the existentialists. One can go back as far as Nietzsche and those advocates of the so-called *Lebens-philosphie* who most often clothed their attack against the historical classification and the "democratic" mania for equalization, with the formula of the "eternal return," according to which humankind was, at all times, divided into two groups: geniuses and the rabble. For them, the task of the critic lay in recognizing other greats and in interpreting their works with supreme sensitivity. Thus, in the *Birth of Tragedy* (1873), Nietzsche already views the historian as the "unproductive theoretician" who simply collects "artistic styles" of all periods "in order to give them names, like Adam to the animals."

To Nietzsche, this type represents the eternally hungering one, the "critic without passion or power," the "Alexandrian," who is "in essence, librarian or proofreader, and is wretchedly blinded by misprints and the dust of books."[4] Similar pronouncements were made around 1900 by Dilthey, Karl Joël, and Georg Simmel. Out of this movement there developed a kind of *Geistesgeschichte* that stressed the Heroic and the Superhuman and which, in the course of the 1920s, became ever more existential by shifting from the concept of "life" to that of "being." Thus, in 1927, Heidegger's *Time and Being* fell on carefully prepared ground and supported all tendencies toward the static, toward "pure being," which can only be illuminated but never classified.

The existentialist approach gave rise to a strong prejudice against all conceptions of style which place the individual in the framework of a historically determined field of action. One senses that critics of this persuasion are desperately trying to reclaim the identity they felt they had lost in the modern mass age. By rejecting contemporary society, these critics are cultivating the past—always an ominous sign, for the past can never substitute for lost religion, nor can identification with one great poet of the past mitigate this isolation. But perhaps we should not pass only negative judgment on this trend, for this existentially oriented cult of the great individual reveals a genuine discomfort with the growing power of bureaucracy, which meets every personal emotion with suspicion. For this reason, existentialists used epochal concepts of style only on a trivial level, and avoided applying them to "significant" artists whose greatness they saw only in their individuality. Like the monographs produced by the circle around George, their work transforms artists into mythical figures. The greatness of art here represents the power to stand outside of time, which the art historian Sedlmayr once termed "the stepping beyond history."[5]

All of these tendencies could have been overcome by a well-founded "literary history." But when these countermovements made themselves felt, the study of literature was still far from being a methodologically refined discipline, and therefore was open to every attack from without. For this reason, toward the end of the 1920s, many were already pushing for a "new scholarship" and fighting against the blurred concepts of style associated with *Geistesgeschichte* and the previous crossing of boundaries. They sought to replace literary history which necessarily rests on a total conception of history with a literary scholarship that concerned itself solely with so-called "inner-literary" phenomena. Among the first to be sacrificed were the epochal concepts borrowed from art history, which were considered "foreign to literature." Epochal concepts derived from expressionistic abstractions, clichés taken from *Geistesgeschichte*, and purely formal visual modes were now, by a more autonomous approach, protecting literature from all cultural and historical connections.

Behind this "intrinsic" study of literature, consciously or unconsciously, there stands the previously mentioned desire to emulate the exactness of the natural sciences. Therefore, within this mode of thought, the scholar is urged toward strict specialization and methodological narrowness. Furthermore, he is given the feeling that knowledge has become so vast that he should no longer dare step beyond the bounds of his own field, and that even within his own field, he should confine himself to a single author or genre. Of course, this fear of the nonspecialist has its roots in a genuine problem, one which, in recent years, has increased, rather than diminished. While previously we still had Goethe specialists, today there are only *Wilhelm Meister* or *Faust II* specialists. Scholars generally seem to feel that if they work in limited areas and occupy themselves with fixed facts that cannot be made historically relative, they can attain greater certainty. But how far can this process really be carried before the discipline that concerns itself with the human spirit is deprived of its "humane" quality? It is not difficult to understand why this is happening; not only for the sake of exactness, but because in this "age of anxiety," scholars want to have something to hold on to.

Because of these trends toward nationalism, individualism, existentialism, and specialization, scholars are ready to do without the former concepts of periodization. Thus René Wellek, in his *Theory of Literature*, designates the entire history of styles before new criticism as alien to literature and urges an "intrinsic" approach that only describes, but no longer explains anything in historical terms. When the adherents of this school do avail themselves of older concepts of style, they usually use them ironically, in quotation marks, or with a supplementary label, "so-called" romanticism, "so-called" expressionism. As a result, the previously established concepts of style are used as purely regulative, generic terms or approximate working hypotheses, which have lost their historical meaning as well as their "essence" as conceived by the older *Geistesgeschichte*.

Most German histories of literature since the 1930s and 1940s no longer use concepts of style for chapter headings, but instead divide literature eclectically according to genres or geographical regions, or else return to purely mechanical devices, such as annals of time. Thus, for example, Ernst Alker orders his *History of German Literature from the Death of Goethe to the Present* (1949) into chapters like "Young Germany," "Austrian Literature before 1848," "Aesthetes," "The Beginnings and Rise of Realism," "Eclectics, Epigones, Opportunists, and Syncretists." That is, he combines, in colorful array, aesthetic, stylistic, political, and regional features. Even more confusing is the escape into the annalistic. One need only think of the voluminous *Annals of German Literature* (1952) prepared by Heinz Otto Burger, which consciously avoids a total view of history. How grotesque such a division can be, is shown by the following chapter headings, which once again cover the early nineteenth century: 1805–1808, High Points; 1809–1815, Nationalistic Romanticism; 1815–1820, Romantic Climaxes; 1821–1826, Anti-Romantic Restorational Spirit; 1827–

1832, Epilogue; 1832–1836, After the Death of Goethe; 1837–1842, After the Death of Büchner; and so on, as you like, *ad infinitum.*

In the meantime, what happened to the older epochal concepts? In studies of the middle ages, one comes across them only in exceptional cases. Almost no one any longer speaks of "romanesque" literature. Even the concept of "classicism of the 12th century" has noticeably retreated to the background. The stylistic designation "gothic," which was particularly favored in the 1920s, is considered equally problematic. The same is true for the concept of the renaissance, which is hardly ever applied to literature. Scholars simply speak either of the sixteenth century, or use terms like humanism or the period of the reformation. Even the word "baroque," which was generally accepted around 1930, is being questioned today.

Both de Boor/Newald and the Collective for Literary History (a writers' group in East Germany) speak only of the seventeenth century, and reject the stylistic concepts of art history. Similarly controversial is the situation of the rococo. Classicism and romanticism, in general, have continued to be accepted, even if not as unassailably as in the 1920s. Books like those of Strich or Korff could hardly be written today. Even the concept of Biedermeier, which originated in art history, still meets with harsh resistance. "Poetic realism" has been replaced by a view of realism which emphasizes the self-enclosed quality of the work of art. In contrast, ever since the period of naturalism, epochal concepts have become entirely confused. Most scholars simply lump together various terms like naturalism, impressionism, art nouveau, symbolism, expressionism, and the *neue Sachlichkeit* under some general heading, such as "The First Phase of the Modern," in order convincingly to balance concepts like classicism or realism and, at the same time, to prepare the way for a consciously "modernistic" study of literature.

Appealing as such an approach might be, we must not overlook the dangers of such a position, for this rejection of epochal concepts results in an increased atomization of knowledge, and turns literature into a disconnected series of single works. Such strong insistence on the individual work leads to a theology of literature or an exaggerated formalism which gives greatest value to the existential personal response. Whoever looks only at the single work, no longer sees even that correctly. How can we grasp the specific, when we ignore the general? Only if we study the single work of art within the corpus of a particular writer, as well as within the framework of its epoch, do we avoid turning literary scholarship into ontology. The absence of comparisons almost always leads to false conclusions; by ignoring the historical, one can easily interpret general characteristics of a given period as peculiar to the writer under discussion. Such an ahistorical perspective often results in exaggerated admiration for a few greats. But is such canonization at all legitimate? Even a brief look at literary history speaks against it. Without our interest in the unknown or the obscure, we would never have discovered Kleist, Büchner, Stifter, or Eichendorff—to cite only a few nineteenth-century names— and we would still be stuck with Geibel, Freytag, and Scheffel, the "canonized" greats of that period.

Thus, in spite of the apparent gains brought about by the newly-won "objectivity" and the confinement to individual works seen as a whole, this narrow focus leads to a considerable decline of historical awareness; for even the existential "response" or the detailed analysis of "structures of words" cannot obscure the fact that by means of these approaches literary criticism is degraded to a purely private occupation. Granted that in the humanities some judgments and opinions will always be subjective, but hostility toward history will only strengthen, rather than weaken this trend. Let us speak out against those who oppose the historical approach, without mincing words. For them, the consciousness of history, which includes the recognition of epochal styles, leads only to misconceptions. Thus, some followers of Heidegger refer to the historical approach simply as the "pathway to error" or as a "philosophy of hippopotami." On this point, Gottfried Benn speaks with similar condescension, "What is history—*bons mots*, arabesques, tiny whirlpools in *panta rhei!*"[6] The mere recognition of epochs is denounced by these people as an idle game enjoyed by those who specialize in classification and labeling. This aversion to history often hides a deep disappointment: sincere intellectuals have lost faith in the idea of progress; simple opportunists have entirely misunderstood what is meant by "history." Some are no longer even aware of the changes in their own opinions. For as soon as one stops thinking in historical terms, one necessarily loses all perspective.

But the greatest danger is the loss of possibilities for comparison, which led to the temporary victory of literary criticism over literary scholarship. As a result of this emphasis on the subjective, criticism tends to focus on the "modern," which has some advantages but all too often becomes a merely modish exercise. For in the meantime, the concept of the "modern" has lost much of the progressive impulse that it still had in the 1920s. Today the term rarely incorporates that which "points ahead," but refers to a latent mannerism, a fascination with the decadent, the grotesque, and the absurd, which are seen as existing in all epochs. The very word "modern" has been taken over by those who stand diametrically opposed to revolutionary conceptions of modernity, as envisioned by the Young Germans, the naturalists, or the expressionists. Thus, many formalists study the past only to find precursors for this kind of "modernism." Their search is as invalid as the Marxist's search for precursors of socialist realism. Both of these efforts represent attempts to justify particular ideologies —the one inclining toward realism, the other toward anti-realism—which are equally ahistorical.

III

Fortunately, a number of voices, which do not approve this ahistorical opposition to the history of styles, have recently been heard. While up to the mid-fifties scholars concerned themselves primarily with single works of art, these newer groups are once again trying to achieve an inner balance between the whole and the part. In any case, it is becoming increasingly obvious that phenomenology, existentialism, formalism and new criticism have passed their peak and that a renewed emphasis on broader connections is inevitable. In place of narrow studies, satisfied with a "special twist," those who feel a genuine responsibility are again demanding universal methods.[7]

And it is within the framework of the efforts made by those who are not satisfied with the withdrawal into the purely private that the much-abused study of styles and epochs could once again fulfill a meaningful function. However, this should not signify a return to the clichés of *Geistesgeschichte*. Instead, we should heed all the doubts raised since that era and take into account all the previous concepts of epoch. With these, we could forge a new definition which would view style neither as a mere label nor as a form imposed from without. For this reason, the question, "What is style?" must advance a structural unity that tries to combine within itself all the perspectives of a particular era. And to this end, neither the positivists' love of statistics nor an intuitive phenomenology will suffice; what is needed is a concept of epoch that tries to situate itself midway between abstraction and empiricism.

Such questions are, of course, not new and were already raised in the 1930s—when *Geistesgeschichte* was first rejected. Thus, in 1933, Benno von Wiese wrote in his essay, "Toward a Criticism of the Epochal Concepts of *Geistesgeschichte*," "The concept of epoch does not mean simply bringing together disparate elements under a single heading, but implies a synthesis of factors that are organically related to one another. For this reason, in spite of its insistence on finding a common denominator for each period, the theory of epochs necessarily remains tied to the material plenty of historical fact." He thus emphasizes the fact that concepts of epoch must remain "historical categories" and must not depend only on the "genius of the scholar" and his "originality of vision." He finds all "metaphysical-ontological" stretching of historical categories odious. Instead of identifying particular styles with the absolute "essence of their epochs," he views them as ordering principles in the "endless progressive pathway of historical awareness," as Troeltsch before him had argued. For the same reason, and with justice, Wiese is against interchanging epochal concepts, that is, he opposes the bad habit of speaking of the gothic-baroque or of medieval romanticism. In order to avoid such inflation of terms, he decries all concepts of epoch as no longer viable and views them only as working aids.[8]

This position is echoed by all who have remained true to the older concepts of epoch. Wherever terms like baroque, rococo, Biedermeier, or bourgeois realism are still current, they function as regulative norms, overriding conceptions, or collective terms, used merely as a labeling device. Theoretical arguments about these concepts have long since ceased. The terms continue to be used because they have insinuated themselves, not because anyone believes in their intrinsic value. This habitual use often creates a bad conscience, which scholars try to conceal with ironic quotation marks. And so it happens that concepts of style often appear in book titles, which no one takes very seriously anyhow. For some, they merely serve as effective trademarks, maintained because of their marketability but scoffed at in private.

It is in the very sphere of epochal concepts that a new approach must be put into action. What is the use of perpetuating terms to serve only as "working titles"? Are these not empty labels or noncommunicative generalizations? Perhaps we should first ask ourselves in which epochs the above-suggested "total view" is even possible and whether it is really meaningful to speak of styles or closed epochs for all periods. We are probably safe in doing so only until the collapse of the baroque world view around 1750. Before that time, the various realms of culture can be coordinated with relative ease, since we are dealing with "closed societies" which stood under the banner of authoritarian powers. After that, one can hardly speak of real styles, for the rising subjectivism and liberalism necessarily created a "loosening" of social norms, which in the realm of art gave rise to a number of competing movements.

Here one must speak of currents or modes, at the heart of which lies a highly complex style pluralism. But even the early epochs are by far not as homogeneous as had previously been believed. Already in the period of the gothic and the baroque, the two showpieces of *Geistesgeschichte*, we find numerous countercurrents, so that any cultural harmony, as suggested by the popular representation of gothic or baroque Man, must actually be ruled out. For ultimately, the belief that style is more than a simple cross section of a particular era perhaps holds true only for the very early periods of history, where the individual stages of style encompass hundreds, sometimes even thousands of years. With the acceleration of cultural changes an even greater number of styles comes into existence simultaneously. Whenever this occurs one can speak only of "phases." Here investigation of styles is more or less a question of finding the dominant stylistic factor of a given work.

Obviously the most varied theories already exist in this area. One of the first was the so-called generation theory, which concerned itself with the coexistence of various age groups within a single epoch,[9] that is, what Wilhelm Pinder once called the "contemporaneousness of noncontemporaries."[10] From a sociological or Marxist perspective, scholars always pointed to the various social strata, the existence of which made such a cultural homogeneity implausible. Thus Arnold Hauser writes, "One can never speak of a unified style that dominates an entire epoch, for every era has as many styles as it has artistically productive social groups."[11] A similar attitude underlies Lenin's principle of the "two cultures." In folkloric studies, scholars distinguish between "high" and "low" culture, as if a decade later intellectual fashions were sold in the bargain basement. Others pointed to phenomena like epigones, the seemingly eternal continuation of trivial literature, bohemians, and avant-gardists, in order to call into question the older concepts of epoch. Some of their objections are quite legitimate. But does this mean that every search for epochal unity necessarily signals an idealistic orientation?

We could make a new start in this direction if we were to tackle the problem of the dialectical interrelationship of the various "strata of style" within a given epoch. In so doing we would come to realize that even competing movements are often in a mysterious way related to one another, in what could be called the principle of "friendly enemies," for the battle often leads to similar tactics and techniques. For example, it is astonishing how closely the movements labeled Biedermeier and Young Germany resemble one another. In spite of their fundamentally disparate liberal and conservative attitudes, the two movements often caught hold of the same literary forms, showed the same eagerness to proselytize and in addition, advocated the same universalism, which after 1848 gave way to a skeptical relativism. Or we can cite Ernst Bloch's essay, "West, East, and the Same Epoch," in which he refers to this inner affinity as "sitting in the same boat." His example is "humanist socialism," "blocked in the East by orthodox communism and blocked in the West by capitalism," which creates a kind of symmetry, if only in a negative sense. The same is true for the relationship of apparent outsiders to their time.

In this context, opponents of epochal concepts point to figures like Nietzsche or George, who do not seem to fit anywhere. Since they are generally viewed in mythical singularity it is, of course, not difficult to strip them of all time-bound elements. If, however, Nietzsche were once seen as spokesman of the 1870s or George as representative of the period around 1900, both would suddenly look quite different. That these men, in their high-flown ambition, viewed themselves as "unique beings," is forgivable, if not exactly engaging; to take them at their word, in our scholarship, would be foolish.

From this perspective, the troublesome problem of "style pluralism" is not nearly as insoluble as it appears to be on first glance. But in contrast to earlier efforts, we should concentrate on smaller epochs. Broad concepts, such as the nineteenth century or the modern make as little sense here as in other areas. For example, how questionable it is to speak of romantic music and to mean by it a historical complex which reaches from Schubert to Pfitzner, that is, from 1820 to 1940. Therefore it is the more modest concepts of style, such as the rococo, storm and stress, Biedermeier, or art nouveau, which have the most to offer. Most of the others are still too broadly conceived to give us genuine insights. Here we must thoroughly revise the older concepts. So, for example, we could refine the broad concept of bourgeois realism between 1848 and 1889 by viewing the nationalist tendencies of the 1870s as the expression of the "period of unification"; we could also use the term art nouveau in literature and, thereby, gain a useful designation for the stylized impressionism around 1900. On the other hand, the styles at the turn of the century could be differentiated into phases such as aestheticism, national monumentalism, and formalism. The same goes for the 1920s, where a highly dramatic fluctuation between expressionism, constructivism, and the *neue Sachlichkeit* can be observed.

However, this leads us to the far more important question, "How are such 'layers of style' laid bare in the first place?" It should be clear by now that what is needed is a certain ability to combine and connect. But this is exactly what the advocates of *Geistesgeschichte* also claimed—only they were satisfied with two or three examples, and left everything else to the creative imagination. Today, scholars take a different approach and raise the question of epochal style only after they have examined a great deal of evidence. For only then can one begin to see what is specifically "new" in a given style, that is, to single out those aspects which distinguish a particular movement from all previous ones. The discovery of this particularity is, therefore, not only an intuitive act of the mind, but one which demands a complex historical knowledge of different cultural domains. We should therefore not restrict ourselves to a single discipline. This is demonstrated by our previous example of the term romantic which in music encompasses an entire century. This concept would have to be qualified, if

Lortzing were viewed as a composer of the Biedermeier period, and the late Wagner as a representative of the period of unification. In other eras, for instance between 1890 and 1920, when the visual arts were more prominent, stylistic concepts should be derived from them. In general, one should always ask which art was the actual "style determinant" within a given epoch. Such a fact can never be determined simply by means of statistics, but demands a methodological "crossing over."

Furthermore, we must rid ourselves of the idea that we can ever define a particular style definitively. Style is always only an idea, an approximation that, in reality, is present only in fragments. The idea of "pure styles" is as absurd as that of "pure races." To say that a given romantic also displays unromantic characteristics is no proof that romanticism did not exist. The determining factor should not be harmony, but the inner congruence of the various elements within a given epoch. Therefore, style must be viewed as an integrating element of the total culture. Perhaps style could best be defined as the totality of all the "new" tendencies working against the stagnating influence of previous styles.

But who are the real representatives of such a style? Here too we must rid ourselves of mere statistics. For often it is only a small group, or a few scattered individuals who give birth to a new style, forseeing what is to come, sooner than the epigones or run-of-the-mill artists, whose works still reflect the influence of the declining epoch. Therefore, the peculiarities of a particular elite, or of seemingly isolated geniuses, in no way contradict the *Zeitgeist* of a period, as is frequently suggested. Quite the contrary. In this connection, the very phrase "avant-garde" is misleading. It is not they who are the vanguard; the others have simply remained behind. Externally, they often appear to be misunderstood outsiders. The forces of opposition can also be seen as representative of a certain period, in the same way the position of the sun can be determined by means of shadows. Therefore, it is sometimes not the popular works that are most representative of their time, but rather the great ideas, or the style of those works in which the creative spirit of a particular segment of society manifests itself. Eras in which the masses play a decisive role, as, for example, periods of revolution, are especially marked by these mass experiences. On the other hand, in other eras, the creative forces arise as a result of the interrelationship of an individual genius with the masses, as, for example, the era of Napoleon, or Lenin and the Russian Revolution.

Thus, it becomes clear that what is "new" in a given epoch can never be determined purely quantitatively. Although a style is frequently found in the work of only a few prominent figures, it can nonetheless still be representative. The masses sometimes take on such styles only years or decades later. Understood in this fashion, research into styles is more than vulgar materialism, which leaves no room for individual factors; it is a discipline in which personal judgment as well as external factors play a decisive role. After all, styles are not mere epidemics that spread from a single case; they usually depend on a genuine breakthrough, carried out by those trying to forge a new path. Moreover, these breakthroughs are seldom the work of younger artists, as the popular imagination would have it, but are more often carried out by older ones who already have youth behind them. Only they have the perspective necessary for making comparisons; the younger ones, for whom revolutions are often only part of their own development, merely follow.

Of course, this does not mean that the new should be valued for its own sake. Such a perspective would stress only what is modish and quickly fades. Hermann Beenken writes, "Not the 'new' *per se*, but only that which is 'new' in connection with the development of style has intellectual worth," and thereby "historical depth."[12] For this reason, the new style is forged only by those who stand within the general dialectics of cultural movements, who react to change by continual metamorphosis and do not glorify change for its own sake. Therefore, the new is not to be found either in the commercially promoted "avant-garde," nor in the trivial dregs of a period, but only in those creative spirits who, by virtue of their knowledge, have gained enough freedom to keep themselves from being sucked into the current of commercially managed culture.

Viewed more closely, there are simply no "outsiders" as some artists, in their rage against those who have remained behind, like to claim. Every person stands in direct or indirect relation to his or her epoch, and therefore, how they perceive themselves in terms of this dialectic, determines their intellectual rank. For this reason, recognition of styles may well also imply recognition of values. For it is very questionable whether the "small" are really better representatives of their time than the "greats," as has so often been suggested. Perhaps it is only that the former adhere longer to one established style, while the latter are already moving on. Thus, we must distinguish modish opportunists from the real progressives. In this area, hasty generalizations would be dangerous. Sometimes the truly worthwhile achievements appear at the beginning of an era, sometimes at the end, and at times directly in the period of transition from one phase of development to another. Historically, each case is different. Therefore, those who undertake the study of styles should be especially aware of the fact that history can never repeat itself.

Chapter Four

CONCERNING THE DIALECTICS OF CULTURE

"Only that which arises out of the dialectics of culture is new in the good sense of the word."

—Gottfried Keller

I

The one thing that remains constant is the fact of change. But what determines this continuous fluctuation? Are we here dealing with a phenomenon like perpetual motion, which, like a pendulum, swings back and forth along the same axis? Anyone who subscribes to this position places himself outside history from the very start. For this reason, any attempt to establish some kind of mathematical formula to explain the numerous changes in style, is highly questionable. We have seen how problematic abstract constructions like Spengler's morphological cycles or Wölfflin's basic principles of "visual perception" are. We have also seen the shortcomings of the idea, cherished by some Marxists, that there is constant fluctuation between revolution and reaction, as well as the limitations of the thesis-antithesis scheme of the Old and New Hegelians. The study of style must never assume the primacy of either purely ideal or purely materialistic concepts. While from time to time such a one-sided approach may fulfill a polemic function, it is untenable as a methodological basis. For ultimately, everything living is not only determined, but also determining, and therefore can only be understood as part of a dialectical tension between all the factors in society.

Therefore in asking the question, "How do styles originate?" it would be totally insufficient to confine ourselves to purely sociological elements that assume the absolute supremacy of socio-economic factors over the intellectual and artistic products of a given epoch. Such a viewpoint can be justified to a degree, for all too often these aspects are suppressed by scholars with an existential, idealist, or religious orientation, who still view art and culture as the creation of isolated geniuses—a position that often leads to exaggerated interpretations of an ontological, poetic-ecstatic, or simply sentimental nature. The prestige that these interpretations enjoy hardly needs comment. "Alas, in the sphere of German letters, he who deems himself anti-Marxist, or who disdains psychoanalysis is still not ridiculed," writes Alfred Andersch of those who make a show of their "anti-materialistic" attitude.[1] Therefore, the responsible scholar must always take the socioeconomic basis into account. However, in dealing with questions of art, we must be careful not to fall prey to materialistic oversimplification, which would simply identify base and superstructure. We must always keep the dialectic in mind, difficult though it may be to decipher.

Let us cite an example of Richard Hamann's that may appear irrelevant, yet leads to the very heart of the matter.[2] In the Paleolithic era, people lived as hunters and gatherers almost on the same level as certain animals who engaged in the same activities. Their products, even the artistic ones, must be understood in terms of their economic situation. As evidence, we have not only the bow and arrow but also the stone axe and mallet, which served as weapons or were used for domestic tasks such as cracking nuts. The hunter's skill and his keen eye help to explain the amazing realism of the cave paintings and the magical significance of their art, for these people believed that their luck in hunting would be influenced by the possession or recreation of the objects of the hunt. These paintings were also thought to hold magical value for their descendants. We know of tribal dances, in which people dressed themselves in the skins of animals and took part in rituals supposed by them to insure their material success. It is therefore virtually impossible to understand the "spiritual" life of these people without some knowledge of their "material" existence.

But can we hope to explain, on the basis of purely material factors, why man developed beyond other animals precisely to this form of spiritual, artistic, and economic life? Did not other mammals live in the same circumstances? We could argue equally convincingly that it was the spiritual potential within human beings which determined their more developed economic status as compared to apes, for instance. We could further argue that this inherent spirituality resulted in religious rites, in the belief in magic objects, in the creation of drawings and paintings which were executed with extraordinary skill. These many aspects of spiritual life cannot possibly be understood solely on the basis of material factors. On the contrary, it is clear that they played an important part in determining the material practices developed for the purpose of controlling nature. This interrelationship reveals what is peculiarly "human" in this course of events and which can only be understood in dialectical terms.

If the people of the Stone Age banded together into nomadic tribes which were in constant search of new hunting grounds, if they felt the need for leaders to promote cooperation within the tribes, or if they created a language to ensure communication among themselves, then these factors clearly demonstrate how closely the economic situation is tied to social organization and to the products of the mind; yet even they do not offer decisive proof of any ultimate causality. Here we could ask, to what degree the societal and psychological factors bring about a spiritual condition without which it would be impossible for us to understand the economic situation of that period. In fact, such questions concern not only the Stone

Age, but can easily be applied to all styles and stages of culture. Even in the realm of the gothic or the baroque one could ask, "Which elements are actually determining and which are determined? What changes what? Does the underlying material basis determine the spiritual superstructure or does the spiritual superstructure determine the underlying material basis?" On this point Arnold Hauser once expressed himself in the following way, "A reversal occurs when the general historical, that is, social, economic conditions complete their development in a certain direction and alter their tendencies. A change of style can only be determined by external factors; it has no inner autonomy."[3] This is quite a useful, well-formulated polemic antithesis to Wölfflin's "formalism," but it leaves us with the question, "What actually determines the shifts in social and economic circumstances?"

An even greater dilemma develops if we try to interpret all spiritual or stylistic changes in the history of art solely in terms of ideal constructions. If we were to agree with René Wellek that "Literature has its own autonomous development, irreducible to any other activity or even to a sum of all these activities,"[4] we necessarily arrive at an art-for-art's-sake principle that stands outside the spiritual-material dialectic and leads to simple aestheticism. Moreover, no one has as yet convincingly demonstrated that art can really be separated from all "extra-literary" phenomena. And even if it could be, we would immediately be faced with the equally difficult problem of isolating the "inner determinants" of this apparently autonomous development.

Is the spiritual created by pure spirit? From this perspective, the entire process of man's artistic development would consist only of a series of avant-garde experiments, each so far ahead of its own era that it would be senseless to try to see any of them in relation to a particular "spirit of the time." It is easy to see to what ridiculous consequences such a premise leads. For example, how can we hope to understand Egyptian pyramids, Greek temples, or gothic cathedrals without any knowledge of the religious or historical circumstances surrounding these structures? The same holds true of the renaissance palaces and baroque castles. To attribute these monuments to an artistic avant-garde would be to think in much too modernistic terms. This concept is not even valid in interpreting the art of the last hundred years. Was any artist ever so autonomous that he developed independently?

It is perhaps only possible to construct a really convincing concept of epoch or style, one that would give equal weight to basis and superstructure, by means of a method that could best be described as a "materialistic history of the spirit." Only in this way would the study of styles or epochs lead to the fundamental question concerning what actually determines the continuous changes in artistic form: are these factors intellectual, political, economic, social, religious, or some combination of these? Thus, the question concerning the style of an epoch becomes a question concerning the very meaning of history. At first, this suggestion may seem highly exaggerated, and will, no doubt, be rejected by those who oppose a thoroughgoing historical method. They will object that from this perspective the individual is totally lost in the general. They will ask: is the individual left any freedom at all, or is everything predetermined from the start? What happens to the so-called "eternal truths" in this process of continuous change? If we emphasize only the dialectic of epochal structure and ignore individual artists, are we not degrading art into an absolutely faceless anonymity?

If we wish to make some progress in answering these questions, we have to come to terms with the specific historical place of all works of art. In order to do this, we must limit ourselves to what is singular and unrepeatable, and we must be careful to avoid all the manipulations and false analogies of *Geistesgeschichte*. Even if it becomes evident that certain things do repeat themselves, it is far more important for us to focus on what is really new, than on what is mere repetition. For this reason, the frequent talk of constants and revivals has become meaningless. The same goes for the many period concepts which begin with "neo," such as neoromanticism. Here it would be much better to take the "new" as our point of departure, rather than the "romantic." If we wish to discover the real style determinants of a given period out of the multiplicity of converging tendencies, only a total analysis of the particular epoch will serve. For without knowing which elements represent the "stagnating" and which the "progressive" forces within the chaos of conflicting artistic and spiritual tendencies, we can hardly hope to reach any valid conclusions. Therefore, any true dialectical way of thinking must always begin with the recognition of what is "new," which tries to break through historically accepted traditions. The consequences of such an approach for research into styles should be obvious.

But first, we need to do more work in the periodization of epochs, in order to get beyond isolated facts. What have we really gained by creating concepts like Biedermeier, bourgeois realism, the period of unification, or art nouveau? the imagined opponents of this method will no doubt ask. Does not the awareness of the extreme complexity of epochal styles ultimately forbid slogan-like oversimplifications and shallow "isms"? This is certainly an embarrassing question, which should by no means be summarily dismissed. Whoever starts with exclusively formal, or purely individual characteristics, will always find some methodological objection to a scholarly approach that inclines toward the universal, that seeks to create a synthesizing unity within a given epoch, out of the changing relations between its spiritual and material elements.

If, however, we forego such conceptual abbreviations altogether, we entirely obviate the possibility of communication on the level of a universal perspective of history. And does not such a position present even greater difficulties? What Kurt Hiller, in his essay "The Role of Activism," once said with true expressionist fervor, in 1916, still holds today: "No position or idea worth mentioning can ever be simple; only those who consider it in all its complexity can do it justice. But the necessity of separating one idea from another forces

one to cram the fullness of life into the narrowness and rigidity
of a designation. In competition with others, no idea can afford
to carry subtle distinctions; this would mean certain defeat. . . .
Therefore, it is not the catchword that is 'flat.' It is neither 'flat'
nor 'deep'; only the ideology that stands behind it can be flat
or deep. While popular laughter over 'isms' is often entirely
appropriate, even more appropriate would be laughter over the
arrogance of those who cannot differentiate at all."[5]

II

So we see that for better or for worse we can easily answer
this kind of criticism. More difficult to dismiss is the objection
to our emphasis on the new, the singular, the unrepeatable.
Does not this merely represent a new version of that evil "historicism" which, it was widely believed, had been definitely
overcome since the 1920s? Against our thesis, critics will level
the much overworked phrase "general relativism." They will
ask: Why should we be interested in the momentary "new,"
if it only represents an unrepeatable phase that will soon give
way to a newer trend? Does not this turn history into a
chamber of curios, which do not concern us as people of today?
And would not those opposed to a historically oriented study
of literature be right in objecting to the misuse of literature as
the "handmaiden of history"? Of what use is the past, if history only teaches us that it is irrevocably past?

Such voices have already been heard since the late nineteenth
century. Nietzsche and Dilthey had spoken out in this fashion
against positivism. But the ranks of the opposition swelled
only in the neoidealism around 1900, as shown in the writings
of Eucken, Münsterberg, Spranger, and Nohl. In contrast to all
leveling and democratizing historicism, they demanded eternal
values derived from the Absolute. And thus, in his well-known
tract, *Historicism and Its Defeat* (1924), Ernst Troeltsch, with
a side glance at the George circle and the youth movement,

declared himself for a "system of value" which would stand as an everlasting monument that not even "relativism" could touch.[6]

At first glance, such a thesis seems quite impressive. However, this avowal of the permanent and the eternal, in most cases, signifies a return to the past and represents conscious enmity to progress. It stands opposed to all ideological positions based on a concept of development. Disappointed by the "modern" and its pseudo-progressiveness, some have become unable to overcome the perversions of the previous concepts of progress and have either remained locked in hopeless contradictions or have become unequivocally reactionary. The much proclaimed "revision of relativism of values" in Troeltsch's sense, usually turns against the so-called "liberal anarchy" of the late nineteenth century, whose humanistic and cosmopolitan tendencies had little in common with the eighteenth-century enlightenment and were thus easily exposed as mere facades. Because the neoidealists singled out only that which appeared in a state of the most extreme corruption, they lost the possibility of developing a genuine awareness of history or a genuine humanitarianism.

No wonder, then, that in the wake of this reaction false standards and false alternatives surfaced everywhere. One contradiction followed another. New values were set up, new eternal verities postulated. In spite of their aversion to the anarchy of individualism, few were willing to give up their own subjectivity. Wherever one looks, concepts of the eternally beautiful, the eternally good, the eternally true, even existential and religious truths and revelations thought to have been defeated long ago, now reappear in strangely individual interpretations. Once again, everyone thinks of constants, but in fact professes only a private world view. We might well ask how universal these "eternal truths" really are. For once we have given up all hope of progress, the idea of the "eternal" can only be an ideological vestige within the domain of stagnating or slowly declining cultures.

This playing with "eternals" usually takes one of two forms:

either the eternal is interpreted as truth embedded in the content, or as truth expressed in aesthetic formal elements. Let us first consider the existential or religious enthusiasm which leads those affected by it to practice literary theology or practical ontology instead of literary history. For behind this attitude there is usually some revelation or illumination that can only be experienced in a mythical or religious way. Thus Heidegger repeatedly calls poetry the "expression of Being in words," in which every reduction to the psychological, historical, or the predetermined, appears impossible from the start. According to his scale of values, art ranks almost higher than philosophy, in that the "revealed" image proffers far greater illumination than the purely rational idea. No doubt such assertions seem highly flattering to some literary scholars, for their profession thus takes on the character of an all-embracing "grand view" of existence. And in accordance with the existential response, which assiduously avoids any and all entanglements with history, they glorify only those prime experiences and eternal truths in which man triumphs over history and moves forward into the sphere of the eternal, wherein he finally perceives "true knowledge."

Those who follow Heidegger determine the value of poetry solely by its eternal appeal. For them, real masterpieces do not age, but become increasingly deeper in the course of time, and gain in existential substance what they lose in the richness of historical connections. These critics always behave as if no history of the human soul or spirit ever existed, as if emotions like love, hate, and the desire for power are purely abstract, *a priori* categories that mean the same today as they did three thousand years ago. But do "eternal" human responses really exist at all? Are these not decoys intended to distract us from underlying problems? Is not all understanding without historical perspective not necessarily *mis*understanding, or even worse, a sign of extreme constraint and ignorance that forces us to push aside all critical objections and urges us to identify with a purely "emotionally" felt past? Would it not be outright blasphemous to assert that we can still share with a sensitive artistic understanding Dante's adoration of Beatrice, the world of the *picaro*, or even Goethe's *May Song* without some mediation? Whoever claims this and longs for a timeless emotional response is also bound to pay homage to the principle of the "eternal recurrence of the same," which necessarily leads to a reactionary submission to the past.

One could well ask these same questions from an aesthetic perspective. For in this domain, those who subscribe to T. S. Eliot's belief in the simultaneous existence of all great works of art are also taken with the idea of eternal beauty. For them, world literature consists only of a series of disconnected masterpieces, which have been so removed from all historical connections that they can be enjoyed on a purely aesthetic basis. But is not such search for aesthetic perfection an absurd undertaking from the start? Does such eternal beauty really exist? In this connection, Friederich Sengle once quoted an extremely appropriate passage from Schiller's letter of January 21, 1802, to his friend Körner, in which Schiller attacks the prevailing literary pietism and opposes the ahistorical "blah-blah" of perfection with the thesis that art only moves toward perfection as an idea, and that in its empirical manifestation it is never free of artistic flaws.[7] The tendency toward aesthetic escapism is largely the product of increased mechanization and the resulting "uglification" of the modern world, which have given rise to a whole series of resigned or pessimistic reactions. In trying to reorient themselves, some have completely lost sight of the collective hopes of the eighteenth-century enlightenment and thus no longer view art as an integral part of the larger process of development, but see it as an autonomous "artificial paradise," reserved for ultrasensitive beings. Romanticism, symbolism, art-for-art's-sake, and the numerous recent manifestations of the "esoteric" are the most familiar stages in the course of this development.

Does not this retreat into "art for its own sake" necessarily lead to snobbish connoisseurship that ultimately views even life itself as a form of art? Warnings in this direction are legion. Did not Nietzsche, one of those best acquainted with this kind of aesthetic decadence, once assert, "Art for its own sake, perhaps: the virtuoso croaking of cold-blooded, desexed frogs despairing in their swamps."[8] But even more effective than this metaphor was his image of the artist as a tightrope walker that culminated in the figure of the Aesthete around 1900. While Tolstoy disavowed a poet like Shakespeare on ethical grounds, these aesthetes propagated a kind of snobbery which gave equal value to a champagne breakfast and a night at the opera. Is it not the case that every autonomous, that is, purely aesthetic theory of art, necessarily leads to hedonism? And thus, to this very day, art is often merely tested for its formal perfection by those with an exclusively aesthetic orientation, and in the process, is sentimentalized.

How many still speak only of masterpieces, great books, and immortal works of the past? This attitude has resulted in a far-reaching victory of literary criticism over literary history. Since it lacks all historical perspective, and therefore offers no opportunity for comparison, this boundless overestimation of aesthetic values leads to grotesque superlatives. Everywhere we find scholars searching for the greatest, the best, the most perfect, as if literature dealt only with badges of merit. Some go so far as to allow only one great accomplishment in each area and disdain all works of the second rank. One is reminded of those journalists for whom there was only one Toscanini or one Caruso. How different was the judgment of a man like Kleist, who also tended to think in extremes, and yet was able to assert, "It takes more genius to appreciate a mediocre work of art than an obviously superior one." Or even more explicitly, "Whoever praises Schiller and Goethe does not, as he may believe, convince me of his superior or exceptional sense of beauty; but he who is, on occasion, satisfied with Gellert or Cronegk . . . convinces me that he possesses understanding and sensitivity, and both, at that, to a rare degree."[9]

Let us not blush at such pronouncements and let us advance our goals a little further. Imagine the many works that could be included in the sphere of literature, if we were to break away, once and for all, from the kind of aestheticism that only accepts the epic, lyric, and dramatic as worthy of inclusion in the realm of literature. Travelogues, memoirs, diaries, biographies, aphorisms, letters, *chansons*, essays, and all manner of "applied" literature would be redeemed and finally recognized as equally valuable documents of the human spirit, sometimes even more important than the works of epigones.[10] Instead of always focusing on the formally perfect, we should extend the circumference of literature and finally give the "nonaesthetic" its due.

From a truly historical perspective, which will not allow itself to be blinded by any imagined autonomy of art, everything is of interest, even the obscure and the uncomfortable, all that has previously been neglected and therefore seems to be inferior. But the further we move in this direction, the louder the voices of opposition will sound their objections of "general relativism." Let us, therefore, first come to terms with this concept, which is widely conceived as a term of sheer negation, disintegration, and disillusionment. What do people really have against such relativity? Do they oppose it because they sense in it a more "critical" spirit or an inner affinity with progressive tendencies? If this were the case, then this concept would be a mark of distinction, or at least a synonym for a thoroughgoing historical perspective.

Therefore, if we approach this problem without any preconceptions, we could easily attribute a series of highly useful characteristics to the concept of "relativism." One positive result would be our giving up normative models. For example, we should consider how long the term "German classicism" simply hid a multitude of smaller periods, and as a result, deprived these epochs of scholarly study. It took almost a century before any interest was shown in the baroque, the romantic, Biedermeier, or bourgeois realism. Only by means of a relativizing perspective can we possibly free ourselves from those concepts that authoritarian scholars held to be inimitable. Therefore, we could equate relativism with the unfettered freedom of opinion that Goethe supported in the aphorism, "True liberalism lies in tolerance."[11]

This relativization of the past can equally well be characterized as the gradual abandonment of myths and legends or as
the self-realization of humankind. For it is precisely the much-
abused relativity that keeps us from holding fast to a narrow
world view, that opens our eyes, and allows us a degree of
freedom. We could go even further and ask whether without
such a continuous process of relativization it would be possible
to progress to a genuine universalism? Did not the increased
awareness of other nations, religions, and moral codes, which
developed in the eighteenth century, shake the foundations of
the ruling powers and, at the same time, question the sanctity
of previously held opinions? In this connection, let us keep in
mind the significance of the first great explorations, including
the discovery of Australia and Tahiti. In the sudden con-
frontation with other religions, social forms, and economic
systems, people were forced to make comparisons.

From this perspective, we could just as well characterize
relativism as the great cultural educator. It is relativism that
gives us intellectual breadth, promotes spiritual empathy, and
keeps us from retreating to the past, or making an idol of the
"modern." Only by means of a relativistic perspective do we
gain historical distance. Emil Staiger once wrote, "He who is
well acquainted with history is the freest, most judicious being."[12] These words, which could possibly still be interpreted
as escapism into the past, were formulated more concretely by
Friedrich Sengle, "Tolerance developed with historical thinking; it seems to me that it rises and falls with it."[13] Only those
who agree with the above can keep from falling prey to the
many forms of absolutism that constantly threaten us; it makes
little difference behind which masks these claims to pseudo-
totality hide.

III

Those who do not wish to have anything to do with historical
relativism will continue to view such a position as a regrettable

loss of values, to put it mildly. In truth, however, this relativism offers one of the few possibilities for a new scale of values, in that it forces us to give up previously fixed conceptions and compels us to make a concrete decision. Seen from this perspective, it is precisely this disreputable "relativism of styles" that gives us aesthetic freedom, makes it impossible for us to hold derivative opinions, and continuously confronts the individual with the inexorable mutations of history. In this way, all conceptions of golden ages, classical periods, and climaxes fade, and open the way to a broad panorama of entirely different horizons. In this respect, relativism could be extremely salutary. It might free us from the usual talk about "loss of center" and lead us to an objectivity that should not be counted as a loss but as a triumph, especially if it leads to the dismantling of outmoded values. In short, a relativistic view of art and literature is simply a necessity, if ever we hope to stand in a truly productive relationship to our own time.

These few remarks should have made clear that by "relativistic" we do not mean a "scholarship free of values" à la Max Weber. We have no intention of now going to the opposite extreme. Instead of preaching absolute freedom of values, we seek values in other directions: not in beauty, nor in eternity, but within the framework of so-called developmental factors in history. But perhaps this would only be workable if, once and for all, we stopped viewing art as an existential modality, valuable in its own right. For ultimately, art, like everything human, is only an interesting, albeit imperfect, instrument in the frame of broader connections, whose significance stands or falls with our ability to make these connections meaningful.

For this reason, art cannot fulfill the aesthetic education of mankind nor transcend the historical-concrete into the category of the existential or generally human. Examined closely, even the greatest works of art are only small paving stones in the mysterious pathway of humanity, whose course is often so sinuous one could easily despair. Therefore, it would make more sense to see these works as fragments of an incomplete entelechy, whose noblest task consists in giving us a small "foretaste" of circumstances more worthy of human dignity, and strengthening our hopes for gradual improvement. In this way, even within time-bound circumstances there arise non-time-bound elements, which contain the actual seed of development, which function in the present and yet are connected to the future. For the sake of truth, we must devote ourselves to the idea of wholeness, which more idealistically inclined epochs once called the *hen kai pan* of human knowledge, and not allow ourselves to become seduced by the specialized and the technical. Only after this task has been fulfilled, will art be able to help us see through the clichés of our own time, and make us ready for a progressive consciousness.

This does not sound like much, and yet it is a great deal. For what we take away from art on the one hand, we freely give back to it with the other. But we can only arrive at such a position if we understand by art neither revealed existential truths nor aesthetic reflections of eternal beauty. But after the historical perceptions of the last two hundred years, such viewpoints are no longer tenable. Garve, Schiller, and Hegel had gone so far as to assert that art, as a purely aesthetic phenomenon, was already a thing of the past, since it had been superseded by the philosophical discoveries of the eighteenth century. "The wondrous days of Greek art, like the golden days of the middle ages, are past," asserted Hegel in his *Lectures on Aesthetics*. Elsewhere he writes more explicitly, "In all these respects art, in its highest destination, is and remains something that belongs to the past," for it contains too many external elements and therefore no longer represents the "highest form of the spirit."[14] Leaning on such observations, Heine once spoke of art as a "lovely inessential," inferior to philosophy or politics.[15] Of course, this does not mean that Heine and the liberals of the 1830s wished to "do away" with art entirely. They were simply trying to give it a different function. They believed that art, instead of lending religion its beautiful cloak or placing itself in the service of sensual beauty, should devote itself to the concerns of real life.

Little in this situation has changed since then. In the realm of art we are still faced with three possibilities. First, we can counteract the rising tide of intellectualism by embracing the principle of the autonomy of art and trying to separate ourselves as best we can from the rest of the world. Second, we can bid farewell to art entirely and devote ourselves to the modern world of technology as, for example, the Bauhaus or the movement of *literatura facta*. Both aestheticism and utilitarianism boast an impressive following and on occasion the one merges with the other. Without a doubt, however, the most important direction is the one that resist both of these trends and strives for a new principle of wholeness. Its ideal can neither be existentialism nor formalism, but an uncompromising engagement that stands in a critical, dialectical relationship to its own time. Therefore, it seems best to avoid immersing oneself only in the past and also to avoid empty activist acclamations that bear no relationship to history. By and large, the central concern of art must be to diminish our belief in the eternal by constantly confronting us with the unrepeatability of history. Instead of allowing us to muddle along in a philistine fear of the "new," it should prepare us for true freedom by making us more fully aware of the current situation.

For this reason alone, the goal of art cannot be either beauty or originality, the aesthetic norms of the nineteenth century, but that which is "new" in a provocative sense and calls for radical change. As previously suggested, the "new" here is not meant to refer to the "modish," to a narrow expression of any "abstract otherness," or to a conformism that goes in the dress of nonconformity, typical of certain avant-garde phenomena.[16] The "new" should consist of a synthesizing response to the contradictions of our time, which is truly epoch-making. The value of such art lies primarily in its developmental quality, that is, in its uncovering that historical spiral or cultural dialectic without which we would be absolutely incapable of understanding ourselves. Seen in this light, this third direction would provide no more and no less than an aesthetic guide enabling us to recognize, in our own time, the potential opportunity for development in the progressive self-realization of humankind. For only in this way can art really affect us as contemporaries and, at the same time, put us in accord with the always only-intuited future.

This suggestion will probably meet with sharp resistance and will only strengthen the desperate pleas for "that which endures." For if this position is taken to its extreme, does not everything become outmoded, not only art but also our perception of art, and all of culture? But does not even this also have its "positive" features? For this thesis not only points to change, but also to the fact that art, like all other intellectual, political, and social phenomena, is changed by man. In this way, historical thinking and a relativizing perspective go hand in hand. Thus, Brecht once wrote in his *Little Organon*, "The field must be marked out in all its historical relativity. We should leave [the various ages] their differences, and keep their transitoriness in mind, so that we will also perceive our own time as transitory."[17] Everyone knows how untiringly Brecht tried to achieve critical distance in the productions of his plays, in order to counteract the average theatergoer's propensity (so difficult to eradicate) to become so "moved" by the characters that he completely identifies with them and, in the process, loses all historical perspective.

This is how we ought to approach *all* works of art. Instead of wanting to "relive" them completely, which always leads to false conclusions, we should try to point out their historical, dialectical nature, and in this way, transform the world of art into an arena which reveals the development of humankind. In such a world theater, we need fewer enthusiasts and more critical observers, who would view the changes in the form and content of art as part of their own prehistory. Martin Walser's dictum to the effect that "old plays" should only be performed "to show us how it once was," tends in this same direction. In sharp contrast to those critics who search everywhere for "general validity and immortality," Walser believes that every work of art represents an "unrepeatable moment of history." And so for him, a character such as Luise Miller in Schiller's *Intrigue and Love* is not an eternal model of renunciation but merely someone who is ruined by the contemporary code of morality. He is, therefore, right to speak out against staging such a work in a contemporary setting, which ultimately diverts us from the problems of our own time. Like Brecht, Walser is against undistanced appreciation; he urges us to become more fully aware of the fact that history continually destroys traditional patterns of thought and thus forces us to make new decisions.[18]

In line with these observations, literary history could also teach us to view every individual work of art as an essential part of that endless process of reflection which actually never reaches its goal but nonetheless moves in a certain direction, or at least ought to move in that direction. For only in this way can all revolutions in style, and all historical innovations be seen as part of the historical process. Thus, in spite of all relativity, the processes of change gain a "touch of eternity" by becoming integrated into the apparently unending process of human self-realization. Thereby we will have arrived at an important point of departure for a new value system within the world of continually "aging" artistic forms. For such a perspective would make clear to us that all works of art that seriously confront their own age and attempt to overcome its contradictions are as caught up in currents of history as works of the second rank or the unequivocally inferior. They move us by displaying a genuine breakthrough to higher levels of consciousness, and thus offer us undeniable encouragement. And why should an experience that appeals to our historical sense as well as our ideological engagement be less valuable than a purely aesthetic or existential identification with feelings which are often falsely assumed to be eternal? Let us, therefore, value works that fully express their epochs, and not those artifacts that have been honed and polished for purely aesthetic reasons. For only that which has really lived in its own time can also live in ours.

True historical thinking, then, would reside in the awareness that, while everything becomes outmoded, nothing is lost so long as we can keep the "whole" in proper perspective. From such a point of view, even works or ideas that seem to be antiquated are sublated* into humanity's ever-increasing consciousness. In this connection, let us think of works like *The Critique of Pure Reason*, in which Kant proved all previous metaphysical possibilities absurd, but still did not simply write off the entire past as "false," but gave it its appropriate place in the history of the human mind. Hegel then dealt with Kant in a similar fashion. Today hardly anyone doubts that even Hegel's position was only a relative one, as radical as it may have appeared in its own day. All this is an essential part of the process of human reflection, which will only cease when the human species finally dies out. In this sense, literary scholarship should not forget that even its own best accomplishments are merely "acts of history, designated only for the present as the ultimate stage of historical reflection, but in no way fixed in stagnant finality."[19]

IV

True historical thinking therefore only has meaning if we are determined to preserve the idea of progress, at least as a postulate, or an "as-if" proposition. It should be clear by now that we do not have in mind a concept of progress that walks through the centuries like an automaton, inspired by an Hegelian *Weltgeist*. Whoever still believes in this not only appears ridiculous, but is actually slandering the concept of real progress. After two world wars, after Hitler, Stalin, and Hiroshima, such conceptions simply have no place. Only the most vulgar materialists and followers of Darwin who have never moved beyond the nineteenth century can possibly believe in an automatic evolution. If we wish to outlive the cur-

---

* Eliminated during the dialectical process but simultaneously elevated and preserved. In this way, it is passed on into the resulting synthesis.

rent world situation (and who would reject such a hope?) then all the terror to which we continue to be subject should not diminish, but strengthen the need for a new summons to progress. Even failure and regression into "dark centuries" are not evidence to the contrary. "How long it will take [for humankind to reach self-realization] is entirely relative," Hegel once wrote, in speaking of the "goal of history," that is, man's attainment of freedom.[20]

Therefore let us not despair too quickly, even if the way seems burdensome, long, and at times unending. Everyone knows how easy it is to make fun of the idea of progress in the light of our experiences, to make it sound cheap or absurd, and so fancy oneself more profound than the so-called optimists. But such a denial of progress should make us suspicious, for it is always the political, philosophical and religious reactionaries who, in fact, enjoy all the comforts of the modern world, who nonetheless, in theory, mock the idea of progress. Those who wish to make things still easier for themselves need only label this idea of progress as "Marxist." A Britisher once said with apt sobriety, "It would be just as absurd to say that mankind has made no progress, as absurd indeed as to maintain that a man who had fallen off the north face of the Matterhorn had not started to climb it."[21]

For only by means of the postulate of progress could the much-maligned historical approach once again appear in a different light. When viewed from this perspective, it directs attention not only to the transitory nature of all human efforts, but also to the human will to change, which is always closely allied to the principle of historical relativism. Ultimately we must be able to free ourselves from traditions, be they ever so strongly ingrained in our consciousness. For only after we have freed ourselves from the fetters of the past, are we ready to be real contemporaries, who view their own present in the light of the past as well as the future. Without this dialectical relationship to the three "ecstasies of time," as Heidegger once called them, it would be difficult to get beyond the widespread tendency to imitate the past. We would thus impede humanity's self-realization—to use these grandiose words once again. A person's intellectual level is determined by his ability not to lose sight of any of these three dimensions. "Chronicles are only written by those who value the present," wrote Goethe.[22] Achim von Arnim once expressed himself similarly, "There is a future of the spirit, as there is a past, as well as a present; without the former two, who has the latter?"[23] Even Nietzsche once asserted, "Only he who builds the future has a right to judge the past."[24]

In the spirit of these maxims, only those who have really grasped history and come to terms with it are able to free themselves from the *morte main* of the past and thus become purveyors of style in their own time. How true this is, is shown by a brief glance backward at the purely antiquarian "historicism" preferred by the nineteenth century. That this era leaned toward a conspicuously imitative style, particularly in the pictorial arts, has always been interpreted as an excess of historicism. In reality, we would have to argue the exact opposite. Whoever allows himself to be so strongly seduced to imitation, clearly shows that he does not understand the workings of history. For him, everything "great" in the artistic past is something "eternal," and therefore worthy of imitation. Such a person is unaware of the fact that even the most brilliant works of art can never be repeated, and do not allow themselves to be transplanted from one era to another. It is precisely these unsuccessful imitations that are the best evidence against the thesis of the "eternal" or generally human in art. If there really were an existential response, we would still be able to create sculpture like the Greeks or build gothic cathedrals. That we cannot do it, and will never be able to in the future, has nothing to do with inferior ability, but lies in our metamorphosed spirit.

Therefore, in viewing the past, literary criticism should never lose sight of its universal historical function. Instead of searching everywhere for constants in form or content, it must turn its attention more strongly to the elements of historical development and thereby contribute to the raising of humanity's consciousness. Ideally, it would put us in touch with the entelechy of all humanity and thus offer us the possibility of becoming truly of age. Moreover, in line with such thinking, the difference between the eternal and the transitory would become increasingly less important and might even disappear completely. It would do away with old fixations. "Is it not narrowness," Gervinus once asked, "to attribute purpose-in-itself to a discipline that stands in the river of life?" Elsewhere, he describes the historian as a "partisan of destiny" or a "natural champion of progress," whose task it is to support those who hold progressive ideas.[25]

We fully subscribe to all of this. But how can we recognize the goals of our own time? How can we become proponents of that "progressiveness" demanded by Gervinus? This question is always met with skepticism. Thus Karl Löwith writes, "To expect to orient ourselves by means of history, when we are standing in the midst of it, would be like trying to hold on to the waves in a shipwreck."[26] Similar assertions abound in all the humanities. Who any longer feels obliged to uncover the dialectical contradictions of his time and thereby relativize them historically? We can reach such a position only when we no longer acquiesce to that fatal cycle of "eternal return." Of course, this does not mean that we can consciously *create* a new style. A genuine style, one that is historically significant, cannot be willed into existence, but only comes about when the individual and the general converge in the direction of progress. Forcing styles artificially, usually leads to mere stylization, as the cramped efforts of art nouveau around 1900 show. In the framework of our own present, we can only give impulses. The styles that grow out of these are only recognized after the fact. This is not to suggest that we ought to consider ourselves part of that ominous *Zeitgeist* by reflecting only the currents of the present situation. We become real "carriers of style" (in contrast to Tucholsky's "apes of time" who are swept along by every commercially created fashion),[27] only if it is clear to us what must "go," and if we oppose the clichés of yesterday and today with new perspectives.

In this connection, the study of styles could be an enlightening and freeing influence, since it interprets the succession of styles as stages in humanity's contradictory and ever more circuitous path to self-realization. Such an emancipating spiral or "dialectics of culture" as Gottfried Keller once put it,[28] would make us more fully aware of the many "levels of style" that often play quite a tyrannical role within our "household" of ideas. Understood in this way, research into style can do for literary scholarship what sociology is doing for the mechanics of social life, and psychoanalysis for the mechanics of the unconscious. According to this line of thinking, even the research into style could contribute to the "awakening of humanity from its dreams about itself" by "explaining its own actions to it," and as a result, "bring it to self-awareness."[29] Not only would study of styles show us the unrepeatability of history and the resulting impossibility of imitation, but would also illuminate the many levels of style within our own minds. For undoubtedly, we are governed not only by archetypes and social dynamics, but also by spiritual, artistic, and historical factors. Thus there are still those who have remained in the period of Biedermeier with respect to morality but have already reached bourgeois realism in the sphere of art; socially they behave slightly Wilhelmenian while in their political thinking they have already progressed as far as the 1920s. Some say that in technological matters we live in the present, but that our politicians are still caught up in the concepts of nationalism of the nineteenth century.

On the whole, most people seem to be anachronisms in their own epoch, as if they had been born posthumously. How many really live in that oft-extolled "here and now"? If these contradictions merely mirrored the generation gap, such tensions could be resolved with relative ease. But the "old and the new do not simply divide people into two heaps," Brecht once said, "not even into people of old and new stamp; for the new fights the old within each one of us."[30] And Brecht was well aware of the tenacity of old ideologies. When someone objected to his *Puntila/Matti* on the grounds that the play no longer possessed actuality (because in East Germany there were no big landowners), he defended it with these words, "We do not only learn from the battle, but from the history of battles. The remains of past epochs continue to live in the souls of humans for a long time."[31]

And with that, we will have reached the furthest point that a relativistically oriented study of styles can attain. For only such a perspective could keep our examination of the past from leading to the spiritual crippling that Nietzsche described so strikingly in his tract, *Concerning the Use and Abuse of History for Life*. On the other hand, historical thinking would help us avoid the equally dangerous tendency to achieve a false actualization of the past, which would be less an asset than a liability in our search for new solutions. This undeniably raises more questions than can be answered in a single book. But that too is part of our theory. Every era will have to answer these questions anew for itself.

Notes

Part I: The Pluralism of Methods Since 1900

Chapter One: The Rise and Fall of Positivism

1. Quoted in Hans-Egon Hass, "Das Problem der literarischen Wertung," *Studium Generale*, 12 (1959), 728.

2. See Jost Hermand, "Schillers Abhandlung 'Über naive und sentimentalische Dichtung' im Lichte der deutschen Popularphilosophie des 18. Jahrhunderts," *PMLA*, 79 (1964), 428–41.

3. Hegel, *Jubiläumsausgabe*, 3rd ed. (Stuttgart, 1953), XII, 37.

4. Ibid., XI, 88, 221.

5. Georg Gottfried Gervinus, *Geschichte der poetischen Nationalliteratur der Deutschen*, 2nd ed. (Leipzig, 1840–44), I, 12.

6. Gervinus, *Grundzüge der Historik* (Leipzig, 1837).

7. Leopold von Ranke, *Geschichte und Politik: Ausgewählte Aufsätze* (Stuttgart, 1940), p. 140.

8. Wilhelm Scherer, *Kleine Schriften* (Berlin, 1893), II, 67.

9. See Werner Krauss, "Literaturgeschichte als geschichtlicher Auftrag," *Studien und Aufsätze* (Berlin, 1959), p. 32.

10. Wilhelm Scherer, *Vorträge und Aufsätze zur Geschichte des geistigen Lebens* (Berlin, 1874), p. 411.

11. Friedrich Nietzsche, *Werke* (Leipzig, 1899 ff.), I, 306, 308.

12. Cf. Richard Hamann/Jost Hermand, "Der Gedankenkreis der

'fortschrittlichen Reaktion,' " *Stilkunst um 1900* (Berlin, 1967), pp. 40 ff.

Chapter Two: The Impact of Geistesgeschichte

1. Julius Petersen, *Literaturgeschichte als Wissenschaft* (Heidelberg, 1914), p. 15. How sharply Dilthey must be distinguished from his "disciples" is convincingly demonstrated by Kurt Müller-Vollmer in his book *Toward a Phenomenological Theory of Literature: A Study of Wilhelm Dilthey's "Poetik"* (The Hague, 1963).

2. Petersen, *Die Wesensbestimmung der deutschen Romantik* (Leipzig, 1926), p. 7.

3. Rudolf Unger, *Gesammelte Studien* (Berlin, 1929), I, 154.

4. Emil Ermatinger, *Das dichterische Kunstwerk* (Leipzig, 1921), p. iii.

5. Fritz Strich, *Deutsche Klassik und Romantik* (Munich, 1922), p. 5.

6. Oskar Walzel, *Gehalt und Gestalt* (Berlin, 1923), p. 18.

7. Fritz Brüggemann, "Psychogenetische Literaturwissenschaft," *Zeitschrift für Deutschkunde*, 39 (1925), 756.

8. Werner Marholz, *Literaturgeschichte und Literaturwissenschaft* (Berlin, 1923), pp. 7, 10.

9. Jean Paul, *Werke*, ed. R. Wustmann (Leipzig, n.d.), IV, 114.

10. Cf. Jost Hermand, *Literaturwissenschaft und Kunstwissenschaft*, Sammlung Metzler, 41 (Stuttgart, 1965), p. 24 ff.

11. Richard Hamann, *Der Impressionismus in Leben und Kunst* (Cologne, 1907), pp. 25, 319, 19.

12. Oswald Spengler, *Der Untergang des Abendlandes* (Munich, 1918 ff.), I, 8.

13. Herbert Krauss, *Das Wellengesetz in der Geschichte* (Bern, 1929), pp. iii, 114.

14. Cf. Walter Vogel, "Über den Rhythmus im geschichtlichen Leben des abendländischen Europa," *Historische Zeitschrift*, 129 (1924), 1–68.

15. For details of these theories refer to the following: Erwin Panofsky, "Über des Verhältnis der Kunstgeschichte zur Kunsttheorie," *Zeitschrift für Ästhetik*, 18 (1925), 129 ff.; Gerhart Rodenwaldt, "Wandel und Wert kunstgeschichtlicher Perioden," *Zeitschrift für Ästhetik*, 21 (1927), 151 ff.; Edgar Wind, "Zur Systematik der künstlerischen Probleme," *Zeitschrift für Ästhetik*, 18 (1925), 438 ff.; Dagobert Frey, *Gotik und Renaissance* (Augsburg, 1929), p. 38 ff.; Frederik Adama van Scheltema, *Die altnordische Kunst* (Berlin, 1923), p. 224; Paul Frankl, "Der Beginn der Gotik und das allgemeine Pro-

blem des Stilbeginns," *Wölfflin-Festschrift* (Munich, 1924), pp. 107–125.

16. Cf. Albert Erich Brinckmann, *Plastik und Raum als Grundformen künstlerischer Gestaltung* (1922).
17. Strich, *Deutsche Klassik und Romantik*, p. 255.
18. Arthur Hübscher, "Barock als Gestaltung antithetischen Lebensgefühls," *Euphorion*, 24 (1922), 522.

Chapter Three: National, "Volkish," and Racial Aspects

1. Emil Ermatinger, *Krisen und Probleme der neueren deutschen Dichtung* (Zurich, 1928), p. 353.
2. Ermatinger, "Die deutsche Literaturwissenschaft in der geistigen Bewegung der Gegenwart," *Zeitschrift für Deutschkunde*, 39 (1925), 258.
3. Ermatinger, *Das dichterische Kunstwerk* (Leipzig, 1921), p. v.
4. Paul Kluckhohn, *Die Auffassung der Liebe in der Literatur des 18. Jahrhunderts und in der deutschen Romantik* (Halle, 1922).
5. Rudolf Unger, *Herder, Novalis und Kleist: Studien über die Entwicklung des Todesproblems in Denken und Dichten vom Sturm und Drang zur Romantik* (Frankfurt/Main, 1922), p. 144. In his *Gesammelte Studien* (Berlin, 1929), Unger subsequently suggested that the methods of *Geistesgeschichte* were the most decisive and most characteristic achievement of German literary criticism (I, 138).
6. Oskar Hagen, *Deutsches Sehen* (Munich, 1920), p. 6.
7. Herbert Cysarz, "Das Periodenprinzip in der Literaturwissenschaft," *Philosophie der Literaturwissenschaft*, ed. by E. Ermatinger (Berlin, 1930), pp. 94, 106, 111.
8. Cf. Richard Benz, "Die Renaissance, das Verhängnis der deutschen Kultur," *Blätter für deutsche Art und Kunst*, 1 (1915), 1 ff.
9. Spengler, *Untergang des Abendlandes*, I, 333.
10. Wilhelm Worringer, *Formprobleme der Gotik* (Munich, 1911), p. 57.
11. Spengler, *Untergang des Abendlandes*, I, 291.
12. Hans Much, *Vom Sinn der Gotik* (Dresden, 1923), p. 16.
13. Wilhelm Hausenstein, *Vom Geist des Barock* (Munich, 1920), p. 113.
14. Heinrich Wölfflin, *Kunstgeschichtliche Grundbegriffe* (Munich, 1915), p. 113.
15. Carl Neumann, *Rembrandt*, 3rd ed. (Munich, 1922), p. 552.
16. Fritz Strich, "Der lyrische Stil des 17. Jahrhunderts," *Muncker-Festschrift* (Munich, 1916), pp. 33, 44.
17. In his book on Grimmelshausen, Rudolf Lochner simply puts

forward the figure of Simplicissimus as *the* representative of the Germanic (Reichenberg i.B., 1924).

18. See Arthur Hübscher, "Barock als Gestaltung," and Willi Flemming, "Die Auffassung des Menschen im 17. Jahrhundert," *DVLG*, 6 (1928), 403–46.

19. Willi Flemming, *Deutsche Kultur im Zeitalter des Barocks* (Potsdam, 1937), p. 324.

20. Karl Viëtor, *Probleme der deutschen Barockliteratur* (Leipzig, 1928).

21. Max Deutschbein, *Das Wesen des Romantischen* (Köthen, 1921).

22. Strich, *Deutsche Klassik und Romantik*, p. 253.

23. Julius Petersen, *Die Wesensbestimmung der deutschen Romantik*, p. 107.

24. Ernst Bertram, "Norden und deutsche Romantik," *Zeitwende*, 2, 46 ff.

25. Richard Benz, *Die deutsche Romantik* (Leipzig, 1937), p. 481.

26. Wilhelm Pinder, *Das Problem der Generation in der Kunstgeschichte Europas*, 2nd ed. (Berlin, 1928), pp. xv, 15.

27. Julius Petersen, *Die literarischen Generationen* (Berlin, 1930), pp. 32, 53.

28. Eduard Wechssler, "Die Generation als Jugendgemeinschaft," *Breysig-Festschrift* (Breslau, 1927), I, 66–102.

29. See Janet K. King, "The Generation Theory in German Literary Criticism," Diss., Wisconsin, 1965, p. 124 f.

30. See Richard Hamann/Jost Hermand, *Stilkunst um 1900* (Berlin, 1967), p. 58 ff.

31. See Conrad Müller, *Altgermanische Meeresherrschaft* (Gotha, 1914), and Ludwig Wilser, *Die Überlegenheit der germanischen Rasse* (1915).

32. Otto Seeck, *Die Geschichte des Untergangs der antiken Welt* (Berlin, 1895–1920) 6 vols.

33. Ludwig Woltmann, *Die Germanen und die Renaissance in Italien*, (Leipzig, 1905), p. 16.

34. Willibald Hentschel, *Vom aufsteigenden Leben* (Leipzig, 1910), p. 10.

35. Guido von List, *Die Namen der Völkerstämme Germaniens* (Vienna, 1908), p. 5.

36. Paul Schultze-Naumburg, *Kunst und Rasse* (Munich, 1928) and *Kunst aus Blut und Boden* (1934).

37. Ludwig Ferdinand Clauss, *Die Nordische Seele* (Halle a.S., 1923).

38. Walther Linden, "Deutschkunde als politische Lebenswissenschaft," *Zeitschrift für Deutschkunde*, 47 (1933), 337, 339.

39. Karl Viëtor, "Die Wissenschaft vom deutschen Menschen in seiner Zeit," *Zeitschrift für deutsche Bildung*, 9 (1933), 344.

40. Max Wehrli, *Allgemeine Literaturwissenschaft* (Bern, 1951), p. 19.

41. Hermann August Korff, "Die Forderung des Tages," *Zeitschrift für Deutschkunde*, 47 (1933), 342.

42. Ludwig Büttner, *Gedanken zu einer biologischen Literaturbetrachtung* (Munich, 1939), p. 10.

43. Heinz Otto Burger, "Die rassischen Kräfte im deutschen Schrifttum," *Zeitschrift für Deutschkunde*, 48 (1934), 476.

44. See the work of Franz Koch, Walter Linden, Helmut Langenbucher, Albert Soergel, Karl Justus Obenauer.

45. Herbert Cysarz, "Das Periodenprinzip in der Literaturwissenschaft," p. 106.

46. See Eberhart Lämmert, *Germanistik—eine deutsche Wissenschaft*, edition suhrkamp, 204 (Frankfurt/Main, 1967), p. 18 f.

Chapter Four: The Influence of Psychoanalysis

1. See Richard Hamann and Jost Hermand, *Naturalismus* (Berlin, 1959), p. 51 ff.

2. Otto Behaghel, *Bewußtes und Unbewußtes im dichterischen Schaffen* (Leipzig, 1907), pp. 4, 5, 21; and Wilhelm Waetzoldt, *Das Kunstwerk als Organismus* (Leipzig, 1905), p. 23.

3. Sigmund Freud, *Gesammelte Werke* (London, 1941 ff.), XIV, 333 ff.

4. Freud, VII, 216, 221.

5. Freud, VIII, 417.

6. Freud, XIV, 439.

7. Cf. Ludwig Marcuse, "Freuds Ästhetik," *PMLA*, 72 (1957), 446–63.

8. Otto Rank, *Der Künstler* (Vienna, 1907), pp. 35, 37.

9. Otto Rank, *Das Inzest-Motiv in Dichtung und Sage* (Vienna, 1912), pp. 13, 31, 681, 683.

10. Wilhelm Stekel, *Dichtung und Neurose* (Wiesbaden, 1909), pp. 13, 7, 12.

11. Otto Rank/Hanns Sachs, *Die Bedeutung der Psychoanalyse für die Geisteswissenschaften* (Wiesbaden, 1913), p. 85.

12. Cf. Jost Hermand, "Spittelers 'Imago.' Über das Verhältnis von Dichtung und Psychoanalyse," *GRM*, 36 (1955), 223–34.

13. Walter Muschg, *Psychoanalyse und Literaturwissenschaft* (Berlin, 1930), p. 11.

14. Frederick J. Hacker, "On Artistic Production," *Explorations in Psychoanalysis*, ed. by R. Lindner (New York, 1953), p. 129.

15. Freud, XIV, 436, 472.

16. Bertolt Brecht, *Stücke* (Berlin, 1955), III, 275.
17. Carl Gustav Jung, "Psychologie und Dichtung," *Philosophie der Literaturwissenschaft*, ed. by E. Ermatinger (Berlin, 1930), pp. 322, 330.
18. Carl Gustav Jung, "Über die Beziehungen der analytischen Psychologie zum dichterischen Kunstwerk," *Seelenprobleme der Gegenwart*, 2nd ed. (Zurich, 1931), pp. 63, 67, 70.
19. See Heinrich Goldmann, *Katabasis: Eine tiefenpsychologische Studie zur Symbolik der Dichtungen Georg Trakls* (Salzburg, 1957), p. 96.
20. Maud Bodkin, *Archetypal Patterns in Poetry* (London, 1934), p. 23.
21. Ernest Jones, *Hamlet* (London, 1947).
22. Bodkin, p. 325.
23. Richard Chase, *The Quest for Myth* (Baton Rouge, 1949), p. 131.
24. Leslie A. Fiedler, "Archetype and Signatures," *Art and Psychoanalysis*, ed. by W. Phillips (New York, 1957), pp. 454–72.

Chapter Five: Sociological and Marxist Literary Scholarship

1. Max Weber, *Wirtschaft und Gesellschaft* (Tübingen, 1925), p. 9.
2. Arnold Hirsch, "Soziologie und Literaturgeschichte," *Euphorion*, 29 (1928), 74–82.
3. Levin L. Schücking, *Soziologie der literarischen Geschmacksbildung*, 3rd ed. (Bern, 1961), p. 55.
4. See Chapter Three, footnotes 26–29.
5. Karl Mannheim, "Das Problem der Generationen," *Kölner Vierteljahrshefte für Soziologie*, 7 (1928), 172.
6. Walter Muschg, *Tragische Literaturgeschichte* (Bern, 1948), p. 272.
7. The attention currently being given to trivial literature is proof of this. See W. Killy, *Deutscher Kitsch* (1961), W. Nutz, *Der Trivialroman* (1962), M. Beaujean, *Der Trivialroman in der zweiten Hälfte des 18. Jahrhunderts* (1964), G. Schmidt-Henkel, H. Enders, F. Knilli und W. Maier, *Trivialliteratur* (1964), W. Langenbucher, *Der aktuelle Unterhaltungsroman* (1964), M. Greiner, *Die Entstehung der modernen Unterhaltungsliteratur* (1964), among others.
8. Hugo Kuhn, "Dichtungswissenschaft und Soziologie," *Studium generale* 3 (1950), 622–26.
9. *Soziologie und Leben*, ed. by C. Brinkmann (Tübingen, 1952), p. 199.

10. See Martin Greiner, "Literatur und Gesellschaft," *Deutsche Universitätszeitung* XII, 7 (1957), 14–17.
11. Hans Norbert Fügen, *Die Hauptrichtungen der Literatursoziologie und ihre Methoden* (Bonn, 1964), pp. 108, 166 ff.
12. Cf. Franz Mehring, "Die Literatur im deutschen Reiche" (1874), *Meisterwerke deutscher Literaturkritik*, ed. by H. Mayer (Berlin, (1956) II, 899 ff.
13. See Peter Demetz, *Marx, Engels und die Dichter* (Stuttgart, 1959), pp. 243 ff.
14. See Ursula Münchow, *Aus den Anfängen der sozialistischen Dramatik* (Berlin, 1964), I, xii.
15. Georg Lukács, *Probleme des Realismus*, 2nd ed. (Berlin, 1955), p. 202.
16. Georg Lukács, *Schicksalswende* (Berlin, 1956), p. 230.
17. Hans Kaufmann, "Lukács' Konzeption eines 'dritten Weges,'" *Georg Lukács und der Revisionismus* (Berlin, 1960), pp. 322–39.
18. *Materialistische Wissenschaft* (Berlin, 1971), I, IV, and II, 36.
19. Georg Lukács, *Ästhetik* (Neuwied, 1963), I, 843 ff., 614, 701, 702.
20. Ernst Fischer, *The Necessity of Art* (Baltimore, 1963), p. 101.
21. Hans Kaufmann, *Heinrich Heine: Werke und Briefe* (Berlin, 1961 ff.), X, 8.
22. Lukács, *Ästhetik*, I, 230.
23. Paul Reimann, *Über realistische Kunstauffassung* (Berlin, 1952), pp. 93, 62.

Chapter Six: Literature in the Service of "Being"

1. Ernst Troeltsch, *Gesammelte Schriften* (Tübingen, 1922), III, 26.
2. Ernst Bertram, *Nietzsche* (Berlin, 1918), 1.
3. Emil Utitz, *Grundlegung der allgemeinen Kunstwissenschaft* (Stuttgart, 1914–20), II, 65 ff.
4. Ludwig Coellen, *Der Stil in der bildenden Kunst* (Traisa, 1921), p. 10.
5. Coellen, *Über die Methode der Kunstgeschichte* (Traisa, 1924), p. 28.
6. Ernst Cassirer, *Philosophie der symbolischen Formen* (Berlin, 1923–29), II, 320.
7. Martin Heidegger, *Hölderlin und das Wesen der Dichtung* (Munich, 1937), p. 12.
8. See Kurt May, "Über die gegenwärtige Situation einer deutschen Literurwissenschaft," *Trivium*, 5 (1947), 299.
9. Hermann Pongs, *Das Bild in der Dichtung*, 2nd ed. (Marburg, 1960), p. 453.

10. Pongs, "Neue Aufgaben der Literaturwissenschaft," *Dichtung und Volkstum*, 38 (1937), 324.
11. Horst Oppel, *Die Literaturwissenschaft der Gegenwart* (Stuttgart, 1939), p. 169.
12. Johannes Pfeiffer, *Umgang mit Dichtung* (Leipzig, 1936), pp. 41, 90.
13. Martin Heidegger, "Der Ursprung des Kunstwerkes," *Holzwege*, 2nd ed. (Frankfurt/Main, 1950), p. 28.
14. Ibid., "Wozu Dichter?", p. 294.
15. In recent years, Sartre has gone even further and asserted that writing is not enough, that the artist must also engage in direct social and political action. As is well known, he continues to follow his own advice.
16. Heidegger, "Der Ursprung des Kunstwerkes," p. 28.
17. Herbert von Einem, "Fragen kunstgeschichtlicher Interpretation," *Studium generale*, 5 (1952), 105.
18. Kurt Bauch, "Die Kunstgeschichte und die heutige Philosophie," in *Martin Heideggers Einfluß auf die Wissenschaften* (Bern, 1949), p. 93.
19. Ibid., Erich Ruprecht, "Heideggers Bedeutung für die Literaturwissenschaft," p. 137.
20. Bernhard von Arx, *Novellistisches Dasein* (Zurich, 1953), p. 11 f.
21. Johannes Pfeiffer, *Über das Dichterische und den Dichter* (Hamburg, 1956), pp. 14, 181, 178.
22. Theodor W. Adorno, *Jargon der Eigentlichkeit: Zur deutschen Ideologie*, edition suhrkamp, 91 (Frankfurt/Main, 1964).
23. Arnold Gehlen, "Der Betrachter wird zum Problem," *Merkur*, 18 (1964), 64.

Chapter Seven: Formalistic Trends

1. Alois Riegl, *Stilfragen* (Berlin, 1893), p. 24.
2. Gottfried Semper, *Der Stil in den technischen und tektonischen Künsten* (Frankfurt/Main, 1860–63).
3. Riegl, *Stilfragen*, p. 3.
4. Heinrich Wölfflin, *Klassische Kunst* (Munich, 1899), pp. viii, ix.
5. Wölfflin, *Kunstgeschichtliche Grundbegriffe* (Munich, 1915), p. vii, 11.
6. Arthur Hübscher, "Barock als Gestaltung antithetischen Lebensgefühls," *Euphorion*, 24 (1922), 517–62.
7. Fritz Strich, *Deutsche Klassik und Romantik* (Munich, 1922), p. 6.

8. Karl Viëtor, *Geschichte der deutschen Ode* (Munich, 1923); Günther Müller, *Geschichte des deutschen Liedes vom Zeitalter des Barock bis zur Gegenwart* (Munich, 1925); Wolfgang Kayser, *Geschichte der deutschen Ballade* (Berlin, 1936); Friedrich Beissner, *Geschichte der deutschen Elegie* (Berlin, 1941).

9. Karl Viëtor, *Geist und Form: Aufsätze zur deutschen Literaturgeschichte* (Bern, 1952), p. 12.

10. Karl Viëtor, "Deutsche Literaturgeschichte als Geistesgeschichte. Ein Rückblick," *PMLA*, 60 (1945), 915.

11. Horst Oppel, *Morphologische Literaturwissenschaft* (Mainz, 1947), p. 108.

12. Ernst Robert Curtius, *Europäische Literatur und lateinisches Mittelalter* (Bern, 1948), p. 20.

13. Walter Höllerer, "Methoden und Probleme vergleichender Literaturwissenschaft," *GRM* N.F., 2 (1951/52), 124.

14. Kurt May, "Über die gegenwärtige Situation einer deutschen Literaturwissenschaft," *Trivium*, 5 (1947), 300.

15. Wolfgang Kayser, *Das sprachliche Kunstwerk* (Bern, 1948), pp. 5, 18, 24.

16. Emil Staiger, *Die Kunst der Interpretation* (Zurich, 1955), p. 31.

17. Emil Staiger, *Die Zeit als Einbildungskraft des Dichters* (Zurich, 1939), pp. 12, 13 f., 15, 17.

18. Cleanth Brooks and Robert Penn Warren, *Understanding Poetry* (New York, 1938), pp. iv, ix.

19. Archibald MacLeish, *Collected Poems* (Boston, 1952), p. 41.

20. See Victor Ehrlich, *Russischer Formalismus* (Munich, 1964), pp. 51, 191.

21. Boris Eichenbaum, *Aufsätze zur Theorie und Geschichte der Literatur* (Frankfurt/Main, 1965), p. 13.

22. René Wellek and Austin Warren, *Theory of Literature* (New York, 1949), pp. 66, v.

23. T. S. Eliot, *The Sacred Wood*, 4th ed. (London, 1934), p. 42.

24. Wellek and Warren, *Theory of Literature*, p. 290 f.

25. Staiger, *Die Zeit als Einbildungskraft des Dichters*, p. 17.

26. See Fritz Lockemann, *Literaturwissenschaft und literarische Wertung* (Munich, 1965), p. 128.

27. Cf. the article "Philologische Methode," *Fischer-Lexikon, Literatur* II, 2 ed. by W. Friedrich and W. Killy (Frankfurt/Main, 1965), p. 411.

28. *Die Kunst der Interpretation*, p. 10.

29. *Die Kunst der Interpretation*, p. 12.

30. Horst Rüdiger, "Zwischen Interpretation und Geistesgeschichte," *Euphorion*, 57 (1963), 233, 234.

31. Wolfgang Iser, ed., *Immanente Ästhetik* (Munich, 1966).
32. Friedrich Nietzsche, *Werke* (Leipzig, 1899 ff.), XVI, 11.
33. Gottfried Benn, *Gesammelte Werke* (Wiesbaden, 1958 ff.), I, 474.
34. René Wellek, *Concepts of Criticism* (New Haven, 1963), p. 255.
35. For a critical survey see Robert Weimann's *"New Criticism" und die Entwicklung der bürgerlichen Literaturwissenschaft* (Halle, 1962).
36. Susanne Langer, *Problems of Art* (New York, 1957), p. 132.
37. Max Bense, "Zusammenfassende Grundlegung moderner Ästhetik," *Mathematik und Dichtung* (Munich, 1965), pp. 313–32.

Chapter Eight: The dernier cri *of Structuralism*

1. For further information the following studies and collections should prove useful:
   Serge Doubrovsky, *The New Criticism in France* (Chicago and London, 1973); John K. Simon, ed., *Modern French Criticism* (Chicago and London, 1972); Laurent LeSage, ed., *The French New Criticism: An Introduction and A Sampler* (University Park, Pennsylvania and London, 1967); Richard Macksey and Eugenio Donato, eds., *The Languages of Criticism and The Sciences of Man: The Structuralist Controversy* (Baltimore, 1970); Jacques Ehrmann, ed., *Structuralism* (New York, 1970); Edward M. Jennings, ed., *Science and Literature: New Lenses for Criticism* (New York, 1970).
2. On these grounds it has been attacked by Alfred Schmidt in "Der structuralistische Angriff auf die Geschichte," *Beiträge zur Erkenntnistheorie* (Frankfurt, 1969), p. 231.
3. Beda Alleman, "Strukturalismus in der Literaturwissenschaft," *Ansichten einer künftigen Germanistik*, ed. by J. Kolbe (Munich, 1969), pp. 143, 149.
4. Thus Helga Gallas tries to utilize the structuralist approach on a Marxist basis. See the introduction to her anthology, *Strukturalismus als interpretatives Verfahren* (Neuwied, 1972), pp. vii–xxx.
5. Cf. Günther Schiwy, *Der französische Strukturalismus* (Reinbek, 1970).
6. Quoted in Günther Schiwy, *Neue Aspekte des Strukturalismus* (Munich, 1971), p. 57 f.
7. *Spiegel* (July 27, 1971).

PART II: POSSIBILITIES OF A NEW SYNTHESIS

Chapter One: The Dilemma of Over-Specialization

1. Herbert Cysarz, *Geschichtswissenschaft—Kunstwissenschaft—Lebenswissenschaft* (Vienna, 1928), p. 48 f.
2. Georg Gottfried Gervinus, *Grundzüge der Historik* (Leipzig, 1837), p. 85.
3. Cf. Edgar Wind, *Art and Anarchy* (London, 1963), pp. 9 ff.
4. Levin L. Schücking, *Soziologie der literarischen Geschmacksbildung*, 3rd ed. (Bern, 1961), p. 75.
5. Hegel, *Jubiläumsausgabe*, XII, 77/78.
6. Friedrich Gundolf, *Goethe* (Berlin, 1916), p. 27.

Chapter Two: The Voices of Methodological Reintegration

1. Fritz Martini, "Wieland-Forschung," *DVLG*, 24 (1950), 278.
2. Friedrich Sengle, "Zum Problem der modernen Dichterbiographie," *DVLG*, 26 (1952), 102, 103.
3. Erik Lunding, *Strömungen und Strebungen der modernen Literaturwissenschaft* (Aarhus, 1952), p. 55.
4. Cf. Heinz Otto Burger, "Methodische Probleme der Interpretation," *GRM*, 32 (1950/51), 81.
5. Heinz Otto Burger, *Annalen der deutschen Literatur* (Stuttgart, 1952), p. i.
6. Erich Trunz, "Literaturwissenschaft als Auslegung und Geschichte," *Trier-Festschrift* (Meisenheim, 1954), pp. 50–87.
7. Clemens Heselhaus, "Auslegung und Erkenntnis," *Gestaltprobleme der Dichtung* (Bonn, 1957), pp. 259–82.
8. Hugo Friedrich, "Die Dichtung und die Methoden ihrer Deutung," *Neue deutsche Hefte*, 40 (1957/58), 676–88.
9. Friedrich Sengle, "Zur Einheit von Literaturgeschichte und Literaturkritik," *DVLG*, 34 (1960), 327–37.
10. Emil Staiger, "Das Problem des Stilwandels," *Euphorion*, 55 (1961), 229–41.
11. Benno von Wiese, "Geistesgeschichte oder Interpretation?" *Die Wissenschaft von deutscher Sprache und Dichtung* (Stuttgart, 1963), pp. 239–61.
12. Horst Rüdiger, "Zwischen Interpretation und Geistesgeschichte," *Euphorion*, 57 (1963), 227–44.
13. Peter Demetz, *Marx, Engels und die Dichter* (Stuttgart, 1959), p. 294. This turning toward the "universal" shows itself even more clearly in his essay, "150 Jahre Germanistik," (*Neue Form*, 14 [1967], 176–82), in which Demetz advocates giving

greater attention to comparative, anthropological, psycho-analytical, and sociological factors within the individual disciplines of literary scholarship.

14. Wiese, "Geistesgeschichte," p. 245.

15. Staiger, "Das Problem des Stilwandels," p. 241.

16. René Wellek, *Concepts of Criticism* (New Haven, 1963), p. 20.

17. Walter Muschg, "Germanistik? In memoriam Eliza M. Butler," *Euphorion*, 59 (1965), 18.

18. Karl Otto Conrady, *Einführung in die Neuere deutsche Literaturwissenschaft* (Reinbek, 1966), p. 30.

19. Hans-Egon Haas, "Literatur und Geschichte," *Neue deutsche Hefte*, 5 (1958/59), 309.

20. Friedrich Sengle, "Aufgaben und Schwierigkeiten der heutigen Literaturgeschichtsschreibung," *Archiv für das Studium der neueren Sprachen und Literaturen*, 115 (1963), 243.

21. Lunding, *Strömungen und Strebungen*, p. 8.

22. Muschg, "Germanistik?", p. 19.

23. Walter Abell, *The Collective Dream in Art: A Psycho-Historical Theory of Culture Based on Relations between the Arts, Psychology, and the Social Sciences* (Cambridge, Mass., 1957), p. 30.

24. Leslie A. Fiedler, "Archetype and Signature," in *Arts and Psychoanalysis*, ed. W. Phillips (New York, 1957), p. 427.

25. Frederick J. Hacker, "On Artistic Production," in *Explorations in Psychoanalysis*, ed. R. Lindner (New York, 1953), pp. 134, 135.

26. C. Hugh Holman, "More Recent Trends," in *The Development of American Literary Criticism*, ed. F. Stovall (Chapel Hill, 1955), p. 239.

27. Ernst Troeltsch, "Der Historismus und seine Probleme," *Gesammelte Schriften* (Tübingen, 1922), III, 33.

28. Ibid., VIII.

29. *Mathematik und Dichtung*, ed. H. Kreuzer and R. Gunzenhäuser, sammlung dialog, 3 (Munich, 1965), p. 17.

30. Muschg, "Germanistik?", p. 19. This trend toward "pluralism of methods" is also observable in some series. Compare the more formalistic series, *Literatur als Kunst*, with the more pluralistic *Schriften zur Literatur* (Göttingen, 1961 ff.).

31. Stanley Edgar Hyman, *The Armed Vision* (New York, 1948), p. 405.

32. Troeltsch, "Historismus," p. 700.

33. Max Wehrli, *Allgemeine Literaturwissenschaft* (Bern, 1951), p. 145.

34. Karl Lamprecht, *Zur jüngsten Vergangenheit* (Leipzig, 1912), I, 137.
35. Troeltsch, "Historismus," p. 701.

Chapter Three: The "Epochal" as a New Collective Concept

1. In regard to the following see Jost Hermand, "Über Nutzen und Nachteil literarischer Epochenbegriffe," *Monatshefte*, 58 (1966), 289–309.
2. Julius Wiegand, *Geschichte der deutschen Literatur* (Cologne, 1922).
3. Cf. Herbert Cysarz, "Das Periodenprinzip in der Literaturwissenschaft," p. 94.
4. Friedrich Nietzsche, *Werke* (Leipzig, 1899 ff.), I, 130.
5. Hans Sedlmayr, "Die Kunstgeschichte auf neuen Wegen," *Kunst und Wahrheit* (Reinbek, 1948), p. 8 ff.
6. Gottfried Benn, *Gesammelte Werke* (Wiesbaden, 1958 ff.), II, 248.
7. See Sengle, "Aufgaben und Schwierigkeiten," p. 260.
8. Benno von Wiese, "Zur Kritik des geistesgeschichtlichen Epochebegriffs," *DVLG*, 11 (1933), 132, 137, 134, 140. A similar point of view is found in Hermann Beenken's essay, "Geistesgeschichte als System geistiger Möglichkeiten," *Logos*, 19 (1930), 216.
9. Cf. Janet K. King, "The Generation Theory in Literary Criticism," Diss., Wisconsin, 1955.
10. Wilhelm Pinder, *Das Problem der Generation in der Kunstgeschichte Europas* (Berlin, 1928), p. 1.
11. Arnold Hauser, *Sozialgeschichte der Kunst und Literatur* (Munich, 1953), I, 463.
12. Beenken, "Geistesgeschichte als System," p. 262.

Chapter Four: Concerning the Dialectics of Culture

1. Alfred Andersch, *Die Blindheit des Kunstwerks und andere Aufsätze* (Frankfurt/Main, 1965), p. 69.
2. Richard Hamann and Jost Hermand, *Gründerzeit* (Berlin, 1965) p. 11.
3. Hauser, *Sozialgeschichte*, I, 463.
4. René Wellek, "Periods and Movements in Literary Criticism," *English Institute Annual 1940* (New York, 1941), p. 80.
5. Kurt Hiller, "Ortsbestimmung des Aktivismus," *Die Erhebung* (Berlin, 1920), p. 360 f.
6. Ernst Troeltsch, *Der Historismus und seine Überwindung* (Berlin, 1924), p. 3.

7. Friedrich Sengle, *Arbeiten zur Literatur, 1750–1850* (Stuttgart, 1965), p. 117.
8. Nietzsche, XVI, 236.
9. Heinrich von Kleist, *Sämtliche Werke*, ed. K. Siegen (Leipzig, n.d.), III, 281, 282.
10. Cf. Wolfgang Ruttkowski, *Die literarischen Gattungen und Grundbegriffe* (Bern/Munich, 1967), and Friedrich Sengle, *Die literarische Formenlehre* (Stuttgart, 1967). Both called for a reevaluation of so-called "applied" literature.
11. Goethe, *Gesamtausgabe* (Munich, 1961 ff.), XXI, 5, 103.
12. Emil Staiger, *Geist und Zeitgeist* (Zurich, 1964), p. 15.
13. Friedrich Sengle, "Zur Einheit von Literaturgeschichte und Literaturkritik," *DVLG*, 34 (1960), 337.
14. Hegel, *Jubiläumsausgabe*, XII, 31, 32, 35.
15. See Heine's letter to Karl Immermann, December 24, 1822.
16. Georg Lukács, *Ästhetik* (Neuwied, 1963), I, 19.
17. Bertolt Brecht, *Schriften zum Theater* (Frankfurt/Main, 1964), VII, 29.
18. Martin Walser, *Erfahrungen und Leseerfahrungen*, edition suhrkamp, 109 (Frankfurt/Main, 1965), 69, 71.
19. Benno von Wiese, "Zur Kritik des geistesgeschichtlichen Epochebegriffs," p. 143.
20. Hegel, *Jubiläumsausgabe*, XI, 151.
21. J. H. Plumb, *Crisis in the Humanities* (Baltimore, 1964), p. 42.
22. Goethe, *Gesamtausgabe*, XXI, 32.
23. Achim von Arnim, "Von Volksliedern," *Des Knaben Wunderhorn*, ed. K. Bode (Berlin, n.d.), II, 476.
24. Nietzsche, *Werke*, I, 338.
25. Georg Gottfried Gervinus, *Schriften zur Literatur*, ed. G. Erler (Berlin, 1962), pp. 600, 102.
26. Karl Löwith, *Die Hegelsche Linke* (Stuttgart, 1962), p. 38.
27. Kurt Tucholsky, *Gesammelte Werke* (Reinbek, 1961), III, 366.
28. Gottfried Keller to Hermann Hettner, June 26, 1854.
29. Karl Marx to Arnold Ruge, September, 1843.
30. Brecht, VII, 313.
31. Brecht, *Theaterarbeit* (Dresden, 1952), p. 46.

Bibliography

List of original titles cited in the text
in English translation

Alker, Ernst. *Geschichte der deutschen Literatur von Goethe's Tod bis zur Gegenwart*, 1949.

Barthes, Roland. *Sur Racine*, 1963.

Benn, Gottfried. *Statische Gedichte*, 1948.

Bertram, Ernst. *Nietzsche: Versuch einer Mythologie*, 1918.

Bloch, Ernst. *Geist der Utopie*, 1918.

Brecht, Bertolt. *Kleines Organon für das Theater*, 1948.

Burger, Heinz Otto. *Annalen der deutschen Literatur*, 1952.

Büttner, Ludwig. *Gedanken zu einer biologischen Literaturbetrachtung*, 1939.

Cassirer, Ernst. *Philosophie der symbolischen Formen*, 1923–29.

Chamberlain, Houston Stewart. *Grundlagen des 19. Jahrhunderts*, 1899.

———. *Arische Weltanschauung*, 1905.

Coellen, Ludwig. *Der Stil in der bildenden Kunst*, 1924.

Croce, Benedetto. *Poesia e Non-Poesia*, 1923.

Cysarz, Herbert. *Literaturgeschichte als Geistesgeschichte*, 1926.

Dessoir, Max, ed. *Zeitschrift für Ästhetik und allgemeine Kunstwissenschaft*, 1906 ff.

Deutschbein, Max. *Das Wesen des Romantischen*, 1921.

Dilthey, Wilhelm. *Einleitung in die Geisteswissenschaften*, 1883.

————. *Die Einbildungskraft des Dichters*, 1887.

————. *Das Erlebnis und die Dichtung*, 1906.

Ermatinger, Emil. *Das dichterische Kunstwerk*, 1921.

————. *Philosophie der Literaturwissenschaft*, 1930.

Fischer, Ernst. *Die Notwendigkeit der Kunst*, 1959.

Flemming, Willi. *Deutsche Kultur im Zeitalter des Barocks*, 1937.

Fontenelle, Saint-Pierre. *Digression sur les anciens et les modernes*, 1688.

Foucault, Michel. *Les Mots et les choses*, 1966.

Freud, Sigmund. *Das Unbehagen in der Kultur*, 1930.

Gervinus, Georg Gottfried. *Geschichte der poetischen Nationalliteratur*, 1835–42.

Hamann, Richard. *Impressionismus in Leben und Kunst*, 1907.

Hausenstein, Wilhelm. *Vom Geist des Barock*, 1920.

Hauser, Arnold. *Sozialgeschichte der Kunst und Literatur*, 1953.

Hegel, Georg Wilhelm Friedrich. *Ästhetik*, 1835.

————. *Vorlesungen über die Philosophie der Geschichte*, 1837.

Heidegger, Martin. *Sein und Zeit*, 1927.

————. *Hölderlin und das Wesen der Dichtung*, 1937.

————. *Holzwege*, 1949.

Hentschel, Willibald. *Vom aufsteigenden Leben*, 1910.

Herder, Johann Gottfried. *Ideen zur Philosophie der Geschichte der Menschheit*, 1784–91.

Hettner, Hermann. *Geschichte der deutschen Literatur im 18. Jahrhundert*, 1862–70.

Hocke, Gustav René. *Die Welt als Ladyrinth*, 1959.

Husserl, Edmund. *Ideen zu einer reinen Phenomenologie und phenomenologischen Philosophie*, 1913.

Ingarden, Roman. *Das literarische Kunstwerk*, 1931.

Iser, Wolfgang, ed. *Immanente Ästhetik: Lyrik als Paradigma der Moderne*, 1966.

Jauss, Hans Robert. *Literaturgeschichte als Provokation der Literaturwissenschaft*, 1967.

Jean Paul. *Vorschule der Ästhetik*, 1804.

Kant, Immanuel. *Kritik der reinen Vernunft*, 1781.

Kayser, Wolfgang. *Das literarische Kunstwerk*, 1948.

Kommerell, Max. *Geist und Buchstabe der Dichtung*, 1939.

————. *Gedanken über Gedichte*, 1943.

Korff, Hermann August. *Der Geist der Goethezeit*, 1923–40.

Krauss, Herbert. *Das Wellengesetz in der Geschichte*, 1929.

Kretschmer, Ernst. *Körperbau und Charakter*, 1921.

Lamprecht, Karl. *Deutsche Geschichte*, 1891–1909.

————. *Zur jüngsten Vergangenheit*, 1912.

Laube, Heinrich. *Geschichte der deutschen Literatur*, 1839.

Lévi-Strauss, Claude. *La Pensée sauvage*, 1962.

Lombroso, Cesare. *Genio e Degenerazione*, 1864.

Lublinski, Samuel. *Literatur und Gesellschaft im 19. Jahrhundert*, 1899–1900.

Lukács, Georg. *Theorie des Romans*, 1916.

————. *Geschichte und Klassenbewusstsein*, 1923.

————. *Goethe und seine Zeit*, 1947.

————. *Deutsche Realisten des 19. Jahrhunderts*, 1951.

————. *Zerstörung der Vernunft*, 1953.

————. *Der historische Roman*, 1955.

Lux, Joseph August. *Ein Jahrtausend deutscher Romantik*, 1924.

Mehring, Franz. *Die Lessing-Legende*, 1896.

Münsterberg, Hugo. *Philosophie der Werte*, 1908.

Muschg, Walter. *Tragische Literaturgeschichte*, 1948.

Nadler, Josef. *Literaturgeschichte der deutschen Stämme und Landschaften*, 1912–18.

Nietzsche, Friedrich. *Unzeitgemässe Betrachtungen*, 1874–76.

————. *Geburt der Tragödie*, 1873.

————. *Vom Nutzen und Nachteil der Historie für das Leben*, 1874.

Nordau, Max. *Entartung*, 1892.

Oppel, Horst. *Morphologische Literaturwissenschaft*, 1947.

Pastor, Willy. *Die Erde in der Zeit des Menschen*, 1904.

Petersen, Julius. *Die Wesensbestimmung der deutschen Romantik*, 1926.

Pongs, Hermann. *Das Bild in der Dichtung*, 1935.

Rank, Otto. *Der Künstler: Ansätze zu einer Sexual-Psychologie*, 1907.

————. *Das Inzest-Motiv in Dichtung und Sage: Grundzüge einer Psychologie des dichterischen Schaffens*, 1912.

Reimann, Paul. *Über realistische Kunstauffassung*, 1949.

Rickert, Heinrich. *Die Grenzen der naturwissenschaftlichen Begriffsbildung*, 1896–1902.

Riegl, Alois. *Stilfragen*, 1893.

Sartre, Jean-Paul. *Qu'est-ce que la littérature?* 1947.

Spengler, Oswald. *Der Untergang des Abendlandes*, 1918–22.

Spoerri, Theophil. *Renaissance und Barock bei Ariost und Tasso*, 1922.

Staiger, Emil. *Grundbegriffe der Poetik*, 1946.

———. *Die Kunst der Interpretation*, 1955.

———. *Die Zeit als Einbildungskraft des Dichters*, 1939.

Stekel, Wilhelm. *Dichtung und Neurose*, 1909.

Strich, Fritz. *Deutsche Klassik und Romantik: Vollendung und Unendlichkeit*, 1922.

Schemann, Ludwig. *Die Rasse in den Geisteswissenschaften*, 1931.

Schmidt, Julian. *Geschichte der deutschen Literatur*, 1890.

Schücking, Levin L. *Soziologie der literarischen Geschmacksbildung*, 1923.

Tönnies, Ferdinand. *Gemeinschaft und Gesellschaft*, 1887.

Troeltsch, Ernst. *Der Historismus und seine Überwindung*, 1924.

Utitz, Emil. *Grundlegung der allgemeinen Kunstwissenschaft*, 1914–20.

Vico, Giovanni Battista. *Scienza nuova*, 1725.

Voltarie, *Essai sur l'histoire générale*, 1756.

Walzel, Oskar. *Wechselseitige Erhellung der Künste*, 1917.

———. *Deutsche Literatur seit Goethes Tod*, 1918.

———. *Gehalt und Gestalt*, 1923.

Wechssler, Eduard. *Esprit und Geist*, 1927.

Weinreich, Harald. *Literaturgeschichte des Lesers*, 1967.

Wölfflin, Heinrich. *Klassische Kunst*, 1899.

———. *Kunstgeschichtliche Grundbegriffe*, 1915.

Worringer, Wilhelm. *Abstraktion und Einfühlung*, 1908.

INDEX